THE BIRTH OF TERRORISM IN MIDDLE EAST

Muhammed Bin Abed al-Wahab, Wahabism,
and the Alliance with the ibn Saud Tribe

MUHAMMAD NE'MA AL-SEMAWI
TRANSLATOR: SABAH EL-ALI

PARAGON PUBLICATION

ISBN: 0989594106
ISBN-13: 9780989594103

Copyright © 2013 by: Muhammad Ne'ma al-Semawi
Paragon Publications
All rights reserved. No part of this publication may be reproduced, distributed, or transmitted in any form or by any means, including photocopying, recording, or other electronic or mechanical methods, without the prior written permission of the publisher, except in the case of brief quotations embodied in critical reviews and certain other noncommercial uses permitted by copyright law.

Published by:

Paragon Publications LLC
P.O. Box 2584
Dearborn, Michigan, 48123 United States of America

Printed in the USA

Dedication

This book is dedicated to those who were brutally massacred by the Wahhabi-Saudi alliance. These innocent individuals were free of any crime according to both Islamic and secular law. And yet, their fellow Muslims showed them no mercy. My hope is that this book will light a candle on the path of safety and peace worldwide and prevent such hatred in the future.

Publisher's Introduction

It pleases Paragon Publications to present this work to the reader. It provides a missing link in the chain of research related to one of the greatest challenges of this age, one which is deeply entrenched in the history of both Arab and Islamic civilizations and their nations.

This work is not a biography, or the history of a tribe, or a guide to a geographic region. Rather, it is the result of research designed to reach the root of a problem and find its solution. That problem is a form of terrorism that has become especially prominent after September 11, 2001. Wahhabism has grown and given birth to terrorist groups that are spreading like wildfire, such as Jabhat Al-Nusrah and Daʿish (ISIS/ISIL) and others that have mercilessly and inhumanely murdered, burned, raped, and mutilated the innocent, including children and the elderly.

Unforeseen circumstances have delayed the publication of this valuable research. Otherwise, the discerning reader will recognize that in more than one instance, the author predicts events that, by the time of publication, may have already taken place. This is a direct result of his meticulous research and analysis. The author also gives preventative solutions. There remain a number of predictions that are expected to occur unless a realistic treatment of this cancer is embraced.

Paragon Publishing hopes the present work helps readers form a clearer understanding of Wahhabism and its roots through its use of tangible

The Birth of Terrorism in Middle East

documentation and strong evidence. In addition, Paragon invites counter-terrorism agencies and those involved and interested in such a topic to examine and contemplate key points in this study.

Table of Contents

Publisher's Introduction vii
Introduction. 1
Chapter 1: Early Life 9
   1: The Beginnings 9
   2: Birthplace of Ibn Abd al-Wahhab and His Mission 15
   3: The Religious Situation 22
Chapter 2: The Great Mission 32
   1: Prior to Declaring the Mission. 32
   The First Story. 36
   The Second Story. 37
   The Third Story 39
   The Fourth Story 40
   2: The Pedigree of Ibn Abd al-Wahhab. 49
   3: Historians Who Favored the Shaykh 51
   4: Mr. Hempher 57
   5: The Memoirs of Hempher 59
   6: Ibn Abd al-Wahhab's Escape from Basra. 63
Chapter 3: Declaration of the Mission 66
   1: In Huraymalah 66
   2: In Uyaynah (Yamamah). 67
   3: Ibn Abd al-Wahhab's First Sponsor and the
   Retribution of Sennemar [111] 70

>   Observations About the Beginnings of the Mission and the
>   Personality of Ibn Abd al-Wahhab 75
>   The Controversy Surrounding the Death of Ibn
>   Abd al-Wahhab's First Ally. 79
>   Revisiting the Shaykh's History as Portrayed by the Author of
>   *Lam al-Shahab* and Hempher 84

Chapter 4: The Village of Diriyah and Al Saud 94
>   1: The Village of Diriyah: The Capital of Wahhabism 94
>   2: The Saud Family: Rulers of the Wahhabi State. 97
>   3: Muhammad Ibn Saud 98

Chapter 5: The Third Journey to Diriyah 103
>   The Alliance Between the Shaykh of the Village and the
>   Shaykh of Religion. 103
>   The Meeting of the Allies: A Meeting with No Prior Notice. 105
>   The Terms of the Alliance 109
>   The True Motives Behind the Alliance 111
>   Diriyah Before and After the Alliance 116
>   The Puzzle of Ibn Suwaylim. 118
>   Other Mysteries in the Life of Ibn Abd al-Wahhab. 124
>   The Interests at Stake for the Two Shaykhs. 126
>   The Shaykh: A Totalitarian Leader and Expert in Weapon
>   Manufacturing and the Affairs of War 128

Chapter 6: The Strategic Objectives of the Allies. 132
>   The Strategic Goals and Methods of the Allies 132

Chapter 7: Wahhabi Terror Tactics Used to Establish the State 156

Chapter 8: Wahhabism: A System of Violence and Estrangement . . 167
>   1: Impressions and Conclusions. 167
>   2: The Logic of Self-Interest. 168
>   3: Unjust Punishments. 170
>   4: False Likening Unto Authentic Prophetic Knowledge 171
>   5: A Tendency Towards Heresy and Estrangement. 172

6: Polishing the Reputation of Ibn Abd al-Wahhab to
Confirm the Legitimacy of the State 172
7: Criticizing Early Muslims is Forbidden 174
8: Using Polytheism as a Pretext to Dispose of Others 174
9: A Flawed Understanding of Islam 175
10: Using Islamic Pretexts to Subjugate Others 176
11: Wahhabi Violence and the Motives for Raids. 177
12: The Manufacture of Extremism 178
13: Ibn Abd al-Wahhab at the Forefront of the Salafis 180
14: Declarations of Infidelity 181
15: Between Severity for the Committed and
Tolerance of the Deviant 182
16: The Manufacture of Terrorist Sleeper Cells 183
17: The Link Between Wahhabism and al-Qaeda, the Taliban,
and Other Radical Extremist Movements. 184
18: Legitimizing Terrorism in Wahhabi Discourse 186
19: Addendum: Ahmad Ibn Abd al-Halim Ibn
Taymiyyah (1262–1328 CE) 187
References 189

Introduction

Since its inception, Wahhabism has been a source of sectarian violence. Intolerance grounded in dogma dismissive of the precedence of the Islamic schools of law is at the core of what distinguished the founder of Wahhabism, Shaykh Muhammad ibn Abi al-Wahhab al-Najdi (1702–1792), from his contemporaries. And such intolerance has been continued to this day by Ibn Abd al-Wahhab's sympathizers, who simply refer to him as "the Shaykh." While some Wahhabis, or, as they prefer to be called, "Salafis," may clothe their works in the language of reform and enlightenment, the bloodshed done in the name of their cause speaks for itself.

Regardless of their different denominations and dispositions, the subsequent generations of Wahhabis continued violating traditional geographical faith boundaries in order to infiltrate the areas most sympathetic to their beliefs and vision. They diligently searched for clusters in neighboring areas most compatible with, and most receptive of, their beliefs all in an attempt to broaden their control and gain followers with the eventual goal of eradicating any who held a different approach to Islam.

Since the first days of Ibn Abd al-Wahhab's campaign, Wahhabis employed confrontational behavior in an organized manner typical of a collaborative faction. They relied upon intimidating displays of attacks and retreats, armed invasions, and daily educational sessions aimed at spreading Ibn Abd al-Wahhab's ideologies and particular understanding of monotheism. They also closely

The Birth of Terrorism in Middle East

observed how the communities under their control reacted to what was initially perceived as being a strange, new ideology.

The Shaykh was a central figure and a source of legitimacy for a movement that would have otherwise faded due to its radical tenets. Wahhabis held fast to his role as the bearer of a pure form of Islam. However, because of Ibn Abd al-Wahhab's shortcoming as a *mujtahid* (jurist), Wahhabis adamantly adhered to a less sophisticated methodology in Islamic law characterized by rigidity and prejudice. And their preconceived notions, free of substantial proof, dictated that they passionately dismiss other sects and religions and dole out unjust penalties without due process.

The first Saudi state, with an army headed by the Shaykh and his followers, was established by way of religious warfare; the Wahhabis raided their Muslim neighbors who had allegedly apostatized. It was then that a strong connection was established between the ruling line (the Saudis) and those who accused others of infidelity (the Wahhabis). This connection resulted in a permanent marriage between the factions of extremism and violence, two attributes now unfairly attributed to Muslims at large.

The Saudis and Wahhabis fought until they established an emirate in their native Najd,[1] which is located in Central Arabia. From the Wahhabi perspective, they were successful in establishing a sort of utopia in which Islam was abided. In their literature and in historical records, the Wahhabis are documented to have employed language that depicts their emirate in Diriyah in a most positive light, such that Ibn Abd al-Wahhab and the founder of the first Saudi state, Muhammad Ibn Saud,[2] re-established Islam through their conquests. In such books, comparisons are made to the Prophet Muhammad's government in Medina as well as the governments of the four "rightly guided" caliphs (*al-khulafā' al-rāshidūn*).[3]

In addition to attacking surrounding towns and local rulers, the Wahhabis extended their violence to other parts of the Islamic world. Over two centuries ago, the Wahhabis raided Karbala, Iraq and plundered the shrine of the

Introduction

Prophet's grandson, Husayn.[4] The wealth acquired and the blood that was shed are mentioned with great pride in the works of early Wahhabi historians.[5] But this was not an isolated incident; the earliest primary sources describing the establishment of the first Saudi kingdom mention the slaughter of hundreds of thousands of people.

Contemporary Wahhabis in Afghanistan, Pakistan, and elsewhere gain inspiration from the founders of the original Wahhabi state and regard Ibn Abd al-Wahhab as a redeemer who approached the status of the Prophet. Wahhabi jurists issue verdicts calling for the eradication of a large percentage of the global population.[6] Wahhabism continues to spread in universities, mosques, and Islamic centers due to the funding of the Saudi government. They incite their followers to carry out suicide missions after convincing them that these acts lead to martyrdom and are part of a holy war against modern societies.

This, of course, raises the question: How can Ibn Abd al-Wahhab be perceived as a redeemer who will relieve the world of its afflictions when his ideology contains messages of hatred and intolerance? Nonetheless, affection for Wahhabism continues to grow, which means acts of terrorism will only increase. The likes of Osama Ibn Laden,[7] Ayman al-Zawahiri,[8] al-Mullah Omar[9] and al-Zarkawi[10] have openly attempted to imitate Ibn Abd al-Wahhab's condemnation of modern lifestyles and adopt his policies of violence, including unprovoked raids and beheadings. Unfortunately, modern-day Wahhabis are also armed with more advanced technology, allowing for unprecedented acts of terror.

The Saudis became actively involved in spreading Ibn Abd al-Wahhab's ideals beyond the Arabian Peninsula by funding thinkers such as Muhammad Rasheed Rida[11], and, more recently, the likes of Jouhayman al-Ateebee,[12] Ibn Laden, Ayman al-Zawahiri and al-Mullah Omar. Such individuals, who are strongly influenced by Wahhabism, claim that their movement finds its roots in early Islamic history, which they present as having been a sort of utopia.[13] This is due, in large part, to the fact that Ibn Abd al-Wahhab's principles served as the founding principles of a nation that later became one of the wealthiest and most influential in the world. Wahhabi sympathizers attribute the wealth of Saudi Arabia to the adherence of its founders and leaders to the true principles of Islam as detailed by "the Shaykh." Thus, God rewarded them with plentiful riches on Earth and will reward them in the hereafter as well.

Modern-day Wahhabi extremists look to establish their "Islamic" states wherever they may be, including Tora Bora,[14] the caves and hills of Afghanistan and Pakistan, and the sandy regions of western Iraq. As they attempt to muster the deepest pockets of extremism in lands that express sympathy for their violent ideology, followers of Ibn Abd al-Wahhab seek new arenas to stage their battles. And there are indications that should Pakistan succumb to the Wahhabi movement, widespread chaos will ensue as Pakistan serves as an incubator for al-Qaeda and its extremist ideals influenced by Wahhabism. As for the Wahhabis' desire to establish an emirate similar to Diriyah in Iraq, it has been met with some hurdles as traditional Sunni Iraqis are moderate and unaccepting of the Wahhabi message. For this reason, the Wahhabi agenda can only be established in Iraq by way of great bloodshed.

Meanwhile, Ibn Abd al-Wahhab's ideals have actually begun to wane in the very land in which it was originally founded, despite the fact that it is spreading elsewhere. Ibn Abd al-Wahhab's message has become a burden for the Saudis ever since the Taliban and al-Qaeda adopted it, for, as the world gains awareness of the consequences of Ibn Abd al-Wahhab's ideals, his message is met with increasing opposition and distrust.

• • •

In order to understand the nature of terrorist groups like al-Qaeda, the Taliban, and ISIL (The Islamic State in the Levant), one must understand Wahhabis' fascination with Ibn Abd al-Wahhab, his pernicious personality, and his provocative writings devoid of coherent methodology. Wahhabi accounts of his life present a carefully woven legend of an exceptional and infallible man, seemingly guided by an invisible power. His story is interlaced with precarious situations from which he cleverly escaped. Ibn Abd al-Wahhab is presented as

Introduction

having been the awaited savior who will carry out God's will on Earth and restore it to the purity of the days of the prophets, especially the exemplary early days of Islam.[15]

Wahhabis hold that one must strive to emulate the Shaykh by spreading a revolutionary message of renewal and reform. Some have even adopted the nickname "the Shaykh" or "the Shaykh of Islam," assuming positions of authority similar to Ibn Abd al-Wahhab and Ahmad Ibn Abd al-Halim Ibn Taymiyyah (1263–1328 CE).[16] And Wahhabis are uncompromising in their beliefs, unwilling to debate Wahhabi principles. Ibn Abd al-Wahhab's teachings are, in practice, given sanctity on par with the Quran.

The reform imagined by Ibn Abd al-Wahhab, and practiced by his followers, regards the vast majority of humanity (including most Muslims) as being unbelievers who are hopeless in that they will never be guided and, thus, are destined to be slaughtered at the Wahhabis' hands. The Wahhabis justify their brutish actions with the alleged goal of purifying the Arabian Peninsula and the rest of the world from the unbelievers, even though their violence has no basis in traditional Islamic texts, such as the Quran.[17] They have divided the world into two camps: the camp of faith (exclusively reserved for the Wahhabis themselves) and the rest of the world, or, their enemies, who belong to camp of unbelief and falsehood.

Ibn Abd al-Wahhab declared his mission to be to eradicate what he deemed polytheistic practices in his native Najd and elsewhere. The particular conditions of his time along with the presence of an ambitious partner, in the person of Muhammad Ibn Saud, helped the Shaykh find success. Ibn Saud sought to unify and govern the scattered tribes of Arabia. The odds were stacked against Ibn Abd al-Wahhab as he operated in a greatly fragmented Arabia bearing a message that stood in stark contrast to the inclusive vision of Islam. Ibn Abd al-Wahhab's success was not a result of formal training.

Ibn al-Wahhab's tendency to dismiss a large number of Muslims as being unbelievers was largely due to his definition of monotheism. In this regard, he was greatly influenced by the works of Ibn Taymiyyah. To this day, Ibn Taymiyyah's views on what constitutes monotheistic practice continue to inspire Wahhabi policies; those who hold beliefs other than what the Wahhabis deem acceptable will be out of the scope of "true" monotheists. Ibn Taymiyyah and the Wahhabis believe in anthropomorphism and hold views that are in contrast with mainstream Muslims. Also, in his time, Ibn Taymiyyah was known for his petulance, prejudice, and controversial verdicts as he dismissed large numbers of Muslims as being unbelievers. This entailed that their blood could be shed and their property plundered.

It is worth noting that, despite being a great influence upon him, Ibn Taymiyyah wrote in a far more sophisticated manner than would Ibn Abd al-Wahhab, who did not demonstrate scholarly innovation nor rely upon concrete proof in his methodology. Ibn Abd al-Wahhab, in fact, was willingly opposed to any sort of adaptation or evolution in the Islamic fields of knowledge. At the same time, his works show a lack of proper engagement with the great body of Islamic tradition. Thus, he was opposed to adapting to contemporary society while simultaneously stringently adhering to tradition despite not fully grasping the essentials of that tradition. Furthermore, the Shaykh was not consistent or compliant with any known Islamic school of thought, including the Hanbali school of jurisprudence to which he claimed affiliation. He contradicted its teachings and even those of Ibn Taymiyyah. He justified his particular position by claiming his opinions and decisions were derived directly from the text of the Quran. However, Ibn Abd al-Wahhab was not fully versed in the sciences related to the study of the Quran as he did not distinguish between literal and allegorical verses of the Quran, nor between verses whose application was temporary and those that were to be permanently effective.[18] Ibn Abd al-Wahhab's methods of relating verses without providing true analysis and deriving from verses without any sort of objective and comprehendible proof have been adopted by later Wahhabis. And Ibn Abd al-Wahhab was preceded in this regard by the Kharijites[19] who caused a rift in early Islamic history due to their lack of training in the language and style of the Quran.

Introduction

Ibn Abd al-Wahhab is also emulated by other Wahhabis in terms of his personal habits and behavior. The Shaykh emphasized a strict adherence to the way of life of the time of the Prophet, including habits like eating without utensils, shortening one's clothing, and spreading pebbles on the floors of mosques. He claimed that he imitated the earliest Muslims in his mannerisms and that their way of life was idyllic in its simplicity. And an exaggerated emphasis upon such outward etiquettes is characteristic of Wahhabis today as they impose strictly interpreted tradition at the expense of individual expression (in religion and otherwise) and even original research and independent thinking. In their portrayal of "the Shaykh," the Wahhabis, in fact, elevate Ibn Abd al-Wahhab to a status beyond that of the prophets of God; in Wahhabi sources, it is claimed that prophets made several mistakes, whereas mistakes committed by the Shaykh have not been documented.

• • •

This book covers the early life of Muhammad Ibn Abd al-Wahhab, including his travels before his movement and his invasions in Najd and the surrounding areas of the Arabian Peninsula. It also covers his struggles in establishing an emirate based upon his vision of an ideal society. Furthermore, it documents his daily efforts to monitor the affairs of the emirate as well as impose his thoughts and beliefs in conquered areas. In the eyes of the Wahhabis, the Shaykh was a true reformer and the ideal Muslim. It is thus the goal of this book to clearly demonstrate his thinking and actions. The reader can then decide to what extent the Wahhabis accurately imagine their role model as this book examines Ibn Abd al-Wahhab's mental makeup and behavior. It also provides practical solutions for dealing with Wahhabi extremism in the form of his admirers from among generations of youth today. Lastly, the historical sources cited represent both pro-Wahhabi and anti-Wahhabi agendas, in an attempt to give an objective representation of Wahhabism.

Chapter 1: Early Life

1: The Beginnings

Muhammad Ibn Abd al-Wahhab[20] was born in 1111 AH (1698 CE)[21] in the town of Uyaynah, in the hills of Najd, in the valley of Hanifah. The region is infamous for being the same valley in which Musaylamah al-Kadhdhab[22] was raised and would proclaim his false prophethood towards the end of the Prophet Mohammad's time. Musaylamah issued his claims to prophethood in the form of poetry in an attempt to imitate the style of the Holy Quran. As a result, his movement was able to gain influence in the same region that would later produce the founder of Wahhabism.

Ibn Abd al-Wahhab spent the majority of his lengthy life of ninety-five years tirelessly propagating his understanding of monotheism. He held that misconceptions concerning monotheism had led to deviant practices in the Muslim world such as the care for and visitation of graves and shrines as well as mosques constructed upon such sites. Early Wahhabis were determined to rectify these practices at all costs as they deemed Muslims guilty of such acts to be polytheists.

• • •

The Shaykh would be provided the opportunity to form an alliance with an ambitious local ruler, Muhammad Ibn Saud. The two would combine military and religious authority in what would become the first Saudi state. Ibn

The Birth of Terrorism in Middle East

Abd al-Wahhab was given the title of *imam al-daʿwa* ("Imam of the Message") while Ibn Saud was called *imam al-muslimin* ("Imam of the Muslims"). Since its inception over two and a half centuries ago, this nation has experienced great success despite approximately a century of discord.[23] Significant developments after World War One as well as a booming oil industry later in the century prepared the grounds for Wahhabi success. As a result, a vast number of people were enlisted in the movement, which assumed the guise of reform and a return to early Islam and the successful conquests of the caliphs.

• • •

Historical accounts surrounding the life of Ibn Abd al-Wahhab are not necessarily reliable. Facts are interlaced with a great deal of legend. This is because Wahhabi accounts sought to depict the Shaykh as having been the greatest of Islamic reformers, a man endowed with superior strengths and talent who was guided by God in his decisions and success. Nonetheless, in the following pages, the existent writings concerning the early life of Ibn Abd al-Wahhab will be presented.

Ibn Abd al-Wahhab came from a family of scholarship. His grandfather issued edicts for the entire area of Najd and was recognized for his expertise in theology. His father, Abd al-Wahhab,[24] was a judge in the town of Uyaynah who issued verdicts as well. He taught from his home such subjects as Quranic exegesis, the science of prophetic traditions and jurisprudence in accordance with the school of Imam Ahmad Ibn Hanbal. The young Ibn Abd al-Wahhab enjoyed his father's council and benefitted from the conversations and arguments of the attendees.[25]

According to Abu Bakr Hussein Ibn Ghannam (1811 CE), an early Wahhabi historian who encountered "the Shaykh," Ibn Abd al-Wahhab demonstrated great ability and piety from a young age. Ibn Ghannam reports that Ibn Abd al-Wahhab memorized the Quran by the age of ten. He was reportedly, "quick to comprehend and memorize, earning his parents' admiration for his intelligence and acumen." And after the Shaykh reached puberty, reportedly

Chapter 1: Early Life

his father decided that he was worthy of leading prayers. His father would later allow him to perform the Hajj ritual, which he did completely in accordance with tradition. After the Hajj, he spent two months in Medina, a center of learning at the time. He would then return to Najd to study Imam Ahmad's doctrines in jurisprudence. Ibn Abd al-Wahhab would then embark upon on a journey to other Muslim countries in the pursuit of knowledge. Along the way, he acquired the skill to write at an alarming rate, "capable of writing an entire booklet in a given council."[26]

The anonymous historian and author of *Lam al-shahab fi sirat Muhammad Ibn Abd al-Wahhab*, who lived to see the fall of the Wahhabi movement after Ibn Abd al-Wahhab's death, wrote the following regarding the founder of Wahhabism's exceptional talents:

> It was relayed to us by a trustworthy source who was a contemporary of the Najdi Shaykh Muhammad Ibn Abd al-Wahhab that he pursued knowledge persistently from an early age. Also, he was intelligent, a quick learner, and constantly in the pursuit of knowledge, at first in his own town and then in al-Kaseem, beginning at the age of seven. He then became so proficient that others sought him for edicts.[27]

Dr. Abd al-Raheem al-Rahman, professor of history at the Azhar University wrote:

> During his childhood, Shaykh Muhammad Ibn Abd al-Wahhab preferred to study in groups of students who came from different corners of the Earth simply to study with his father as opposed to studying in gatherings of his peers. Therefore, he grew up with a stronger grounding in than others from his generation. This also helped him memorize the Quran before the age of ten. Additionally, he was very fond of learning and spent his time reading books of [Islamic] law, Quranic exegesis, [Islamic] creed, and prophetic traditions.

The Birth of Terrorism in Middle East

He also read the books and letters of Ahmad Taqi al-Din Ibn Taymiyyah, his source of inspiration in many issues.

> The Shaykh was quick to comprehend and could write quickly. His father foresaw goodness in him, supervised his upbringing, and was very proud of him to the point where he had him lead prayers at a very young age. His father would say, "I have benefitted from my son Muhammad['s opinions] on various edicts."[28] The Shaykh was diligent in his studies and discussions with his father and shined in addressing religious edicts and the legal issues that were brought before him.[29]

According to these testimonies, Ibn Abd al-Wahhab was distinguished since his childhood with rare qualities reserved for geniuses. And these qualities are presented as being the result of divine providence. These qualities included decorum, discipline, and the preparation for a special mission, similar to those of prophets and great reformers.

As for accounts of Ibn Abd al-Wahhab as an adult, it is apparent that his followers sought to make the Shaykh appear to be a brilliant man in order to provide their movement with legitimacy, especially in the face of competing sects and ideologies.

Non-Wahhabi historians, however, provide different accounts.

It should be mentioned that, in the process of researching the history of someone who lived more than two and a half centuries ago under turbulent conditions using only narratives from unknown sources, it is not correct to accept their word without the presence of substantial proofs. These proofs must be corroborated by documents, deeds, or personal memoirs from his contemporaries who either interacted with the Shaykh or witnessed his actions. These items are missing in most of the research about Ibn Abd al-Wahhab.

Let us now consider some of the accounts by other historians:

Chapter 1: Early Life

Muhammad Ibn Abd al-Wahhab was born in 1111 AH and died in 1207 AH, thereby living for ninety-six years. In the beginning, he learned from the jurists of Mecca and Medina, but they soon saw in him aberrance and misdirection. His father, Abd al-Wahhab, a virtuous scholar, used to observe his son, frequently rebuke him and warn people of him. His brother also rejected that which he [Muhammad Ibn Abd al-Wahhab] brought forth and authored a book in response to him. The Shaykh was initially fond of reading the reports of proclaimers of prophethood such as Mousaylemeh, Sajjah, al-Aswad al-Anasi, Taleehah al-Assadee,[30] and others.[31]

Another account reads:

Initially, [Muhammad Ibn Abd al-Wahhab] was among the seekers of knowledge, frequently visiting Mecca and Medina to learn from their scholars, including Shaykh Muhammad Ibn Sulayman al-Kerdee and Shaykh Muhammad Hayat al-Sindi. These two shaykhs and others noticed that he harbored misguidance and blasphemy. They said, "God will allow him to go astray and He will misguide by way of him the wretched among His servants." And this came to be true. His father, a virtuous scholar, noticed in him tendencies towards blasphemy and he warned people about him, as did his brother Shaykh Sulayman.[32]

In the book *Tarikh Najd*, the author Mahmoud Shekri al-Alusi wrote:

The son of Abd al-Wahhab was raised in the town of Uyaynah in the region of Najd. He studied law at the hands of his father according to the doctrine of Ahmad Ibn Hanbal. Even in his early life, the Shaykh used terminology strange to Muslims and condemned much of Islamic practice at the time. The path he chose was completely devoid of guidance. He denied the beliefs of the Muslims in Najd which led his father to proscribe him. But that did not stop him. Rather, it led to discord between them. Many arguments followed between him and the other Muslims in Horaymelah for two years until his father died in 1153 AH. At that point, he dared to openly express his beliefs as well as his opposition of other Muslims. He would gain the following of the dregs of the people.[33]

It is worth noting in the passages above that Muhammad Ibn Abd al-Wahhab's brother (Sulayman) and his father were both Hanbali scholars and both strongly opposed to his message. Sulayman wrote a book entitled *Al-sawa'iq al-ilahiyah fi al-radd 'ala al-Wahhabiyah*[34] ("Divine Lightning in Response to Wahhabism") in which he rejected his brother's beliefs. According to Shaykh Ahmad Ibn Zayni Dahlan, the author of the book *Khulasat-ul-Kalam Fi Umaraa al-Bait al-Haraam* ("The Princes of the Holy Country"), Shaykh Muhammad's father and his brother, Shaykh Sulayman, were virtuous and educated men. They learned about the mission of Shaykh Muhammad through his proclamations and behavior when he was studying in Medina. Both would then admonish and criticize him and warn people about him.[35]

• • •

There are a number of inconsistencies in accounts of "the Shaykh." Further complicating the issue is the fact that the majority of the historians who wrote of his life were not contemporaries of Ibn Abd al-Wahhab. One can, however, assess the position of the scholars of his time, including his father and brother, through documents that have survived. These documents include the aforementioned book his brother wrote, currently published and available on a wide scale. Also, historical events such as Wahhabi invasions of his time convey Ibn Abd al-Wahhab's ideology. His ideas have been adopted today by the wealthiest religious organization in the world, that of the Salafi Wahhabis, which has printed thousands of Ibn Abd al-Wahhab's books and distributed them around the world in its own centers as well as other sympathizing religious centers. This organization has garnered the support of thousands of researchers, universities,

Chapter 1: Early Life

and cultural centers in order to spread Wahhabi doctrine as well as those of the Hanbali sect and Ibn Taymiyyah.

• • •

Miltebron[36] says:

> The origin of the Wahhabi movement begins with a story told by Arabs, especially the Yemenis, in which it is said that a poor shepherd named "Sulayman" dreamt a flame emerged from his body and spread across Earth, burning everything in its path. He related his dream to an interpreter who told him that one of his children would form a strong nation. The vision became true with his grandson Muhammad Ibn Abd al-Wahhab, for when he grew up, he became a respected man in his town...[37]

Some stories claim that Ibn Abd al-Wahhab was of foreign origin and not native to Arabia.[38] However, we have reservations regarding these stories due to a lack of evidence. Furthermore, his father, Abd al-Wahhab was a judge and Hanbali jurist who had a good reputation among the Muslims in his area and it is difficult to attain such status in such a society when there is doubt about one's heritage. And his jurist grandfather Sulayman had a reputation of being moderate and dedicated to seeking knowledge and being educated in jurisprudence. Finally, Muhammad Ibn Abd al-Wahhab's brother, Sulayman, was also a respected scholar in the region. Thus, it is difficult to imagine such a distinguished group of scholars could have fabricated their family tree in eighteenth century Arabia.

2: Birthplace of Ibn Abd al-Wahhab and His Mission

Ibn Abd al-Wahhab was born and raised in Uyaynah[39] which was located in the Najdi oasis of Ared. In the middle of a rough and sandy dessert, Uyaynah, at the foot of Mountain Touwaik, was considered to be of relative beauty. It had fresh water springs and wells in addition to palm trees and other vegetation.[40]

Ared[41] was a region that also included the city of Riyadh, the modern-day capital of Saudi Arabia, and Diriyah, the first center of the Saud family emirate. And it was in this region that the Shaykh and Muhammad Ibn Saud began their operations before expanding to other parts of the Arabian Peninsula. Najd lies in the middle of the Arabian Peninsula and is bordered by the Western Hills, Hijaz, Dahna', and Ahsa'.

According to the author of *Al-Dawlah al-Saudiyah al-Ula,*[42] the inhabitants of Najd were not ethnic Arabs. They lacked proper use of the Arabic language and did not write any proper Arabic poetry. Their contributions consisted of simple rhyming lines of poetry and widespread hymns in booklets and schools or Nabatean folkloric poetry. These are not comparable to the works found in *Diwan al-Arab*, for example. Furthermore, Najd was a melting pot of races and ethnicities from the Middle East and Africa in which foreigners married into native families.[43] Thus, claims of "pure" Arab ancestry made by Najdis are questionable.

• • •

Najd was an impoverished area in which the main concern for many was survival. The standards and practices of the desert ruled, even among the more affluent in residential areas. These standards were similar to those of the Bedouins who were scattered all over the oases and untracked desert.

In a desert society, the tribe is the source of power and authority. Adhering to its rules and norms is perceived as being the only possible way to protect oneself and absolutely necessary for survival. Thus, tribal members are not particularly concerned with the direction of their tribe and whether it is ethical or not. A famous line of poetry conveys this concept:

وهل انا الا من غزية ان غوت غويت وان ترشد غزية ارشد

"I am nothing but one who belongs to the tribe of Gazyah. If it deviates, so do I. And if Ghazyah is guided, I will be as well."

Chapter 1: Early Life

In these tribes, Islamic principles were observed only insofar as they did not conflict with tribal customs. Even then, knowledge of Islam was superficial.

• • •

A legendary desert motto says, "Support your brother, whether he is the oppressor or the oppressed." The reasoning was as follows: If you do not support your brother, you will be defeated. And if you deter him from oppressing others, you in turn will become oppressed. Conquering the land of others was a preventive measure and a way of ensuring one's own safety. Despite the emphasis upon justice and ensuring the rights of the oppressed in Islam, sociological studies of the desert regions in Arabia reveal that much of the desert culture remained.

• • •

The leader of the tribe is normally one who is admired for his generosity and courage by his fellow tribesmen as well as other tribes. In a demonstration of his noble traits and his power, he will provide feasts for his people. However, he extracts the price of such feasts (oftentimes many times over) by means of his share of war spoils, which is always guaranteed.

Tribesmen viewed each other as family, despite their social standing or whether they were Bedouins or city dwellers. Other than this bond, social ethics were not prevalent. Wherever they lived, these tribes would apply the rules of the desert. For instance, in the pursuit of arable land and water, disputes would be resolved by way of the sword. Left with no resources, the defeated would then look to defeat weaker groups. Thus, the culture of the desert is that of raids:

واحيانا على بكر اخينا اذا ما لم نجد الا اخانا

"Sometimes we attack our own brother, Bakr, if we cannot find someone else to attack."

The spread of Islam did not eradicate Bedouin laws, which were deeply rooted in their society. Alexei Vassiliev in *The History of Saudi Arabia*, writes concerning the primitive and prevalent practices of the Bedouins:

The Birth of Terrorism in Middle East

In the absence of a strong central government, the Bedouins often attacked others. Livestock was often a target for plundering. The looting targeted material for building tents, weapons, clothing and slaves. Items belonging to merchants were also pillaged just like harvests and farming equipment were pillaged from settlers.[44]

John Lewis Burkhart (d. 1817) said:

The Arab tribes were almost always in a state of war against each other. It was rare for a tribe to enjoy peace with its neighbors. On the other hand, war between two tribes seldom lasted for long, for it was easy to declare a truce. However, truces were broken for the silliest of reasons. The style of fighting was usually guerrilla warfare. Broad wars were rare and usually the main goal for either side in a fight was to surprise the enemy with an unexpected attack and to pillage its camp.[45]

Vassiliev writes of the role of raids in Bedouin society:

Raids were considered noble. The desire to pillage excited the Bedouins. Participation in raids was technically voluntary. However, in reality, the fighters, especially the young men, were unable to refuse participating. Such a refusal was costly, as it would be followed by accusations of cowardliness and loss of respect with the family and the tribe.

After one successful raid, the poor Bedouin could improve his financial situation and perhaps even become financially comfortable. Raids were a source of wealth for the tribe dignitaries, for the biggest and best spoils of raids were reserved for them.

Raids were headed by the tribe shaykhs, or, elders. A shaykh would receive a portion of the spoils even if he did not

Chapter 1: Early Life

participate in the actual raids. It is not a surprise, then, that the spoils of raids were considered among the most important sources of income for the dignitaries of the Bedouins.[46]

A well-known Bedouin phrase is: "Your neighbor does not have the right to be richer than you. If he does, he becomes your enemy and it is your right to attack him and loot his wealth." Thus, looting was an ingrained habit, especially since the direct result for the attacker is immediate wealth after poverty. This mentality was passed along to future generations.

It goes without saying that constant raids create an atmosphere of animosity among competing tribes. Furthermore, the lack of safety was not conducive to the establishment of viable cities or cultures.

• • •

In an effort to justify their raids, such tribes would exhibit courage and pride in non-aggressive situations. For instance, the people of Ared, the oasis that included Uyaynah, were "proud of their courage and patience in unfortunate situations. They boasted of their Arabian merits to their neighbors, the people of al-Quasim, who in turn actually felt superior to the people of Najd due to their education, knowledge, virtues and awareness of world events."[47]

These were considered attributes particular to Arabs.

If a particular deed exhibited a truly nomadic trait, it would be a source of pride for many of the inhabitants of Ared. Such deeds were perceived to have been a demonstration of the importance of a particular tribe by the strength of its sons and the ability to launch raids and wars and hoard grazing lands and water.

A close study of history reveals that the Bedouin tribal society of Arabia at the time of Ibn Abd al-Wahhab had regressed beyond its state before Islam. Strength and conquest were valued above all else. And these tribes succeeded in breaking off from the central governments of the Caliphate (the latest of which

The Birth of Terrorism in Middle East

was the Ottoman Empire) due to their distance from the capitals, centers of influence and civilization, as well as its lack of economic relevance.

According to Sate Al-Houssari:

> Around the first half of the eighteenth century, the region of Najd was divided into several small emirates, or, more accurately each town in the region was independent in its affairs, with its own prince who worked diligently to protect and administer. In turn, these princes held the ultimate authority in their emirates.
>
> The region of Najd was not subject to the rule of the Ottoman Empire at that time. This is known due to the fact that Najd did not appear on the lists that demonstrated the regional districting of the Ottoman Empire enacted at the beginning of the seventeenth century and which remained in effect until the nineteenth century. During this period, Najd did not have Ottoman representatives or Turks roaming within its boundaries.[48]

Dr. Abd al-Karim Ghourabiyah writes that this was due to the fact that the Ottoman Empire saw no particular benefit in administering Najd:

> The Ottoman Empire did not care much for controlling the interior region [of Arabia], for it saw no benefit in such control. However, the Ottomans did control the areas bordering Najd in the Hijaz and Ehsa'. But even this control was merely figurative, since its true control was in the hands of Bani Khaled from 1080 AH (1670 CE).[49]

The small emirates in Najd did not enter into political alliances with each other. Rather, the relationships between those emirates were characterized by disaffection and aggression. In Ared, the land that first witnessed the movement

Chapter 1: Early Life

of Ibn Abd al-Wahhab and Ibn Saud, the following families were in control of the most important towns (listed in order of influence):

- The Dawass family in Riyadh
- The Mouamar family in Uyaynah, the birthplace of Ibn Abd al-Wahhab
- The Zamel family in al-Kharej
- The Saud family in Diriyah, the birthplace of Ibn Saud,[50] a village that did not exceed seventy families

In such an environment, it was believed that one would either have to kill or be killed. This culture of violence was justified in lines of poetry, such as the following:

بسفك الدما يا جارتا تحقن الدما وبالقتل تنجو كل نفس من القتل

"It is by spilling blood, oh neighbor, that one's blood is preserved and by killing that one survives."

Furthermore, the lax laws of the desert provided justification for the spilling of blood and aggression under the pretense of providing for those who remained alive. In the absence of central authority, resources were not evenly distributed, meaning, only a portion of the population could be protected and receive access to water and grazing lands. These circumstances resulted in casualties that were normally reserved for times of war.

And it was in this chaotic environment that Muhammad Ibn Abd al-Wahhab was born. His people were one of the few skilled in agriculture and trade, though they were not spared from raids by their greedy neighbors. the Shaykh would provide a confusing and contradictory blend of varied concepts, values, customs, and religious and social practices, such that he arrived at his own particular understanding of the belief in the oneness of God. He called people to follow his understanding by the edge of his sword at the first opportunity. And Ibn Abd al-Wahhab was not concerned with whether or not his conclusions were consistent with those of the seminaries or other institutes of learning across the Muslim world, such as the University of al-Azhar and the seminary schools of Najaf, Karbala, Hilla, and Zaytuna. The son of the desert came to reform the desert according to his understanding and on the basis of his accumulated and inherited beliefs. Ibn Abd al-Wahhab applied the rules of the desert in his raids. Subsequently, entire generations of his admirers followed in his footsteps across two centuries. The Saudi state, which was established based on Ibn Abd al-Wahhab's ideology, dedicated tremendous resources specifically to the spread of his ideals throughout the Arabian Peninsula and beyond. The Saudi state produced tens of thousands of students and missionaries trained in Wahhabi thinking. These missionaries went on to teach Ibn Abd al-Wahhab's directives and his books, which call for violence and hostility on a global scale. In addition, several circles of international politics emphasized that the Shaykh (both during and after the nineteenth century) could serve as a point of balance in the conflicts of the region. These circles were incognizant of the consequences that would from their Wahhabi mentality, which has become the reference for all modern-day movements of extremism and terrorism, movements from which the peoples of the world, both Muslim and non-Muslim, continue to suffer.

3: The Religious Situation

The eighteenth and nineteenth centuries were a time of great conflict in the Muslim world. Islam has witnessed, since its inception, conflicts between the eminent people who were among the companions of the Prophet and those who were in power. It also witnessed the emergence of hereditary, autocratic kingdoms that adopted inhumane tactics in subjugating the Muslim world as they engaged in conquests that swept through vast swathes of the world.

It might be argued that had worthy leaders carried its message and expansion, Islam would have a different status across the globe. But despite the damage done by misguided individuals, this religion maintained its strength and

Chapter 1: Early Life

luster. The Muslim community, as is true for other human societies, does not necessarily reflect the ideals of its religion. It is made up of a people like any other, who have instincts, independent thought, and conflicting desires and are not above submitting to desires, instincts, fears, or ambitions. And adherents of a particular religion are only distinguished by their consciousness and commitment to the value system they inherit.

Historically speaking, there were many more wars amongst the Muslims themselves than there were wars Muslims fought against other religions. In addition, the methods of oppression used by Muslims were no less heinous than those in the attacks made by the Tatars, Mongols, and others. In cases of Muslim-on-Muslim warfare, the end goal was to defend the establishment and its interests. Religion, as is often the case, was but a banner to promote the interests and wishes of the elite and ruling class.

• • •

And deviant forms of Islam accompanied the rule of power-hungry caliphs. Al-Qadriyyah,[51] al-Murji'ah,[52] and al-Mujassimah[53] are just a few of the groups that created waves in the Islamic intellectual world. Earlier in history, challenges were made to Islamic theology by Ka'ab al-Ahbar, Abd Allah Ibn Salam, Wahhab Ibn Mounabeh,[54] and others, who imported the doctrines of other faiths into Islam by way of forged traditions. Furthermore, dream interpretation became of great importance. Some dreams were said to have demonstrated the virtues and exploits of some suspect "caliphs", mercenary scholars, and agents of the authorities.

• • •

Confusion ensued and the scarcity of reliable Islamic sources made it difficult to distinguish reliable information from superstition. Bigotry and bias on behalf of a particular school of thought became commonplace. Sectarian geographic borders began to appear and engulf the map of the Muslim world. Guilds were formed and the acceptable schools of thought were, for all practical purposes, limited to four in the Sunni world. However, the followers of the

The Birth of Terrorism in Middle East

Hanbali Salafi sect inspired by the movement of Muhammad Ibn Abd al-Wahhab reopened the door of *ijtihad* (deriving Islamic law) to every student, even to those who had very little background in Islamic law.

In this climate of controversy, conflict, division, illusions, myths, grave distortions, and gross intolerance of other sects spread in a sea of ignorance. Difficult times inspired some to revert to superstitious beliefs and practices. The remote location of Najd was a place of such ignorance and deviation. It would serve as a breeding ground for backwardness and intolerance.

• • •

According to a number of history books concerning the early days of Wahhabism, heresies and superstitions emerged among the sons of the Peninsula, especially in Najd, thus inspiring the mission of Ibn Abd al-Wahhab and his conquests that employed excessive violence. Below are some excerpts of relevance.

Fareed Mustafa wrote, "The people of Najd began revering their predecessors as saints and performing pilgrimages to their graves. They embraced their tombs, offered vows and pleaded with them to bring good fortune or prevent misfortune. This kind of behavior became ingrained in the people."[55]

Hussein Ibn Ghannam wrote, "The culture of visiting tombs and graves spread across the region. In al-Jabilah, the grave of Zayd Ibn al-Khattab was visited by the people of Najd for their belief that doing so would relieve their distress, fulfill their requests and dissipate their sorrow."[56]

Ibn Ghannam also wrote:

> In Feda, there were male palm trees known as Fahhal (non-fruit bearing trees). Men and women believed such trees had blessings and would visit them to obtain those blessings. The people of Najd believed in one tree called the tree of al-Zayb. Women would visit this tree after they give birth to baby boys and would hang old rags on it in order to prevent envy and

Chapter 1: Early Life

death from befalling their children. Women who were in need of husbands or suitors and women who sought to become pregnant would also visit this tree. Shaykh Muhammad Ibn Abd al-Wahhab would later personally descend upon that tree and chop it down. The people used to also believe that a large cave at the bottom of Diriyah miraculously cracked open for a woman, known as "the daughter of the prince," in order to protect her from torture at the hands of evildoers. People began sending offerings of meat and bread to that cave.

There was a man in al-Kharej named Tajj who people served as they would serve tyrants, such that people started pledging oaths to him, believing that he could bestow benefit or misfortune upon them. They visited him in droves as a sort of pilgrimage and fabricated myths and superstitious stories concerning him. The people of Najd did not stop there. They also slaughtered animals and would leave the meat in the open as offerings, claiming that the demons and devils would come and eat the meat, thereby earning the offering party satisfaction and safety from them.

In reality, such practices were not limited to the people of Najd. Rather, they spread to the rest of the Arabian Peninsula and its neighboring countries in the Arab world. Even the people of the Hijaz did not fare much better, for they deviated from the true religion and mixed religious beliefs with innovations and superstitions. For example, praying at gravesites became a common practice for most people. However, most would be frightened by the practices found at the grave of Khadija in Mou'la and at the dome of Abu Taleb, where worshippers asked these noble personalities for mercy and help.

Meanwhile, the religious situation was no better in places like Egypt, Yemen, Hadar Mouat, al-Shaher, Adan, Makha, al-Hadida, Halab, Damascus, Kurdish Iraq, al-Katif, Bahrain, or Ihsa'. Each of these regions had its fair share of graves, inanimate objects, plants, or shaykhs that were seen as a source of assistance and worthy of glorification.[57]

• • •

No one would argue with the apparent deviance of deifying graves or the belief in the supernatural power of trees, stones, and demons. Such practices are completely unrelated to Islam, and it is our duty to help others see the irrelevance and futility of such forms of worship. So what might be a possible source for these practices? Perhaps a repressed people sought an outlet and means of salvation from the harsh reality they faced in their lives, similarly to what primitive people did prior to being introduced to that which was revealed to monotheistic prophets.

• • •

The Salafi, or Wahhabi, movement condemned Muslims for their rituals. However, to properly assess their stance, it is important to ask some important questions, such as:

- Could reading the Quran and praying at the tomb of the Prophet or in any other mosque and begging God for His mercy and blessings be equivalent to asking for blessings from inanimate objects, stones, trees, or demons in caves and other such places?

- How might Muslims make an appropriate connection with the personality of the Prophet, who carried God's message to them?

- Has any relic from the past come back to life as a result of his death, or does he have a living presence in our mind, conscience, and life?

We will not discuss these matters, upon which a major Wahhabi paradox was based, in this chapter, leaving them for a later chapter as this topic is a major point of contention for the Wahhabis with most other Muslim sects. The

Chapter 1: Early Life

leaders of the Wahhabis confuse the affection that Muslims consign to their Prophet as a living entity with the innovations and superstitions of the ignorant. The Prophet was not a tree, a stick, merely a dead body, or a demon for them to prevent Muslims from visiting his grave, asking for his blessings, and begging for intercession through him to God.

Had this been the argument raised by the Shaykh in his calls for reform and launching raids and wars on his neighbors, despite the fact that only a portion of such neighbors were among those who resorted to stones, trees, and demons, then an objective discussion, using reason and authenticated prophetic narratives and traditions, is the proper gateway for a discussion on the legitimacy of the Wahhabi practices since the time of Ibn Abd al-Wahhab. Subsequently, the next generation of followers of Ibn Abd al-Wahhab were as unwilling as he was to engage in a reasonable discussion that would show that the Wahhabi practices were but an extension of the culture of raids, prevalent in the Arabian Peninsula for centuries — a culture born of the need to acquire gains and to satisfy the internal needs for control and bloodshed.

There is little doubt that the Shaykh resorted to the practice of religious raids as an excuse to establish his control over the region. A new generation of Salafi Wahhabis use similar such methods in order to impose their ideology on others. However, the tools, methods, and pretexts have varied.

Modern Salafis have adjusted their methods due to being faced with the challenge of a world of non-Muslims. The Wahhabi movement became more offensive in nature in the last two decades, especially at the beginning of the last decade of the twentieth century, after the second Gulf War and the Iraqi invasion of Kuwait[58] and its aftermath. This became even clearer after the Taliban and al-Qaeda gained control of Afghanistan and some areas in Pakistan.

But before discussing modern Wahhabi terrorism, we will delve into the Salafi-Wahhabi understanding of the concepts of monotheism and polytheism upon which their movement was built two centuries ago, along with the effects this culture has had on the Muslim world.

• • •

Sectarian geography prior to the time of Ibn Abd al-Wahhab yielded Najd as a district following the Hanbali sect. This area later became the cradle of the ideas of Ibn Taymiyyah upon which Ibn Abd al-Wahhab based and solidified his message.

Ibn Bishar mentioned in his account of early Wahhabi history several names of Hanbali scholars who had lived in the towns and villages of Najd. Students and scholars of this region learned the principles and origins of these sects.[59] Chief among them was Ahmad Ibn Yahya Ibn Atwah Ibn Zayd al-Tamimi al-Hanbali. He lived in al-Jabalyah and died in 948 AH (1541 CE). During his life, he taught the doctrines of the Hanbali sect to a number of future jurists, including Shihab al-Din Ahmad Ibn 'Abdullah, Ahmad Ibn Muhammad Ibn Musharraf, Sharaf al-Din 'Abul-Naga, and Musa Ibn Ahmad Ibn Musa. The latter had a major part in the refinement of Hanbali doctrine as well as its propagation. A great number of Najdi jurists adopted his teachings.[60]

As mentioned earlier, Shaykh Sulayman, grandfather of Muhammad Ibn Abd al-Wahhab, was a Hanbali jurist of Najd. And Muhammad's father, Shaykh Abd al-Wahhab, was a judge and jurist of the city of Uyaynah. Their houses were a meeting place for students of the Hanbali school.

The Shaykh himself also learned the Hanbali doctrine from known scholars as well as from his grandfather and father from an early age, although he did not delve deeply into his studies but, rather, obtaining a superficial understanding of Islamic law.

Despite the fact that the doctrine of Ahmad Ibn Hanbal was not particularly popular in other Islamic countries, it was predominant in the area of Najd to the point where every mention of a judge in Najd describes him as a

Chapter 1: Early Life

Hanbali. Also, every Hanbali jurist in Cairo or Damascus had Najdi teachers or students.[61]

Ibn Taymiyyah, a Hanbali jurist, was particularly popular in the region. In fact, it is possible the arrival of his books to Najd is why the Hanbali school became more popular in this region than in others. This supposition is supported by the fact that this literature had a significant impact on Abd al-Wahhab. He had studied some of these books and embraced the viewpoints of the author at an early stage, before his departure to seek knowledge outside of Najd,[62] as claimed by Wahhabi historians. However, Ibn Abd al-Wahhab would never reach the level of Ibn Taymiyyah.

The author of *Al-Dawlah al-Saudiyah al-Ula* refers to the history of Ibn Bishar when writing that some appeared among the scholars of Najd with tendencies of religious fabrication, known in Muslim culture as *bid'a* ("innovations") before the emergence of Ibn Abd al-Wahhab. Among these men was Uthman Ibn Ahmad al-Najdi (died in 1107 AH / 1685 CE) who authored numerous books in the field of Hanbali jurisprudence.[63] The scholar Marei Ibn Yusuf al-Najdi al-Hanbali (died in 1033 AH), who is also known as al-Azhari ("one who studied at Azhar"), recited the following lines of poetry in admiration of the doctrine of Ahmad Ibn Hanbal:

لَئِنْ قَلَّدَ النَّاسُ الأَئِمَّةَ إِنَّنِي   لَفِي مَذْهَبِ الحَبْرِ ابنِ حَنبَلَ رَاغِبُ
أُقَلِّدُ فَتْوَاهُ وَأَعْشَقُ قَوْلَهُ   وَلِلنَّاسِ فِيمَا يَعْشَقُونَ مَذَاهِبُ[64]

Translation:

> If people emulated different scholarly leaders / then I, indeed, yearn for the school of the scholar Ibn Hanbal I emulate his verdicts and I love his words / And people, in what they love, have various schools

Such literature demonstrates a tendency to blindly accept the Hanbali doctrine, which moved from moderation during the time of its founder, Imam Ahmad Ibn Hanbal, to extremism in later centuries. This extremism has lasted down to contemporary times by way of Ibn Abd al-Wahhab and can be observed in the speeches and practices of the new Salafi generations of this sect.

• • •

The precedents set by some of the followers of the Hanbali school (especially those who were not formally trained in Islamic law) indicate that, until recently, they fought several battles with members of other sects, first in their city of origin, Baghdad, and then in other places. This was not limited to verbal altercations or insults but extended into bloody raging battles.

These attacks oftentimes, due to biases with origins in the Umayyad caliphate, targeted the Shiah, or those who were loyal to the Ahl al-Bayt (the family of the Prophet). The Umayyads imposed severe measures on the imams of the Shiah and set a precedent that would be followed by later generations of authority, including many of the Hanbali school.[65] This could possibly be due to the resentment some Hanbalis felt towards the Shiah and other Muslims who showed great loyalty to the Ahl al-Bayt, which was perceived as being a sort of challenge to the caliphate. Such Muslims displayed this loyalty in the form of scholarship, politics, shrines, and places of worship.

This dedication to the Ahl al-Bayt was portrayed by some as a form of exaggeration or even deviance, arguably planting the seeds for Ibn Abd al-Wahhab's movement which would set out to destroy mosques and shrines built on the graves of the imams of the Ahl al-Bayt and other prominent Islamic figures. It might be argued that the Shaykh targeted such tombs and shrines without exception so as to not make obvious his agenda of diminishing the dedication shown to the Ahl al-Bayt.

Ibn Taymiyyah's interpretation of Hanbali law served as the basis for Ibn Abd al-Wahhab's reform while Najd provided a welcoming environment. Ibn Abd al-Wahhab considered Ibn Taymiyyah's views to be the solution for that which ailed the Muslim world. He was intent on explaining them and writing commentaries on them in an attempt to revive and sustain the call to this doctrine.

Chapter 1: Early Life

When implemented, this call results in a culture of violence. And due to the tremendous backing Salafi movements receive from institutions of terror, Wahhabism continues to spread among Muslims. In fact, it might be argued that the Muslim world is now living in the era of Muhammad Ibn Abd al-Wahhab, for he is present on the scene in a remarkable manner. His followers are ticking time bombs, determined to use terrorism, extremism, and violence to establish their authority.

Chapter 2: The Great Mission

1: Prior to Declaring the Mission

Ibn Abd al-Wahhab's life was dominated by three epic stages. In the first stage, which occurred before he declared his mission, he pursued knowledge of the conditions of the Muslim community. In the second stage, after declaring his mission, he formed a short-lived alliance with the prince of Uyaynah, Uthman Ibn Muammar. This stage lasted until he escaped to Diriyah. The third and final stage begins with his arrival in Diriyah, his alliance with Prince Muhammad Ibn Saud, and the declaration of the state of Saudi Arabia. This stage ended with his death in 1207 AH (1791 CE). These stages shaped the thoughts, ideas, visions, and orientations of the Wahhabi movement as conceived by its founder who spent his life furthering his cause. They also provided the basis for a strict policy as well as harsh methods used in dealing with other sects of Islam, oftentimes using the sword to express their disagreement.

• • •

It is important to note that what is known of the history of the life of Ibn Abd al-Wahhab is not based on verifiable firsthand accounts. Rather, much of that which is written comes from later generations and from anonymous sources. This is to be expected in such conditions as those in which the Shaykh

Chapter 2: The Great Mission

lived. His widespread influence (and the wealth and power of Saudi Arabia) could not have been predicted in his lifetime. Therefore, information about his travels, contacts, and biography (especially the early stages, before his alliance with Muhammad Ibn Saud) is vague and of questionable value, historically speaking.

Furthermore, a number of the historians in question were biased towards the Wahhabi cause. They prescribe to Ibn Abd al-Wahhab's way of thinking and are supporters of the state that sponsors him. Some of the most prominent such historians, whether biased or unbiased, include:

- Hussein Ibn Ghannam who died in 1225 AH (1810 CE), who wrote *Rawdat al-Afkar Wa al-Afham Li Mourtad Hal al-Imam Wa Ta'dad Ghazawat Zawee al-Islam* otherwise known as *Tarikh Najd* ("The History of Najd"). This historian is closest in time to the era of the Shaykh having died twenty years after Ibn Abd al-Wahhab's death. There is no doubt that he was absent during the first half of Ibn Abd al-Wahhab's life as he relied on accounts and hearsay for his work. In fact, it is evidenced in his writings that he may not even have met "the Shaykh" even though Dr. Abd al-Raheem al-Rahman indicated on page 476 of *Al-Dawlah al-Saudiyah al-Ula* that Ibn Ghannam was one of Ibn Abd al-Wahhab's most prominent students. Nonetheless, it is clear that Ibn Ghannam was influenced by his opinions, thoughts, and writings.

- Uthman Ibn Bishar al-Najdi died in 1288 AH (1810 CE), or eighty-one years after Ibn Abd al-Wahhab's death. He wrote *Unwan al-Majd Fi Tarikh Najd*. The accounts in this book begin in the year 1158 AH (1745 CE) which is the year the Shaykh formed his alliance with Ibn Saud, reinforcing the idea that Ibn Bishar was not a contemporary of the Ibn Abd al-Wahhab.

- Ibrahim Fasih Ibn al-Sayed Sibghat Allah al-Haydari, from Baghdad, died in 1882 AH, or ninety-three years after the death of "the Shaykh."

The Birth of Terrorism in Middle East

He wrote *Unwan al-Majd Fi Bayan Ahwal Baghdad Wa al-Basrah Wa Najd* in which he relates from Uthman Ibn Bishar al-Najdi. Thus, he could not have been a contemporary of Ibn Abd al-Wahhab. Al-Haydari, though, provided objective criticisms of the Ibn Abd al-Wahhab's doctrines, his thoughts, and his opinions concerning monotheism.

- Ahmad Ibn Zayni Dahlan, author of *Khulasat-ul-Kalam Fi Umaraa al-Bait al-Haraam,* died in 1304 AH (1787 CE), or seventy-seven years after Ibn Abd al-Wahhab's death. His work corroborates some of the content from historical works that are supportive of the Saudis.

- Rassoul Al-Karakoukli most likely lived a half century or more after Ibn Abd al-Wahhab's time for in his *Dawhat al-Wouzara Fi Tarikh Baghdad al-Zawra* he wrote of the events related to the Saudi raids on Iraq, events which occurred almost a half century after Ibn Abd al-Wahhab's death.

- Uthman Ibn Sanad al-Basari al-Najdi died in 1242 AH (1826 CE), or thirty-five years after the death of "the Shaykh." He wrote *Matali' al-Sa'ud bi akhbar al-wali Dawud* which did not cover the early stages of Ibn Abd al-Wahhab's life. However, his book is considered among the important sources recounting the Wahhabi raids on Ihsa' and some Iraqi regions.

- An anonymous author, with no mention of the date of his death, wrote *Lam al-Shahab fi sirat Muhammad Ibn Abd al-Wahhab.* His sources were ambiguous and included such phrases as, "we were told by someone who is trustworthy," "a man from Baghdad told us," and "I heard from some people in Basra…" This book was printed at a later date at the expense of the Saudi state, based on research by Ahmad Mustafa Abu Hakimah. The author was not a contemporary of "the Shaykh." It is most likely that the author was biased towards Ibn Abd al-Wahhab and the Saud family. However, Dr. Abd al-Raheem al-Rahman argues the opposite in his *Al-Dawlah al-Saudiyah al-Ula* (see page 485).

Chapter 2: The Great Mission

- Sulayman Ibn Samhan al-Najdi al-Hanbali died in 1349 AH, or 140 years after the death of the Shaykh. He wrote *Tanbih Dhawi al-Albab al-Salimah* and *Tabriat al-Shaykhayn al-Imamayn,* printed in Egypt in 1343 AH and Riyadh in 1410 AH, respectively.

- The Shaykh's letters, books, and other such documents concerning his beliefs, doctrines, and traditions are another source. It is believed that these documents have been preserved and, thus, reflect his understanding of Islam, particularly his opinions concerning monotheism which he defended by way of the sword. He began circulating his beliefs during his life. They would eventually become the backbone of Islamic culture in Saudi Arabia. Tens of editions of his books have been printed and enormous quantities of these books have been propagated across the world.

- As for other works concerning early Wahhabism, they are dated well after Ibn Abd al-Wahhab's movement and simply rely on other sources. These include Ottoman records and documentation of Muhammad Ali Pasha's campaign against the Saudis after they established their first state.[66] I will examine a number of these sources later on.

In general, I was unable to find a single historian who was a contemporary of the Shaykh and had written of the Shaykh's early life as well as his message before and after declaring his mission. Therefore, we should be cautious in dealing with the information available. However, much can be inferred from the Shaykh's overall mission and its implications and projections as well as from his books, the nature of his work and its social, psychological, and cultural impact.

• • •

By examining the following stories concerning the Shaykh, it is hoped that the reader will gain a better understanding of his life and purpose.

The Birth of Terrorism in Middle East

THE FIRST STORY

This story has been recounted by Uthman Ibn Bishar al-Najdi, the first official historian of the Saudi state, and Hussein Ibn Ghannam, the earliest historian to write about the Shaykh:

> At thirteen years of age, the Shaykh prepared himself to perform the rituals of the minor and major pilgrimages to Mecca. He also visited the tomb of the Prophet in Medina, where he stayed for two whole months. During that time, he saw observed polytheistic practice committed in the name of religion, thereby igniting a spirit of resistance to such acts.
>
> The Shaykh's quest for knowledge motivated him to study in the Hijaz. He would meet the Najdi scholar Shaykh Abd Ibn Ibrahim Ibn Yusuf in Medina. There he would also meet a scholar of great stature, Shaykh Muhammad Hayat al-Sindi al-Madani, who taught him and ordained him as a Shaykh.[67]
>
> The Shaykh returned from Hijaz to Najd where he remained for a short period of time before traveling to Iraq, where he visited Baghdad and Basra and remained for four years. In Basra he studied language and hadith under Muhammad al-Majmu'i, who was from the town of Majmu'ah, located in the heights of Basra. However, his experiences in Basra were not confined to his studies. In this city, the fanatic Shi'ites had the greatest influence, and the Shaykh was mortified when he saw the devotion they expressed towards their spiritual leaders and how they sanctified their graves and shrines under the banner of religion. The Shaykh voiced his criticism of such practices and he became a harbinger of his own beliefs about monotheism in his own councils. He personally described his beliefs by saying, "there were people among the heathens of Basra who came to me telling me of suspicious behavior, so I

Chapter 2: The Great Mission

would tell them that worship can only be made to God, which stunned them to the point of silence."[68]

Dr. Jamal al-Deen al-Shayal writes:

> The people of Basra became fed up with the Shaykh and his opinions. They carried a relentless campaign in opposition to his violent attempts at deterring them from revering revered figures in Islam. After they banished him from Basra, he set out for Syria. However, a lack of sufficient funds deterred him[69] so he chose al-Ahsa as his next destination. There he stayed with the scholar Shaykh Abd Allah Ibn Abd al-Latif al-Shaf'i al-Ahsai for a short period of time. Shortly thereafter, he went back to al-Huraymilah where his father lived. At the time, the Shaykh was about 35 or 36 years of age. He was fully-grown and the breadth of his education had widened. He was also more experienced as a result of his travels.[70]

The Second Story

This story has been recounted by Ibrahim Fasih Ibn al-Sayed Sibghat Allah al-Haydari:

> The Shaykh traveled from the town of Uyaynah to the House of God to perform his pilgrimage. When he was finished with his rituals, he went to Medina, where he studied with one of the leaders of the town of al-Majmu'ah, the knowledgeable Shaykh Abd Allah Ibn Ibrahim Ibn Yusuf al-Sayf. The Shaykh disapproved of the people's calls for help and intercession from the Prophet at his holy gravesite. The Shaykh overlooked the fact that the Prophet was the greatest medium and the best path to God Almighty, in this life and the hereafter, and that there is no difference in asking for the Prophet's help in this

life or the hereafter, during the Prophet's life or after his death. This is especially true since all agreed that the Prophet is alive and receives sustenance despite being in his grave. It has been narrated that the deeds of his community are presented before him. Such actions are not forbidden nor are they restricted, and God blesses the right behavior.

The Shaykh left Medina for Najd and then traveled to Basra with the intent to go on to Syria. After arriving in Basra, he remained there for a while and learned from the scholar Shaykh Muhammad al-Majmu'i from the town of Majmu'ah, a town in Basra. The Shaykh rejected the practices of the people of Basra and thus caused them annoyance. They set out to hurt him and expelled him from their city. In addition, harm also befell Shaykh Muhammad al-Majmu'i for taking in the Najdi Shaykh Abd al-Wahhab.

Shaykh Muhammad Ibn Abd al-Wahhab al-Najdi fled from Basra and was on the road between Basra and the town of Zubayr in the summertime during the intense heat of the season, travelling on foot. He almost perished from thirst. He ran into a man from the town of Zubayr named Abu Humaidan. The latter determined that the Shaykh was learned, so he gave him water and carried him the rest of the way to Zubayr on his donkey.

Shaykh Muhammad al-Najdi then decided to travel again but was short of money. For this reason, he abandoned the idea of traveling to Syria and instead set out for al-Ahsa. There he stayed with the knowledgeable scholar Abd Allah Ibn Muhammad Abd al-Latif al-Shafi'i al-Ahsai'i. He would later leave al-Ahsa for the town of Husaymilah in Najd where his father had moved from Uyaynah in 1139 CE.[71]

Chapter 2: The Great Mission

THE THIRD STORY

Sulayman Ibn Sahman al-Najdi al-Hanbali writes:

> Upon reaching puberty, the Shaykh's father promoted him as one who could lead prayers. The Shaykh then asked to travel to do the pilgrimage to the House of God, and his father accommodated his request. He proceeded to fulfill this obligation in Islam and completed the rituals in full. He then travelled to Medina, may the best of prayers and salutations be upon its inhabitants, where he stayed for almost two months. He then returned to his homeland in a state of contentment. He was preoccupied with reading jurisprudence according to the doctrine of Imam Ahmad. The Shaykh then travelled, seeking more knowledge, and tasted the sweetness of achievement and understanding, and he interacted with grand scholars. He also travelled repeatedly to Basra and Hijaz where he met worthy clerics and scholars.
>
> He arrived at al-Ahasa', which was, at the time, teeming with clerics and scholars. He listened, debated, researched, and benefitted from them and was granted support and success by God. He studied under Shaykh Abd Allah Ibn Ibrahim al-Najdi al-Madani, who ordained him as a shaykh.
>
> The Shaykh remained in Basra for a long period of time. There he studied hadith, jurisprudence and Arabic. He also authored books of hadith, jurisprudence and language to the extent to which God allowed.
>
> The Shaykh invited others to the monotheistic worship of God. He presented his beliefs to those who socialized with him or asked him for advice, saying, "Worship exclusively

belongs to God and it is not permissible to dedicate any of it to anyone but Him."

In his presence, the locals mentioned tyrants or some of the special blessings granted to dignified saints whom they would ask for assistance. He used to forbid them such practices and reprimand them for such behavior by citing proofs from the Quran and hadith. He warned them that to show love for spiritual leaders and the righteous, one merely had to follow their path in guidance and religion, such that they garner more good deeds. They must follow them in that which was presented by the master of the messengers [the Prophet]. Claiming love and affection while violating his tradition and path is not acceptable to the people of thought and truth. He firmly stuck to this belief, God rest his soul.

He later returned to his homeland where he found out that his father had moved to the town of Huraymilah. So he settled there, expounding upon and inviting others to the tradition of Prophet Muhammad."[72]

THE FOURTH STORY

This story was written by an unknown author; however, his book, *Lam al-Shahab Fi Sirat Muhammad Ibn Abd al-Wahhab*, was adopted by Saudi Arabia as a trustworthy source. The author provides his variation of the Shaykh's chronicles, which are slightly different from previous accounts by his colleagues:

> A trusted source said, based on accounts by some contemporaries of the Najdi Shaykh, Muhammad Ibn Abd al-Wahhab, that he pursued knowledge from his youth in an extreme manner. He was quick to understand and keen to learn. He studied under a man named Shaykh Abd al-Rahman Ibn Ahmad

Chapter 2: The Great Mission

from the town of Buraydah, having emigrated from his hometown. He remained in his company for sixteen years, studying Arabic grammar, conjugation and rhetoric. He also read hadith, including the books of al-Bukhari, Muslim and Ahmad Ibn Hanbal. He then followed Shaykh Hasan al-Tamimi in al-Qasim and studied the sciences of law and interpretation with him for seven years, eventually becoming very skilled, to the point that he was sought after for religious edicts.

When he turned thirty-seven years of age, he left Najd for Basra. When he arrived in Basra, he concealed his knowledge, dressed as one who was impoverished[73] and sat with wayfarers at the local mosque, accepting donations from passersby for basic sustenance. It was said that some merchants from Najd encountered and recognized him, but he denied knowing them when they asked him about his well-being and home. They started talking about him at gatherings in Basra saying, "Here we found a Shaykh from Najd with such knowledge, fame and intelligence. We ran into him yesterday and recognized him, but he denied knowing us. Be careful of him doing something in your land." They had become displeased with him as a result of him denying knowing them.

Some spied on him and figured out his identity. They asked about his story, but he would not answer them. So they went and complained about him to the governor of Basra, Umar Agha, who sent the police to follow the Shaykh and collect him. The governor spoke appropriately with the Shaykh and found him to be a rational and intelligent man with knowledge in the sciences and literature. He decided to host him for days and provided him with lodging and provisions. Many in Basra desired his company, among them Shaykh Inis, one of the most prominent men in the town. Being in the Shaykh's company became worthy of envy. The desire for his company was so great and created such large crowds that it is said that he would be seated on a chair and people would surround him, staring at him, as he told of strange narratives and provided bizarre explanations. This continued for four years.

Umar Agha was eventually replaced by Girgis Agha as the governor of Basra. Girgis Agha then appointed Husayn al-Islam Buli as judge of Basra in place of Shihab al-Din al-Musali. Judge Husayn was told of Shaykh Muhammad Ibn Abd al-Wahhab's reputation and decided to send the Shaykh a message saying that he would like to visit him the next day. The Shaykh welcomed the judge's visit.

The next morning, Judge Husayn went to visit Shaykh Muhammad Ibn Abd al-Wahhab, along with his students and followers. When he heard them arriving, the Shaykh went to meet the judge, welcomed him with a hug and seated him in the best seat. The judge told the Shaykh: "Shaykh, I am told that you tell unfamiliar stories, ones that are not in the books of the scholars. And you interpret the Quran in manners not authorized by God. Are you trying to cause conflict in our religion or are you confused about the methods of Muslims? If you do not refrain from such suspicious behavior, your blood will be spilt and your dignity harmed."

The Shaykh apologized and exhibited sincerity in his profession of innocence, showing his helplessness and weakness, saying: "A stranger, seeking knowledge, arrived in your land. If you are kind to him, you are among those who are generous to a guest. If you are not kind to him, there is no harm or shame in that."

When the judge heard these words from the Shaykh, he believed him. The Shaykh then left for his home. Less than

Chapter 2: The Great Mission

three days later, he sent him a message of reconciliation and invited him to live in his quarters. He also offered him the opportunity to teach Arabic and religion under his watch. The Shaykh quickly accepted the judge's offer and moved into his house and started teaching some of his followers the religious sciences. He beseeched the judge to teach him astronomy and engineering, since the judge was well known for his knowledge of mathematical sciences, especially these two disciplines. The judge taught him Euclid's *Elements* as explained by al-Ma'mun al-Abbasi and the astronomy books of al-Majsti and al-Jakmini.

He remained there for two years, after which, he suddenly disappeared from Basra without anyone's knowledge and walked back to Baghdad. Judge Husayn inquired as to the Shaykh's whereabouts. Eventually, a group from Baghdad visited him and gave him the news that the Shaykh was in Baghdad. The judge then said:

"I seek refuge in God from the evil of this man and his opinions. He would have destroyed the system of Islamic law had he not feared for his life. You will hear more of him later."

As for Shaykh Muhammad Abd al-Wahhab, he arrived in Baghdad and stayed at the Minister's school. There he studied theology under Shaykh Abd al-Rahim al-Kurdi al-Shafi'i.

A man from Baghdad told us that Muhammad Ibn Abd al-Wahhab stayed in Baghdad at the Minister's school for two years, never leaving his home, not even for the market. One day, after two years, he went out into a street without knowing where it led and without knowing any of the locals. He passed by a place where he saw a number of people arguing over inheritance, as they did not know how to divide it. He said to them: "I can resolve your conflict and show you the allocations of inheritance."

They decided to accept him as an arbitrator. He then asked them:

"How many heirs are you?"

They said, "Four men and five women."

He said, "How much money is this inheritance?"

He then told him the amount.

After an argument that lasted days and failing to agree to the arbitration of any outsider, Ibn Abd al-Wahhab was able to successfully divide the inheritance among them according to Islamic law. In that location, there was a large mosque with generous endowments. He asked to live with them and lead them in the Friday prayers as well as the rest of the daily prayers. They agreed to his request and provided him a residence. He then married a woman from that group who had both money and beauty. He stayed there for three years. His wife would later die, leaving him with an inheritance of two thousand dinars.

In the sixth year after his arrival in Baghdad, he set out for Kurdistan by foot. I am not sure as to the city or village in which he arrived, as the narrator of this story did not specify the actual name. I am limited in my narration to that which I have heard and have been able to verify. The Shaykh surveyed the Kurds' country town by town and village by village for an entire year. He then left set out for Iran and eventually arrived in Hamadan, where he stayed for two years, teaching and learning.

A strange aspect of the Shaykh's story is that he would change his name in each country. It was said he called himself

Chapter 2: The Great Mission

"Abd Allah in Basra," "Ahmad" in Baghdad, "Muhammad" in Kurdistan, and "Yusuf" in Hamadan. Thus, he repeatedly concealed his identity.

The Shaykh left Hamadan for Isfahan and stayed at the Abbasiyyah school that was built by Shah Abbas al-Safavi. This was toward the end of the Safavid era and the beginning of the sultanate of Nadir Shah. There, Ibn Abd al-Wahhab studied the peripatetic school of philosophy with Mirza Agha Jan al-Isfahani, the author of a commentary on *Sharh al-Tajrid*. He also studied the commentary of Mullah Ali al-Quawshaji on *Al-Tajreed* and the commentary of Sayyid Sharif al-Jurjani on *Sharh al-Mawakif* and *Hikmat al-'Ayn*. Less than four years later, he had completed his philosophical studies and began teaching the peripatetic philosophy. All of this was done while he managed to remain anonymous in Isfahan. The locals would say, "We have not seen an Arab complete the study of philosophy except this man." He then stayed in Isfahan for three years, pursuing studies in the wisdom of illumination and the ways of mysticism.

I heard some people from Basra say, "An A'ajami Isfahani man told us that after Muhammad Ibn Abd al-Wahhab completed his training in the wisdom of illumination and the ways of mysticism, he isolated himself from people for six months. And then, one day, he passed by a market in Isfahan wearing a green garb with his head uncovered as if he had become insane. Some people who knew him stopped him saying, 'Why have you let yourself fall into such a state?'

He answered, 'I used to know only myself before and now I know my Lord, and so I wanted to distinguish between the two states by uncovering my head. Were it not for being embarrassed, I would have stripped myself bare from my clothes and parted with my loved ones.'

He carried on talking and gesturing with both of his hands and a group of ten people followed him until he arrived and settled at his house. They asked permission to enter and, after he granted it, they said, 'Dear guiding mentor and rescuing teacher, enlighten us to what you are experiencing for, at this time, we accept you and at this time, we know you.' He then began teaching them mysticism and its methods. He continued instructing and attracting followers for an entire year. He suspected that if his approach were known, he would be killed and crucified, as he told his followers, 'Nobody is on the right path except us.'

He then left Isfahan en route to Ray. He passed by one of its villages with only a few dirhams. He stopped at a house to buy goods, as the village did not have a market. The owner of the residence invited him into his home. He entered the house and the owner asked him: 'Why do you come here?'

He answered, 'To buy some goods.'

So the owner of the house said, 'Let me go and get you some goods.'

The owner of the house then left and walked to the village chief complaining to him, 'There is an Arab man who had tricked me out of my money when I performed a pilgrimage to Najd and now fate has led him to our town. He is at my house at the moment. He came to buy some goods.' So the village chief told one of his servants to go and bring the man to him.

When the servant brought the man to the village chief, the latter said to him: 'This is your doing, you wicked Arabs.

Chapter 2: The Great Mission

You threaten those who come to your country and forcibly rob them from their rights and money! By God, you will not leave until you return all that you took from this man. Take him and shackle him.'

When Muhammad Ibn Abd al-Wahhab heard this, he said to the village chief: 'Did someone before me arrive to your village, or am I the first?'

He said this in order to cause a delay, allowing him to clear up the situation. He hoped he could get the village chief to take a liking to him and act in a just manner. The village chief answered him: 'This talk is irrelevant and we will not address it. However the money must be returned.'

Then, they brought wood, tied him up and beat him. Muhammad Ibn Abd al-Wahhab then realized that none of his questions would be answered and none of his words would be heard. He was bound and oppressed regardless. He said: 'Ask him about the amount he is demanding.'

So he said, 'such and such.'

It turns out that the amount was large."

The narrator told us that in the end, they took all of the Shaykh's money and possessions, except his books for they had no use for them. So he left that village with one of his followers, a Baghdadi man name Ali al-Kazzaz. He arrived to Qum and stayed there for a whole month without becoming acquainted with anyone. He was needy and had limited resources. He had to sell some of his books for food. He then left, travelling towards Rome, and came across a caravan from Rome, from the town of Abi Libas. They took him with them. They traveled through the desert while he told them stories of the Arabs in Turkish, so that they could understand. They admired him for his Arabic and Turkish eloquence. When he arrived to Abi Libas with them, they honored him and collected a generous amount of money for him so they were able to outfit him and host him properly. Many people in Abi Libas followed his chosen path, that of the doctrine of the scholar jurist Ahmad Ibn Hanbal. This doctrine did not exist in Abi Libas prior to the Shaykh's arrival, for they followed the doctrine of Abi Hanifah as was common in the Roman countries.

The Shaykh then left Abi Libas and went to Halab where he stayed for six months, teaching Arabic. He was asked about philosophy, and he said, 'I know nothing about it.' This was one of his strange behaviors, for he would occasionally reveal his knowledge while concealing it at other times.

He then left Halab, going from village to village until he arrived in Damascus where he stayed for one year. The narrator did not tell me of the events of that year. The Shaykh then left Damascus and went on to Hebron in Jerusalem where he remained for two months. I have been told that Muhammad Ibn Abd al-Wahhab then left Jerusalem and went to Egypt where he stayed for two years. He resided at the Azhar mosque in Cairo and learned the science of astrolabe and numerology at the hands of Shaykh Muhammad, also known as Zayn al-Din, nicknamed Abu Abd Allah al-Maghribi.

He then descended to the Suez and rode a ship to Yanbu'. He entered Medina and stayed there for a few days. This coincided with the time for the annual pilgrimage, so he performed a pilgrimage of the house of God. It is said that he met with Shaykh Abd al-Ghani al-Shafi'i who, at the time, was the jurist of Mecca. They spoke, and Shaykh Abd al-Ghani acknowledged the Shaykh's virtue and positive attributes. This

Chapter 2: The Great Mission

was during the days of the government of al-Sharif Surur, so the latter, along with the elders of Mecca, asked the Shaykh to remain there. But he refused and left Mecca intending on going to Najd.

When he arrived to Buraydah, they recognized and honored him and inquired about his condition and his travels. He told them his story. He then walked to Uyaynah, where he a group of people tried to kiss his hand, though he prevented them from doing so. They called him their master and their safe haven, as was the people's habit in recognition of their scholars and prominent men. He then said to them, "I do not see anyone worthy of that title except God Almighty."

He stayed in Uyaynah no more than a day, and then walked to Arid, as it was his birthplace and hometown. He set foot in a town that was familiar to him, the same town in which Musaylimah al-Kadhib declared himself a prophet during the days of the Prophet Mohammed in the eighth year after the Prophet's migration. [As the story goes,] Bani Hanifah followed him and, by doing so, they saw him as partners with Prophet Mohammed in his message."[74]

2: The Pedigree of Ibn Abd al-Wahhab

The author of *Lam al-Shahab* said about the pedigree[75] of Muhammad Ibn Abd al-Wahhab:

> He was a worthy scholar, as was gathered from his travels. The narrators said:
>
> It was among his characteristics, before his innovations even emerged, that he would cheerfully salute all those he

passed, regardless of their status in society. He would forbid sinful behaviors as much as he could, and he was satisfied with very little in life when more was not easily available.

It was said that one day, before his travels, there was a gathering of people discussing the state of the world and the gathering of money and the creative ways to earn it. A man, named Sulayman Ibn Raid al-Unayzi, a merchant famous for doing good deeds in the area, said to Muhammad Ibn Abd al-Wahhab: "You are a man of little money and many children." At the time Muhammad Ibn Abd al-Wahhab had three wives, two sons, and two daughters. "I am giving you such and such of my money, he said. "Take it and travel to the Roman countries, areas such as Halab and Damascus. You can have half of my profits from trade you conduct, even though I would have given any other man only a third. [I am giving you a larger share in order] to honor you." The others in that group signaled to the Shaykh that he should accept the offer and proceed in his travels. However, he refused saying, "If I become a trader, I will become a captive of humiliation and greed and I will miss out on the peace of mind of seeking knowledge and good deeds. The Provider endows us with subsistence, so I do not pursue it in a manner that distracts and tires." The point is that he was not one seeking to amass abundant wealth.

It has been narrated by some people from Najd that Muhammad Ibn Abd al-Wahhab was very hospitable to guests, and he rarely ate his lunch or dinner in his own house with his children, but rather he used to take his food to a table set up outside of his house. It was commonplace for the people of Najd to build such tables outside of their homes for hosting others. It was also the Shaykh's habit that, if he had a guest who wanted to leave, he would give him some of what

Chapter 2: The Great Mission

he could afford, a practice that was not commonplace in that town. It was also said that he used to prefer his neighbor over himself and that no one ever heard him curse anybody another person.[76]

3: Historians Who Favored the Shaykh

The narrations written by pro-Wahhabi historians concerning his travels before declaring his mission do not amount to more than that which was mentioned above. Those four were clearly biased toward the Shaykh and favored his explanation for the excessive obsession and condemnation of the people's call for intercession by the Prophet at his holy gravesite despite the criticism directed at the Shaykh by Ibrahim Fasih Ibn al-Sayed Sibghat Allah al-Haydari.[77]

One can conclude the following from these texts:

- These historians tend to portray the Shaykh as an exceptional person. Some even depict him as one who was chosen by God to act as a reformer. Later historians would elaborate upon this further. This was done even though the earlier historians were not actually among the Shaykh's contemporaries. Rather they related from unknown narrators.

   It was also noted by these historians that Shaykh Muhammad Abd al-Wahhab possessed great intellect, memorizing the Quran before the age of ten and composing books at a rapid pace. His father acknowledged benefitting from his young son and promoted him as a leader of prayers. The Shaykh supposedly used to silence his opponents with powerful and amazing proofs. He was the victim of multiple assassination attempts but was saved through divine intervention each time.

   On the other hand are stories that seem to contradict this narrative, such as those of his father being concerned for the Shaykh's future and the reservations of contemporary scholars about the Shaykh's inclinations. One such scholar was his own brother, Shaykh Sulayman Ibn Abd al-Wahhab who died in 1210 AH He expressed his concern in the form of a book, *Al-sawa'iq al-ilahiyah fi al-radd 'ala al-Wahhabiyah*, with expressions like the following: "The characteristics of those who will attain salvation have been described by Islamic scholars, and you do not possess any of their characteristics." He also wrote another book in response to the Wahhabi movement called *Fasl al-Khitab fi al-radd 'ala Muhammad Ibn Abd al-Wahhab*.[78]

- The historical authenticity of these texts is highly questionable. This can be observed in *Lam al-Shahab*, a book that provides an account of the formation of the first Saudi state and has recently been printed at the expense of the current Saudi government. *Lam al-Shahab* portrays the period before the Shaykh as one of darkness and the period after the commencement of his mission as an age of successful religious and social reform.

Lam al-Shahab presents questionable narratives as history and, thus, resembles fiction. The author contends his narrators are reliable and contemporaries of the Shaykh and claims he was committed to telling the story based on input from trusted sources. It seems apparent that he was aware that his sources would be questioned and not easily accepted. He begins with phrases such as the following:

"We were told by a trustworthy source on behalf of some of the Shaykh's contemporaries…"

"We were told by a Baghdadi man…" (when the issue was related to the Shaykh's time in Baghdad).

"The narrator did not specify the name of a city in Kurdistan…"

"I am bound in these papers to say only what I heard or confirmed…"

"It was said…"

Chapter 2: The Great Mission

"I heard from some people in Basra…" (when the issue related to the Shaykh's time in Basra).

"We were told by an 'Ajami (Persian) man…" (when he talked of the Shaykh's life in Persia).

"The narrator said…"

"Some who told us stories about Muhammad Ibn Abd al-Wahhab told us…"

"The narrators said…"

"It was told…"

"We were told by some people in Najd…" etc.

Thus, he relies upon uncorroborated content by anonymous narrators.

- The Shaykh appears as a mysterious man. This is perhaps intentional and a dramatic representation intended to impact the imagination of a simple, normal human being. An example is the Shaykh concealing his identity in countries he visited during the twenty years of his lengthy travels from Najd to Basra, Baghdad, Kurdistan, Persia, Turkey, Damascus, Egypt, Jerusalem, and then the Hijaz, before returning to his native Najd.

In addition to creating an element of awe, the ambiguous nature of these stories suggests the Shaykh arrived at the truth about knowledge and monotheism through his endless patience, perseverance, and determination. This made him worthy of restoring the Prophet's mission which was scattered after the infiltration of polytheism in its ranks. He alone was qualified to correct the deviation of Muslims and repair their affairs.

When he arrived in Basra, Ibn Abd al-Wahhab concealed his identity even from Najdi merchants who recognized him as they harbored enmity towards him. However, it was also these merchants who testified to his knowledge and fame. For he was a clever intellectual, and, as the Arabic saying goes, "one's virtue is confirmed when the enemies bear witness to it."

The following phrases found in the texts mentioned above warrant contemplation:

"He left Basra in disguise," "He lived in Baghdad in the Minister's school for two years and did not leave it to go to a market or a street," "A strange thing in the Shaykh's story is that he would change his name in each country," "In Isfahan, he completed the study of all of the peripatetic philosophy in four years and he had started teaching it, all while he remained anonymous," "He isolated himself from people for six months," "He suspected to himself that if his situation became known, he would be killed and crucified," "He arrived in Qum and stayed there for a whole month without becoming acquainted with anyone," and "This was one of his strange behaviors for he sometimes revealed his knowledge in some places and other times, he concealed it."

It is worth asking how Ibn Abd al-Wahhab could teach, attract followers and devotees, and become the focus of the people in cities unfamiliar to him despite remaining unrecognized and not knowing the language of the locals. In the following examples, one observes the contradictory aspects of the story of a man who somehow managed to remain anonymous and, yet, heavily engaged with society:

"Omar Agha, the governor of Basra, found him to be a rational and intellectual man with knowledge in the sciences and literature," "The desire for his company was so great and created such crowding that it is said that he would be seated on a chair and the people would surround him, staring at him,

Chapter 2: The Great Mission

as he told strange narratives and provided bizarre explanation," "The Basra judge offered him a job teaching Arabic and religion... The Shaykh quickly accepted the judge's offer and started teaching instrumental and religious sciences. The judge taught him Euclid's *Elements* as translated by al-Ma'mun al-Abbasi and the astronomy books of al-Majsti and al-Jakmini," "In Baghdad, he studied the science of theology," "He solved a baffling inheritance issue in Baghdad when no one else was able to resolve it," "He became imam for a large mosque with generous endowments in Baghdad and got married without anyone recognizing him," "The Shaykh surveyed the Kurds' country town by town and village by village for a whole year," "Surely, he spoke the Kurd language well," "He lived in Hamadan for two years, studying and teaching," "This would have been in the Persian language, and maybe he mastered it on his way to that country," "In Isfahan, he stayed at the Abbasiyyah school where he sought knowledge in the peripatetic school of philosophy at the hands of Mirza Agha Jan al-Isfahani who has a commentary on *Sharh al-Tajrid*... He studied with him the exposition of Mullah Ali al-Quawshaji on *Al-Tajreed*, and then he studied the writings Sayyidd Sharif al-Jurjani on, *Sharh al-Mawaqif*, followed by studying the book *Hikmat al-'Ayn*. Less than four years later, he had completed the study of the peripatetic philosophy and he had started teaching it. All of this was done while he remained anonymous, and the people of Isfahan did not know from what kingdom he hailed from or to what religion he belonged. They would say, 'We have not seen an Arab complete the study of philosophy except this man.' He then stayed in Isfahan for three years, pursuing studies in the wisdom of illumination and the ways of mysticism," "He was seen as an authority on mysticism, attracting followers for an entire year," "When he travelled to Rome with a caravan, he reportedly told them Arabic stories but in their own language, or, Turkish," "He spread the doctrine of Ahmad Ibn Hanbal among them after they had been following the doctrine of Abi Hanifah," "In Halab, he denied his knowledge in philosophy," "In Cairo, he learned the sciences of astrolabe and numerology," "The jurist of Mecca acknowledged his virtue and perfection and proposed that he reside there," "In Uyaynah, he was surrounded by a group of people trying to kiss his hand and calling him their master and their safe haven, as was the people's habit in recognition of their scholars and prominent men, so he said to them, 'I do not see anyone worthy of that title except God Almighty,'" "He would cheerfully salute all those he passed, regardless of their status in society," "He would forbid sinful behaviors whenever he could," "He was often offered lucrative work but he refused it."

Based on these accounts, the Shaykh was familiar with a number of languages (Arabic, Persian, Turkish) and was well educated in numerous fields. He also impacted the lives of many. However, despite all of this, he was capable of remaining anonymous wherever he went.

• • •

- There is a clear contradiction between the account of the author of the *Lam al-Shahab* and other historians who said that the Shaykh returned from his travels when he was thirty-six or thirty-seven years old. However, the author of *Lam al-Shahab* indicated that the Shaykh actually began his travels when he was thirty-seven and that those travels lasted for approximately twenty-eight years, meaning that the Shaykh returned to his country when he was sixty-five years old.

- That author of *Lam al-Shahab* also stated that the Shaykh had three wives before he started his travels. This was not mentioned by other historians.

Chapter 2: The Great Mission

- According to *Lam al-Shahab*, the Shaykh delved deeply into the fields of theology, mysticism, and illuminationism. He also told his followers in some of his speeches that they alone are on the correct path. And yet, he would later target the Sufis, the Illuminationists, and the people of theology as did his predecessor, Shaykh Ibn Taymiyyah. Furthermore, his knowledge of these sciences has not been made apparent in his works.

- He reportedly mastered the Persian, Kurdish, and Turkish languages to the point where he started teaching locals in their native languages. However, there is no evidence in his works that suggests that he studied these languages.

The contents of *Lam al-Shahab* conformed to the agenda of the first Saudi family. For this reason, this book was adopted as a historically reliable source, regardless of potential fabrications and exaggerations.

4: Mr. Hempher

At the same time of the release of the book *Lam al-Shahab* (which seems to have been developed for the benefit of the Shaykh and his allies from Al Saud and to flatter them) there was another book that was supposedly published by a British intelligence officer simply identified as "Hempher." In his book, he clarified how he managed to recruit the young man, Muhammad Ibn Abd al-Wahhab, to work with him after failed attempts to subdue him with women, alcohol, and the like.[79] This book could potentially explain the mysterious thirty-year disappearance of the Shaykh as mentioned by the author of *Lam al-Shahab*. The dates of the two books seem to be close both in their accounts and in their events, while no other historians speak of that period in the Shaykh's life.

This British officer indicated that he had a direct relationship with the Shaykh after meeting him in Basra. The Shaykh worked with British agents to raise doubts in the minds of simple people about a number of Islamic practices,

The Birth of Terrorism in Middle East

some prevailing customs, and some traditions. He also colluded to stir up trouble and wars in the Arabian Peninsula which later paved the way for the British to infiltrate and extend their influence.

The officer also recounted how he and a number of his colleagues disguised themselves as slaves purchased from Basra by Ibn Abd al-Wahhab. They accompanied him to Najd to spread his theories. These were among the finest British officers, trained in the Arabic language and desert wars, sent there by the Ministry of the Colonies.

Regardless of the political motives of the British, it appears from Hempher's memoirs that they sought to establish entities that would be loyal to them even after the death of the "sick man." The "sick man" presumably is a reference to the Ottoman Empire. The influence of the Spanish, Dutch, and Portuguese in the region was declining, so it was a good opportunity for the British to gain influence. The British had perceived that region as being important and aimed to be next in line to control its resources and wealth in the long term. Their costs for such a move were limited to sending a few warships to accompany their commercial vessels. Perhaps they were vying to control the region, ahead of other nations, after the disintegration of the Ottoman Empire became evident at the beginning of the eighteenth century.

It is natural that after the failure of military actions on the grounds of holy wars, economic and cultural wars would follow. It was also natural for the British Empire to abandon the colonial powers of old and start a new role of invading the Muslim sanctuaries in the area. They infused its experts and researchers from various disciplines, as well as its spies, to better understand the Peninsula whose wealth, topographic, and demographic composition remained almost unknown.

Some historians have written that the meeting between Shaykh Muhammad Ibn Abd al-Wahhab and Shaykh Muhammad Ibn Saud was facilitated by the British intelligence. According to this narrative, the British were preparing the two shaykhs (one as the shaykh of the religion, the other as shaykh of the tribe)

Chapter 2: The Great Mission

to forge an alliance based on the formation of a religious government under their leadership. This was done in an effort to replace the Ottoman Empire with weaker entities after its imminent fall. These new governments would then be subject to control by the competing empires. The British government would, of course, be at the forefront of that control.

There are indications in history that the British government encouraged the Shaykh's movement based on intolerance.[80] Perhaps as a result of British support, the Shaykh was able to attract large groups of nomads who lacked formal education. He would proceed to create doubts concerning Islamic practice and claim that most sects had apostatized. To this day, the Shaykh's movement continues to attract hundreds of thousands of followers throughout the Muslim world, vast numbers of which adopted his militant policies to be used against those they deem deviant on the pretext that such Muslims showed devotion and visited the graves of saints. These behaviors were considered analogous to idol worship as it was in the early days of Jahiliyyah, or The Era of Ignorance.

5: The Memoirs of Hempher

According to Hempher's memoirs, the British worked to infiltrate the heart of the Arabian Peninsula and increase sectarian and tribal conflict. While the Wahhabi movement was, on the surface, motivated by religion, the ultimate goal would have then been to destabilize the region and its tribes and establish a system with primary allegiance to an extremist organization.

According to this narrative, Hempher saw an opportunity in the Shaykh. He was fully aware of the Shaykh's background up until the time of his coming to Basra and staying at the inn of Safia, a Jewish agent for the Ministry of the British Colonies. That inn was also one of the headquarters for the British intelligence. It was reported that Shaykh Muhammad had abandoned the clothes of a religious student at an early age, as his father began to groom him for the judiciary position in his hometown. It is said that Hempher met the Shaykh at

The Birth of Terrorism in Middle East

the inn and that he was a very moody and ambitious young man.[81] It can be deduced that this would have been between the years 1713 and 1720 CE and that the Shaykh's age would have just surpassed eighteen years. Thus, based on this narrative, the Shaykh would have been too young to master the many sciences that he was claimed to have studied by the historians mentioned earlier.

For instance, the author of *Lam al-Shahab* had indicated that before his travels, the Shaykh had studied for sixteen years with a Najdi scholar, and then for another seven years with another scholar in jurisprudence and exegesis. At this point he became so skillful that he was sought out for edicts.[82]

Based on the narrative of *Lam al-Shahab*, the Shaykh would have been a great scholar before his travels and at least thirty-seven years old. This, of course, contradicts the other accounts given, even those of Wahhabi historians. It has been proven that he was a young man when he commenced his travels; or rather when he escaped his father's control. That could be the reason behind the change in his name in Basra to Abd Allah (as per *Lam al-Shahab*) when some Najdi merchants recognized the Shaykh and asked him about his situation and place of residence.[83]

It is possible that Muhammad Ibn Abd al-Wahhab escaped Uyaynah for a relatively distant place, the religiously and culturally diverse city of Basra, due to some urgent matter. In Basra, he could evade those who sought him. The busy city also provided him with anonymity if he wanted to act on his whims. The period of his escape from Uyaynah and his father's supervision lasted more than twenty years, spent in unknown locations. This period was not discussed by any historian other than the author of *Lam al-Shahab*, which is of questionable authenticity. It then appears that Ibn Abd al-Wahhab committed mistakes that were considered to be unforgiveable by his father.

• • •

According to Hempher's memoirs, Ibn Abd al-Wahhab was seen as a worthwhile investment that would continue to produce for decades. For this reason,

Chapter 2: The Great Mission

he encouraged him and convinced him that his movement was a noble one. Hempher writes:

> I forged between myself and Muhammad the most powerful of relationships and links. And I would always inflate his ego and show him that he was more talented than Ali and Umar and that if the Prophet were present, he would have chosen him as his successor without question. I would tell him, "I hope the renewal of Islam happens at your hands, for you are the only savior we can hope for to pull Islam out of its current tumble."[84]

Hempher reportedly posed as a Muslim from Azerbaijan, perhaps in an attempt to gain Ibn Abd al-Wahhab's trust. As a result of Hempher's encouragement, the Shaykh would intensify his efforts for spreading his ideas and increase his criticisms of religious practice in Basra. This led judge Husayn Islambuli, as was reported by the author of *Lam al-Shahab*, to threaten him after hearing the Shaykh's criticisms that were not, by his judgment, grounded in scholarship or the Quran.[85]

Reportedly, Muhammad Ibn Abd al-Wahhab and Hempher engaged in debates and the latter appeared to be quite knowledgeable and well versed in some aspects of Islamic heritage and history. This allowed him to affect young Muhammad's ideas and beliefs as Ibn Abd al-Wahhab was not particularly accomplished in Islamic scholarship. He was eager to criticize Islamic practice and inclined towards extremism as was mentioned by the author of *Lam al-Shahab* as well as the author of these memoirs. The author of *Lam al-Shahab* and Hempher both agreed that Ibn Abd al-Wahhab travelled to Persia during the period of anarchy of the last days of the Safavid state and before the restoration of order by Nadir Shah between 1722 and 1736 CE.[86]

Hempher's agenda was twofold:
- To destroy the remnants of Ibn Abd al-Wahhab's core values

The Birth of Terrorism in Middle East

- To direct him to establish a radical form of Islam. Ibn Abd al-Wahhab was willing to accept such a role, believing that with his intuition and abilities, he would be able to change the beliefs of the Muslims.

Later, the Shaykh would find young Bedouin followers who saw an opportunity in potential raids and the spoils of war and were thus intrigued by the Shaykh's ideas. They were also impressed by the extent of his vast influence. This gave the Shaykh and his Wahhabi followers confidence in their cause.

When comparing *Lam al-Shahab* and Hempher's account, one can recognize a number of similarities though the latter seems to be more direct, perhaps because Hempher's writings were not intended for publication. They rather appear to be personal and private accounts of his mission assigned by the Ministry. It is worth asking why certain details of the Shaykh's life were mentioned in these two sources but not in other accounts, especially since many of these accounts went to great lengths to mention the details of his life before and after the period in question.

• • •

British intelligence may have seen an opportunity in Ibn Abd al-Wahhab while failing to take into account the long-term effects of the Wahhabi movement, which became a cradle for religious terrorism. After sponsoring alliances and apparent partnerships with the leaders of this plan, particularly in the last century, the British have lost the sympathies of a great number of Muslims due to the practices of the Saudi state and its disregard for human rights under the pretext of adhering to Islamic tenets.

Hempher reportedly influenced Ibn Abd al-Wahhab's opinions of jihad. He mentioned in his memoirs that they had many debates on such topics and that the Shaykh would always adopt Hempher's views. He also said that he contacted some Christian women who worked at the Ministry of Colonies. He chose one of them to establish a sexual relationship with the Shaykh on the grounds that it was a temporary marriage. He also encouraged him to drink

Chapter 2: The Great Mission

alcohol since mixing it with water makes it non-intoxicating. It was, therefore, not forbidden by the religion.[87]

Hempher also mentioned that luring Muhammad Ibn Abd al-Wahhab to alcohol and prostitution was based on the advice of the Minister of Colonies.[88]

Hempher's plan was to make Ibn Abd al-Wahhab rebel against Islamic scholarship and interpret the Quran according to his own whims. The Shaykh claimed that his new doctrine was different from all others, Sunni or Shiah, and the only accurate interpretation. He claimed to represent all people with an Islamic heritage. With that, he relied on his fabricated proofs to declare other Muslims, who were led by the Egyptians and the Syrians, as infidels. And, as such, he launched raids and wars against them.[89]

Wahhabism would indeed become the seed of instability and underdevelopment in the region for two centuries. During this time, the confrontational Wahhabi core, with its Bedouin majority, grew by the spoils of increasing raids. These spoils were a great form of financial and psychological incentive. War became the main ingredient in Wahhabi culture despite an alleged embracement of religion. The Wahhabi movement could not have succeeded in regions like Egypt, Iraq, or Syria as such civilizations differ greatly from the culture of the Bedouins.[90]

6: IBN ABD AL-WAHHAB'S ESCAPE FROM BASRA

The authors of books concerning the Shaykh's life, including Ibn Ghannam, the author of *Lam al-Shahab*, and Hempher,[91] agree that Shaykh Muhammad began spreading his message and raising objections to Islamic practice while in Basra. It is also agreed that he was warned about such behavior and was subsequently detained in the judge's house until he was able to escape in 1139 AH / 1727 CE. This is the same date that was mentioned by Ibn Ghannam and then repeated by other historians. It also corresponds to the date given by Hempher.

The Birth of Terrorism in Middle East

Salah al-Deen al-Moukhtar said, in relaying Ibn Ghannam's words about the Shaykh's escape:

> On the way, the Shaykh became extremely thirsty and he ran into a muleteer named Abu Humaidan from Zubayr who was riding his donkey. The Shaykh was at death's door so the muleteer gave him water. He then had him ride the donkey until they reached Zubayr and then doubled his spending money.[92]

Saudi accounts place great emphasis upon Abu Humaydan even though he is only mentioned in passing. It would seem that emphasizing his story was meant to distract from other names that were mentioned in books and memoirs. This causes doubt concerning Abu Humaydan's true identity. Furthermore, one might ask how a poor muleteer, from the lowest echelons of society and who owned only a donkey, could increase the Shaykh's provisions. Also, why would Abu Humaydan be travelling from Basra to Zubayr without having a client to earn some of his money and eat his leftover food? Is it feasible that he was travelling just for recreation until he found a client?

Hempher's account provides some insight into the mystery of Abu Humaydan, who appeared in the Shaykh's path as soon as he was able to escape. Abu Humaydan was loaded with provisions, water, and money for expenses but had no client with him to Zubayr. This means he must have been in a good financial situation. It then becomes clear that Abu Humaydan likely represents one of two people: 1) Safia, the Shaykh's mistress to whom he was married for personal gain and who was an agent recruited by Hempher. She accompanied the Shaykh to Baghdad, Kurdistan, Hamadan, and Isfahan. 2) One of the recruits chosen for this task by others. His job would have been to safely deliver the Shaykh to his birthplace after he fully comprehended his assigned tasks.

It should also be noted here that the author of *Lam al-Shahab* wrote that when the Shaykh went to Yamamah from Basra, he had a number of slaves (perhaps seven or eight) and that each of these slaves was a trained and armed

Chapter 2: The Great Mission

fighter. It was also said that the Shaykh had money with him. This is incompatible with Ibn Ghannam's account in which the Shaykh was alone and almost perished from thirst.

One possibility is that the officers of the British Ministry of Colonies were able to secure the Shaykh's release from the governor's prison in Basra and to deliver him safely to Yamamah. This allowed the Shaykh to carry out the tasks that were asked of him in exchange for safety from his adversaries among various governments and scholars.[93]

According to his memoir, Hempher caught up with the Shaykh in Najd and they agreed that he would present himself as the Shaykh's slave, purchased from Basra.[94] Later on, the Ministry sent another eleven officers trained in the language and desert combat, and they too presented themselves as the Shaykh's slaves.[95] This, to a certain extent, aligns with the story by the author of *Lam al-Shahab* where it was mentioned that the Shaykh had with him a number of slaves, even though the actual number varied. This explanation negates the existence of Abu Humaydan in general and thus stands in contrast to Saudi accounts. It seems implausible that the Shaykh could have come back with abundant money, a wife, and slaves when he was banished from Basra's prison alone and without enough water to last the journey. The appearance of Abu Humaydan at that crucial moment can then be understood to be an attempt at enhancing the credibility of the Saudi narrative.

Chapter 3: Declaration of the Mission

The Second Journey: From Uyaynah (Yamamah) to Diriyah

1: In Huraymalah

Shaykh Muhammad Ibn Abd al-Wahhab returned from his first journey to Basra and Baghdad to Najd and to Huraymalah (his father's adopted place of residence after leaving Uyaynah[96]). It was in Huraymalah that the Shaykh started spreading his message:

> He started denouncing their polytheistic acts and intensified his condemnation of their actions. Soon arguments broke out between him and his father and then between him and the people of Huraymalah. However, the Shaykh humored his father until the latter's death in 1153 AH / 1740 CE.[97]

Perhaps his father's open opposition, as well as that of his brother,[98] could have extinguished the Shaykh's mission in its infancy. As they were close family members, it does not appear that their opposition originated from personal animosity. Furthermore, they presented particularly effective arguments against his

Chapter 3: Declaration of the Mission

cause. Therefore, Muhammad Ibn Abd al-Wahhab was cautious in his behavior and declarations until his father's death.

After his father's death, Shaykh Muhammad openly declared his mission and his position became widely known in the towns of Ared, Huraymalah, Uyaynah, al-Diriyah, and Riyadh. He soon found sympathizers in these lands. He also authored *Al-Tawhid al-ladhi huwa haqq Allah 'ala al-'abid*.[99]

While his father was alive, the Shaykh was protected from the people's anger due to the father's moderation and rejection of the Shaykh's radical ideas. Therefore, as soon as his father died, the Shaykh felt compelled to leave Huraymalah and return to Uyaynah, his birthplace.

It was reported by Fareed Mustafa[100] that living in Huraymalah did not suit the Shaykh. He did not perceive it as the proper environment for spreading his mission, especially since the slaves of one of its two tribes threatened to assault and kill him. It was also noted by Dr. Abd al-Raheem al-Rahman[101] that it was said that the Shaykh's return to Uyaynah was due to an invitation from its prince. The latter sent this invitation after being informed of the intensity of opposition the Shaykh faced from the people of Huraymalah.[102]

Huraymalah was only a small stop (albeit an uncomfortable one), and its memories were not pleasant. The Shaykh's mission was neither heeded nor accepted there, and his father and brother were at the forefront of the opposition.

2: In Uyaynah (Yamamah)

Al-Yamama, or Uyaynah as it was later renamed, was the most famous town in the Ared region, and it was the town from which the Salafi Wahhabi movement was launched. Ared was among the largest and most beautiful oases in Najd, rich with fresh water wells and springs, palm trees, and legumes.[103] It was located near Riyadh, Diriyah, Huraymalah and other towns and villages.

The Birth of Terrorism in Middle East

It was said that at one point more than six thousand households inhabited the area. In the days of Muhammad Ibn Abd al-Wahhab, it had about three hundred households.[104] Nasir al-Saeed writes:

> The area covered by Uyaynah was about forty square kilometers. It was packed so tightly with houses that on days of celebrations or local events women would exchange greetings, conversations and news from their windows. News would travel quickly across town due to the compactness of the houses.[105]

According to *Lam al-Shahab*:

> Al-Yamamah was the town where Musaylamah al-Kadhdhab claimed to be a prophet in the days of the Messenger of God, in the eighth year after Hijrah. He was followed by the people of Hunayfah, who also claimed a share in the Prophet's message. When Abu Bakr assumed the caliphate, he sent an army of his companions and supporters by way of Yemen until they entered into Najd. They fought the people of Hunayfah, who were the followers of Musaylamah in al-Yamamah, and they triumphed over them, killing and capturing many of them, as was told was Ibn Khalkan, al-Tabari, and Ibn al-Jawzi in their historical accounts.[106]

It has been narrated that the Prophet of God predicted the emergence of strife and the manifestation of the devil's horns in Najd. He would say, while looking east in the direction of Najd, "Sedition is right there where the horn of the devil rises."[107] Such traditions are noteworthy as they appeared in books of hadith (narrations from the Prophet) highly regarded by Islamic scholars. Shaykh Sulayman Ibn Abd al-Wahhab, in his answer to his brother Muhammad Ibn Abd al-Wahhab, wrote:

> If the Prophet had realized that the eastern countries, especially Najd, the town of Musaylamah al-Kadhdhab, had

Chapter 3: Declaration of the Mission

become the house of faith, that the victorious sect would be in that region, that faith would appear in that region—even though it is not absent from others—and that the region of the Two Holy Mosques and Yemen would become ones of disbelief where idols are worshipped, rendering migration away from those countries obligatory, he would have informed us of such happenings. He would have prayed in support of the people of the east, especially the people of Najd. He would have prayed against the people of the region of the Two Holy Mosques and Yemen. He would have informed us that they would worship idols and we should absolve ourselves from them. However, the reality from the Prophet was precisely the opposite.[108]

It was in Najd, and especially in Yamamah, that the Shaykh was born and raised. It was here, too, that he later spread his message with the help of its prince, Uthman Ibn Hamad Ibn Muammar. Researchers have noted that the geographic isolation of Najd affected the manners, temperament, and habits of its people such that rebellion, individualism, and Bedouin independence were better documented in Najd and Ared than in other regions.

The factors mentioned above were contributing factors that helped transform Najd to an environment of sedition and cultural upheaval. Raids became commonplace, and the need to prevail persisted through the centuries creating a continuous state of emergency.

The estrangement and harsh treatment of the majority of the Bedouins and town dwellers created a hostile environment. People lived in a near constant state of fear, knowing that the enemy was always watchful. The emergence of a religious movement transformed the culture of raids into a godly struggle. This was seen as a means to achieve two goals: victory and spoils of war in this world and martyrdom. The majority of those who accepted the Shaykh's call tended to be groups in the Najdi society who were not trained in Islamic studies. Thus, their lack of awareness of Islamic law led to them believing that the

Shaykh's understanding of Islam and his ideas about monotheism were the only acceptable opinions. Other interpretations were dismissed as being polytheism or infidelity. And the Shaykh's works promoted a form of Islam that emphasized raids, murder, and theft. According to Ibrahim Fasih Ibn al-Sayed Sibghat Allah al-Haydari, the Shaykh's radical opinions were a result of the Shaykh not learning Islamic law in its proper context, or in the presence of other scholars.[109]

Since there was much to gain in terms of power in the region as well as war spoils, a form of Islam was promoted with the idea that the sword would separate the people of hell and the people of paradise and sedition resulted in bloodshed. Without this belief, it is highly improbable that the Saudi nation would have been founded.[110]

3: Ibn Abd al-Wahhab's First Sponsor and the Retribution of Sennemar[111]

The author of *Lam al-Shahab* writes:

> Uthman Ibn Muammar al-Taymimi was frequently victorious in battle and had scores of soldiers and great wealth, as his city was the largest in Najd. It was also the most productive in crops and exports, and its people were more obedient to their ruler than their counterparts.[112]

Shaykh Muhammad Ibn Abd al-Wahhab sought refuge with this prince:

> They agreed to establish this order and religion and to work according to Islamic law. They also agreed to dismiss all other doctrines and sects in Islam as well as other religions. Many in Uyaynah agreed with them, including the elite who served Ibn Muammar and his court. Some people in Uyaynah did not agree with this order, but Muhammad Ibn Abd al-Wahhab carried on for a while in that town. It is believed

Chapter 3: Declaration of the Mission

that perhaps some people from Najd heard about his activities and came to him in Uyaynah. They pledged allegiance to him towards the end of the year 1150 CE. The other elders in the rest of Najd were not happy about the growth and expansion of that religion.[113]

Prince Uthman Ibn Muammar received the Shaykh "with salutations, open arms, and a full welcome. The Shaykh started spreading the truths of monotheism, and Prince Uthman provided him protection and support against his enemies."[114]

Wahhabi historians have written that the Shaykh returned from his first journey with a mission in mind. This mission, from his perspective, was to incite change that would eradicate established beliefs, concepts, and practices. Thus the quest to destroy mosques and domes built over the tombs of revered figures, including the dome above the Prophet's grave, began.

No one was safe from being declared an unbeliever or idolater. Adopting the Shaykh's view of monotheism was the only protection from the seizure of one's wealth and the spilling of his blood. Thus, those who did not accept the Wahhabi school of thought were considered polytheists or apostates according to his views and were told to repent and join his ranks.

Ibn Abd al-Wahhab presented his mission as one that would take Muslims back to an era of prosperity. He was to save them from impurity and diversions. His understanding was based on traditions that required scrutiny in evaluating the text and the chain of narrators. But he interpreted them based on his own personal opinion.

It is not my intent in this chapter to discuss the details of the Shaykh's mission. I will address his mission in detail in later chapters. However, here I must mention that this mission coincided later on, in the third stage of his epic and difficult quest, with the mission of an ambitious partner. The latter realized that joining forces would lead to the establishment of a vast emirate. There, both could enjoy prestige and power. The Shaykh's ideas provided the needed legitimacy to establish such an emirate on the ruins of tens of small chiefdoms and emirates in Najd and elsewhere, including the emirate of Ibn Muammar in Yamamah and Ibn Dawas in Riyadh.

This mission also coincided with continuous rejection of the Shaykh's ideas in his community and others to which he had traveled in Hijaz and Iraq, among other places. He had been subjected to harassment and assassination attempts from which he supposedly escaped, as mentioned in his biography.

Perhaps these occurrences, and the fact that a number of Bedouins sympathized with him, directly resulted in his insistence on his plan and spreading it. However, these sympathizers were not formally trained in religion. It is important to recall that the men of religion in the Shaykh's community were opposed to his ideas and theories. Most of these religious men were Hanbalis and included his father and brother (Shaykh Sulayman). This is the reason why he did not openly speak up about his ideas while his father was alive. His brother, however, responded to Wahhabi ideas and what he deemed "innovations" with the two books mentioned earlier.

However, the generation subsequently taught by the Shaykh in Diriyah provided mentors, missionaries, and students who accompanied raids and subdued the resistance. This generation would become the inspiration for the large numbers of Wahhabi scholars and jurists that we see today. They are all the product of the Shaykh's school and the product of his unique understanding of religion. Their roots began when he started spreading his ideas by force of arms. This is supported by the testimonies of those who wrote about Ibn Abd al-Wahhab's life, such as Ibn Bishar and Ibn Ghannam.

• • •

Mahmoud Shekri al-Alusi writes in his book, *Tarikh Najd*, that when the Shaykh returned to Huraymalah, he remained by his father's side and studied under his supervision. He would also denounce the people of Najd in regards to their faith. His father forbade him from such behavior, but he would not

Chapter 3: Declaration of the Mission

desist. This led to a dispute between him and his father. There was also much controversy between him and the Muslims in Huraymalah. This went on for two years until his father's death in 1153 CE. At that point, he, along with his followers, dared to show their beliefs and to openly denounce Muslims in their practices. This led to his countrymen becoming fed up with his movement. They planned to kill him, so he moved from Huraymalah to Uyaynah. There he was able to entice its governor, Uthman Ibn Hamad Ibn Muammar, with control over Najd. Uthman helped him, and he too denounced Muslims. Some people in Uyaynah followed him and destroyed the dome of Zayd Ibn al-Khattab in al-Jubaylah, making the Shaykh more prominent. Word of this reached Sulayman Ibn Muhammad Ibn Aziz al-Hamidi, who was governor of Ahsa', Qatif, and their subsidiaries. He sent a letter to Uthman threatening the latter if he did not kill the Shaykh. So Uthman sent for the Shaykh and ordered him to leave his kingdom. The Shaykh then offered him control of Najd in return for his support. Uthman would not listen to him so, in 1160 CE, the Shaykh left for Diriyah, the country of Musaylamah.[115]

The Shaykh acquired collaborators and devotees in Uyaynah and Uthman Ibn Muammar was at their forefront. He proceeded to destroy many domes and mosques, including the dome of the mosque where Zayd Ibn al-Khattab was buried in Jubaylah. He also worked tirelessly to cut down trees that were considered holy to the Bedouin inhabitants of the Najdi territory. Chief among those trees was the famous Zib tree. He also stoned a woman who he claimed had admitted to him that she had committed adultery. In fact, Ibn Muammar participated in the actual stoning, and it was said he was the one to cast the first stone. Such news about this mission and its advocate spread across the Peninsula in a manner that scared the Shaykh's enemies, both scholars and princes.[116]

The story of the stoning of a woman who allegedly admitted her guilt to the Shaykh was not mentioned by most of the writers of the Shaykh's history. Rather, these historians stated that the Shaykh's other acts, such as the demolition of domes and the cutting of trees, led to his infamous reputation.

The Birth of Terrorism in Middle East

Shaykh Sulayman Ibn Samhan writes:

> The Shaykh asked Prince Uthman to cut down a tree that was being worshipped in that town and to destroy the dome of Zayd Ibn al-Khattab, but the prince refused. The Shaykh persisted and eventually persuaded the prince to grant him his request. The Shaykh then asked the prince to march with him to cut down that tree, which he did along with six hundred horsemen. When they arrived at their destination, near the town of Jubaylah, the tree was cut down and the dome was destroyed. This was among the most dangerous undertakings by the Shaykh. After completing it, he became well known. News of his undertakings reached the Prince of al-Ahsa, Sulayman Ibn Muhammad, who was known for his strength and power. He sent a message to Uthman Ibn Hamad Ibn Muammar threatening to cut off his salaries and to march on him if he does not expel the Shaykh from his country. Uthman then permitted the Shaykh to travel to a place of his choosing and he chose Diriyah. When the Shaykh left for Diriyah, Shaykh Uthman sent with him a group of his own men to protect him from his enemies until he reached his destination.[117]

This story contradicts the previous story that indicated that Shaykh Uthman Ibn Muammar sent only one horseman to accompany the Shaykh and that he had ordered that horseman to assassinate the Shaykh on their route. Perhaps the previous story was told in order to prove that Shaykh Uthman was not a believer in the Shaykh's message, to demonstrate his treachery and to illustrate that, from the Wahhabi perspective, he deserved death after that incident.

The author of *Lam al-Shahab* recounted two different stories about the life of the Shaykh in Uyaynah. Both stories mentioned the occurrence of serious controversy, including actual fighting regarding the Shaykh. Both stories also agreed that the elite of the dignitaries and scholars were not on the Shaykh's side, save for the people of Ibn Muammar.[118]

Chapter 3: Declaration of the Mission

Observations About the Beginnings of the Mission and the Personality of Ibn Abd al-Wahhab

In light of what historians wrote about the Wahhabi movement, we can make some observations about his presence and activities in Uyaynah. There, he openly announced his mission, or "religion," as it was sometimes referred to by supporters of its prince, Shaykh Uthman Ibn Muammar al-Tamimi:

- By reviewing the Shaykh's cultural and educational background, we learn that his studies were not based on an accepted curriculum in any of the accredited schools of theology, nor was he taught by renowned teachers.

The Shaykh only spent time in Medina, where he mentioned meeting only two scholars. It should be noted that this account has not been corroborated. Also, two months is not regarded as being sufficient for completing religious studies, even if the two individuals with whom he studied were grand scholars.

The education acquired during his childhood likely consisted of rudimentary reading, writing, arithmetic, etc. Therefore, it cannot be considered adequate to have become a scholar capable of issuing edicts. In addition, we cannot, based solely on his booklets and letters, assume that he possessed an exceptional level of genius, even if Wahhabi historians have made such claims.

He grew up in a family that was familiar with theological issues, but there was no doubt that at such a young age he could not have understood scholarly theological debates. He lived with his brothers, including Shaykh Sulayman. However, none would rise to a position of prominence other than the Shaykh.

I could not find any account that described the Shaykh's teacher in Basra, Muhammad al-Majmu'i, as a famous scholar. Perhaps he would not have been mentioned at all had there not been claims that he taught the Shaykh in the early stages of his life.

The Shaykh's desire to get rid of the shrines and mosques built on the graves of famous Muslims may have been the result of al-Majmu'i's personal experiences in a society that revered the Prophet and his family in a manner that did not agree with his interpretation of Islam. From the time of the Umayyad caliphate, certain extremists have disagreed with such practice. Such schools of thought viewed calling upon the Prophet and his family for help and caring for their mosques and shrines as fanatical exaggeration.

Perhaps al-Majmu'i is also the one who drove the Shaykh, from an early age, to adopt his unmoving beliefs about polytheism and faith and to divide people into two categories based on their views of holy gravesites.

- The Shaykh was greatly influenced by Ibn Taymiyyah who was known as a hardliner and for his bias to Umayyad ideologies. Ibn Abd al-Wahhab was also influenced by Ibn Qayyim al-Jawziyyah.

Perhaps the Shaykh's conflict with his father, Shaykh Abd al-Wahhab, was based on the son's adoption of the radical theses of Shaykh Ibn Taymiyyah and his consideration of them as proper Islamic sciences. In addition, this conflict could have been due to his call to conversion by the sword. This is contrary to the father's approach as he had learned from established scholars.

- Abd al-Wahhab, the Shaykh's father, warned about his son and was opposed to his cause. Additionally, the Shaykh's brother, Shaykh Sulayman Ibn Abd al-Wahhab, responded to his brother with a book, *Al-sawa'iq al-ilahiyah fi al-radd 'ala al-Wahhabiyah*. Sulayman fought off the invasion of the Wahhabi Saudis to the region of Najd. He also instigated the people of Huraymalah and moved them to rebel against the Wahhabis in 1165 CE. A year later, they attacked Diriyah. In 1168

Chapter 3: Declaration of the Mission

CE, Abd al-Aziz Ibn Muhammad Ibn Saud invaded their city and defeated them. He placed Shaykh Sulayman Ibn Abd al-Wahhab under house arrest after he refused to surrender to his brother and refused to convert to his brother's ideas. Other Najdi and Hijazi scholars were also opposed to those ideas, but they were forced into silence or exile after the Wahhabi Saudi forces took control of the area.

- Due to the position of his father, brother, and other Najdi scholars, the people of Huraymalah strived to kill or at least banish the Shaykh in accordance with the desires of the people of Uyaynah. This was in spite of the support the Shaykh received from the prince Uthman Ibn Muammar.[119]

- The Shaykh first declared his mission in his book, *Al-Tawhid wa huwa haqq Allah 'ala al-'abid* while in Uyaynah and he subsequently proceeded to publish and teach it.

- The Shaykh found popular support among a group of Bedouins. They helped him establish a broad coalition that would later become the core of his mission, especially after the move to Diriyah and joining forces with the ambitious Muhammad Ibn Saud. Some people were dazzled by his mission and joined him in Uyaynah. The efforts to attract more people in Diriyah were expanded, and willing soldiers already sympathetic to the Shaykh's ideas were recruited. This group of Bedouins would become a semi-structured coalition under the encouragement of Ibn Muammar and the Shaykh. They evolved into an armed movement that organized campaigns to demolish domes and uproot trees. Their armed movement drew the attention of some admirers in Uyaynah and elsewhere, and those admirers joined their ranks.

Despite their small size in the initial stages of their movement, the Wahhabis drew widespread attention to themselves in all areas of Najd. Many of the inhabitants of those areas perceived them as a possible danger to their tribal customs and the social norms of their clans.

The Birth of Terrorism in Middle East

- The statements of historians confirm that the Shaykh was aware that his path would not be easy. This was established during his first journey to Basra when he was expelled and nearly died on the road. This was further confirmed in Huraymalah where his father and brother were at the forefront of his opposition. They were followed by most of the townspeople who tried to kill him after the death of his father. This was also confirmed later in Uyaynah where the locals fought each other concerning the Shaykh.

  Ibn Abd al-Wahhab knew that he had to use force in order to accomplish his mission. However, he did not put his own life in danger, as evidenced by historical accounts of his raids, battles, and conflicts.

- In Uyaynah, the Shaykh behaved as though he was the head of an Islamic government. This was evident in his punishment of an allegedly adulterous woman, even though the conditions for that punishment stipulated in Islamic law were not met. He also applied his own interpretation in regards to the shrines and mosques. He destroyed the shrine of Zayd Ibn al-Khattab and declared his intent for the other shrines, including that of the Prophet. His radical inclinations raised real concerns and first caught the attention of the Hanbali religious scholars in Najd. They were followed by those in Hijaz, al-Ahsa, and other neighboring towns. These scholars expressed their objections at the outset. Soon objections were raised to the Wahhabi movement across the entire Muslim world.

- According to the author of *Lam al-Shahab*, the Shaykh amassed huge amounts of money both before leaving Uyaynah as well as during his journey: "He had gathered a lot of money during his travels and had purchased seven or eight slaves from Mecca." He was careful with his money and refused to leave Uyaynah without his wealth with him. This is in contradiction to the statements by the same author that the Shaykh was not interested in amassing wealth.[120]

Chapter 3: Declaration of the Mission

- Many historians revealed the Shaykh to be harsh and unforgiving. Regardless of the underlying reasons, this attitude also became characteristic of his followers. They would not show flexibility in dealing with others and were known for their roughness, excessive extremism, and violence.

THE CONTROVERSY SURROUNDING THE DEATH OF IBN ABD AL-WAHHAB'S FIRST ALLY

Uthman Ibn Muammar al-Tamimi al-Najdi, the governor of Uyaynah, was the first sponsor and ally of Shaykh Muhammad Ibn Abd al-Wahhab. It was from his town that Wahhabism was launched and spread to neighboring areas.

Earlier, the events in Uyaynah and the public reaction to those events were mentioned. These events led to the termination of the partnership and the governor's withdrawal of his protection for the Shaykh. The latter escaped with his family to the town of Diriyah, the home of Muhammad Ibn Saud, the Shaykh's new ally.

In the following pages, I will present some of that which has been mentioned concerning Ibn Muammar as well as his subsequent assassination:

- Ibn Muammar was reportedly no less ambitious than the Shaykh or the Shaykh's new ally, Muhammad Ibn Saud. He stood to gain from the Shaykh's mission in terms of conquests and legitimacy.

  Ibn Muammar encouraged his servants, bodyguards, and some of his close associates to join the Shaykh's movement and receive his instructions in monotheism. He even personally participated in the demolition of a known shrine, the uprooting of a tree, and the stoning of a woman. He also invited the residents of neighboring areas to hear the Shaykh's call.

However, despite initially hastening to support the Shaykh, Ibn Muammar would later abandon him. This was due to the condemnation of the Shaykh by influential entities across the Peninsula, from his own people and relatives and from the Shaykh's relatives from Tamim. Some even attempted to kill the Shaykh and exile him. They were on the verge of carrying out the Shaykh's assassination before the Shaykh asked to be allowed to leave voluntarily.

- Wahhabi historians loyal to the Shaykh agreed that the Shaykh tried to persuade Ibn Muammar to allow him to remain in Uyaynah and that he promised Ibn Muammar victory, power, large sums of money, and abundant spoils if he continued to support him and his religion. Such historians presented the Shaykh as a prognosticator who guaranteed his success due to his connection with God. Furthermore, they implied that these promises became a reality for Muhammad Ibn Saud and his descendants after they supported the Shaykh and his mission.

- It would appear from the available historical documents that Uthman Ibn Muammar was compelled to abandon the Shaykh and exile him from his city. This was due to the problems Ibn Abd al-Wahhab caused and the arrival of the message from the governor of al-Ahsa, Muhammad al-Hamidi. It is possible similar such messages were sent from other regions. Ibn Muammar, thus, elected to betray the Shaykh. According to Ibn Bishar, this was because he did not understand the value of monotheism.[121] But Ibn Bishar himself mentioned in another edition (left for his grandchildren in al-Zubayr) that Uthman Ibn Muammar did not harm the Shaykh. He also did not order his companion to kill him along the way to Diriyah.[122]

- After the Shaykh's escape to Diriyah, his influence and strength grew and his raids against the neighboring areas were successful. Ibn Muammar would eventually be forced to participate in such raids as he was concerned that he would be perceived as an infidel, polytheist, or a hypocrite if he did not.[123] Hussein al-Shaykh Khazal writes:

Chapter 3: Declaration of the Mission

In 1159 CE, Uthman Ibn Muammar participated in the attack that Diriyah launched against the city of Riyadh. However, in 1160 CE, he neglected to participate in Diriyah's subsequent attack on Riyadh, so he attacked it by himself. He feared being accused of hypocrisy and betrayal. He went to Diriyah to offer his apologies for not participating, and he promised the Shaykh and Muhammad Ibn Saud that he would support with them whenever asked. They believed him, and they promised him that he would be appointed commander of their next army.[124]

Ibn Muammar was later suspected of conspiring with the two princes of Riyadh and Tharmada'a to fight against Wahhabism. He apparently asked the Shaykh to come to Uyaynah to meet with those two princes, but the latter refused for fear of such a conspiracy.

According to the aforementioned historian, the people of Diriyah did not appear averse to Uthman. Rather they gave him the general command of their campaign against Riyadh in 1161 CE. This campaign involved people from Diriyah, Huraymalah, Dharam, and Uyaynah. They subsequently gave him the general command of another campaign against Riyadh. This one included the people of Manfuha. Prince Abd al-Aziz Ibn Muhammad Ibn Saud was also under his command.

However, despite such support and despite Abd al-Aziz's request to do so, he refused to enter Tharmada'a despite it being empty. He entered the town later but only destroyed its crops and he did not fight its people. The two allies saw his refusal to enter Tharmada'a as evidence of his treason.

In reality, Ibn Muammar was a strong contender to the Saud family. Simply by remaining alive, he could deprive them of their anticipated leadership. Thus, accusations of apostasy and betrayal were only an excuse to murder him and remove a competitor.

The Birth of Terrorism in Middle East

- Two years after leading the last invasion alongside the Shaykh and his ally, Muhammad Ibn Saud, Uthman was assassinated in the mosque of Uyaynah. Ibn Bishar writes:

  Uthman Ibn Muammar was killed in 1163 CE in the Uyaynah mosque following the Friday prayers. The people selected to execute him indicated that they verified that Uthman had betrayed them by working with their enemies. They said that he had received a message from Muhammad Ibn Afalik, a scholar from al-Ahsa, inciting him against the Muslims, or rather, against following the Wahhabi call, and against his allegiance to the two allies. This was at the time that the daughter of Ibn Muammar was married to Abd al-Aziz, and he was the grandfather of his son Saud al-Kabir. When Uthman was killed, Saud was still an infant, less than two years old. When he completed his prayers, his killers went to him and killed him. Some of the more well known of his killers included Hamad Ibn Rashid, Ibrahim Ibn Zayd al-Bahili, and Musa Ibn Rajih. This was in the middle of the month of Rajab in 1163 CE.[125]

Judgment had been passed against him and plans to enact his sentence had already taken place. The reasons given for his sentencing included apostasy, polytheism, and hypocrisy.

One might ask, how could Uthman have been a polytheist and yet been allowed to lead the Friday prayers? Furthermore, how could such accusations be true when he clearly was one of the most important supporters and followers of the Shaykh? The answer is that the Shaykh's other ally had ambitions to expand his control over Najd and its neighbors, and the Saud family did not desire to share the spoils of war.

Uthman was apparently aware of Muhammad Ibn Saud's intentions to subdue Najd, including Uyaynah. And Uthman was not eager to

Chapter 3: Declaration of the Mission

support him in his bloody plans for expansion. Muhammad Ibn Saud, in turn, remained watchful of Uthman's behavior, particularly because of his past oppositions.

The killing of Ibn Muammar was a big scandal for the Shaykh's supporters, and they tried to acquit him of that murder[126] and even blame their enemies for his murder. Of course, the extent to which Ibn Muammar's reputation would be limited due to the existence of his successor and grandson.

- There is no ambiguity surrounding the Shaykh's desire to kill Ibn Muammar, for he clearly stated, "Ibn Muammar is a polytheist and infidel."[127] Furthermore, historians of the early Wahhabi movement have written that "When the people of Islam confirmed this fact, they committed to kill him after he completed his Friday prayers,"[128] and "Uthman Ibn Muammar barely completed his Friday prayers at the Uyaynah mosque when he was surrounded and killed by a group of loyalists to the Wahhabi movement. The most famous of that group included Ahmad Ibn Rashid, Ibrahim Ibn Zayd al-Bahili, and Musa Ibn Rajih."[129]

It was reported by Hussein al-Shaykh Khazal that Shaykh Muhammad Ibn Abd al-Wahhab was dismayed when he received the news about the killing of Ibn Muammar. According to this report, he then personally marched to Uyaynah, arriving on the third day after the killing and calmed the people.

Perhaps the Shaykh wanted to distance himself from this crime and imply that it happened without his knowledge. Or, perhaps, he wanted to accuse the people of Uyaynah of this murder since they had fought, insulted, and expelled him. The Shaykh would then send Abd al-Aziz Ibn Muhammad Ibn Saud with an army to Uyaynah, ordering him to force its people out, destroy its crops, and ruin its homes. Abd al-Aziz carried out those orders, and Uyaynah remains in ruins today as a testament to the bitter fighting in which Shaykh used to subdue his enemies. This approach became a trademark for his followers later when they resorted to the sword when persuasion and subjugation would not work.

Revisiting the Shaykh's History as Portrayed by the Author of Lam al-Shahab and Hempher

Lam al-Shahab and *The Memoirs of Mr. Hempher* are worth considerable attention as the dates mentioned in both books about the Shaykh are seemingly aligned (despite the apparent lack of acquaintance between the two authors).

In the previous chapter, I mentioned Abu Humaydan, the owner of the donkey, who saved the Shaykh. He was described by *Lam al-Shahab* and was referred to as "Safih" by Hempher. Earlier, I mentioned that it was not possible for Abu Humaydan, a poor man, to save the Shaykh's life and then equip him so abundantly. The Shaykh was said to come to him empty-handed and intensely in need of water. Ibn Abd al-Wahhab then reportedly returned to his own town loaded with money and provisions. The author of *Lam al-Shahab* writes:

> Muhammad Ibn Abd al-Wahhab had lots of money that he had gathered during his journey. The people in his hometown knew that fact and that he had seven or eight slaves purchased from Mecca, each of which was a feared fighter.[130]

He later writes, "This was after the people of one of the villages of the Rey region took all of the Shaykh's money and provisions."[131]

The Shaykh would have returned empty-handed had it not been for whatever Abu Humaydan provided him. However, based on the economic status of Abu Humaydan given, his gift may not have exceeded the sustenance of a couple of days.

However, Salah al-Deen al-Moukhtar, author of Tarikh al-Mamlakah al-Arabiyah al- Saudiyah Fi Madihah Wa Haderhah, writes:

Chapter 3: Declaration of the Mission

On the way from Basra, the Shaykh ran into a muleteer named Abu Humaydan, from Zubayr, on his donkey. The Shaykh was at death's door, so the muleteer gave him water. He had him ride the donkey until they arrived at Zubayr where he doubled his spending money.[132]

It should be noted that *Lam al-Shahab* was written in 1817 CE and that the unabridged manuscript remained in Diriyah until it was invaded by Muhammad Ali Pasha in 1818 CE. At that point, the manuscript was moved by a British spy working for Captain Taylor, a British soldier in the Arabian Peninsula, and it remained with him until his death. The manuscript was later sold by his wife to the British Museum in 1860 CE as was recorded on its last page: "This book was purchased from Mrs. Taylor in April, 1860." It remained there until it was published in 1967 CE without any changes, as was confirmed by Ahmad Abu Hakimah.

Hempher noted in his memoirs that he recruited Shaykh Muhammad Ibn Abd al-Wahhab after vigorous efforts, writing:

> I forged between Muhammad and myself the most powerful of relationships. I would inflate his ego and show him that he was more talented than Ali Ibn Abi Talib and Umar and that if the Prophet were present, he would have chosen him as his successor without question. I would tell him that I hoped the renewal of Islam would happen at his hands for he was the only one capable of pulling Islam out of its current tumble. Muhammad and I decided to discuss the interpretation of the Quran according to our own understanding, as opposed to referring to the opinions of the Prophet's companions and other scholars. We would read the Quran and discuss specific points, which I had selected to entrap Muhammad. He would go to great lengths to accept my opinions to prove himself as a liberal and to increase my confidence in him.[133]

The Birth of Terrorism in Middle East

Hempher also mentioned:

> [He would follow him] on every trip and return and I was careful so that the tree in which I had invested most of my precious youth produces fruit. Muhammad and I are forging down the path that we had quickly planned. I was never apart from him and my mission was to instill in him the spirit of independence, freedom, and continuous doubt. I would always predict for him a bright future, and I would praise his vibrant spirit.[134]

The anonymous author of *Lam al-Shahab* indicated that the judge of Basra, Husayn al-Islambuli, detained the Shaykh for two years under the pretense of appointing him as a teacher of Arabic and theology until the Shaykh was able to escape:

> He suddenly disappeared from Basra without anyone's knowledge and walked back to Baghdad. Judge Husayn sought more information about him and could not get it until a group of people from Baghdad visited him and gave him news of the Shaykh and that the latter was in Baghdad. The judge then said: "I seek refuge in God from the evil of this man and his opinions. He would have destroyed the system of Islamic law had he not feared for his life. You will hear more of him in the future."[135]

Lam al-Shahab does not explain how the Shaykh was able to explain from Basra. However, Ibn Ghannam noted that the Shaykh escaped with the help of the poor muleteer, Abu Humaydan. This raises questions about the true identity of Abu Humaydan and Safih, who was mentioned separately by several authors. What were their true roles in the Shaykh's mysterious escape?

Hempher was concerned about his creation, the Shaykh, in Basra after he left for London for an extended amount of time. He was later assured by

Chapter 3: Declaration of the Mission

high-ranking sources that the Shaykh was as he had left him and that a mistress stayed with him for two months. Hempher also mentioned that the recruited woman had accompanied Ibn Abd al-Wahhab on his journey to Baghdad and then to Kurdistan, Hamadan, and Isfahan.

It is possible that this mistress had allies who facilitated the Shaykh's escape and provisions for travel. In addition, it is possible that Abu Humaydan was hired by the British to aid the Shaykh. For, as mentioned earlier, an impoverished muleteer would not normally be able to provide expenses, a secured travel path, and a quick escape from the authorities anxious to capture and follow the Shaykh.

Hempher mentioned that he told Ibn Abd al-Wahhab to go to Isfahan and Shiraz, even though the people of those towns were Shiites:

> I told him, "Be careful of Shiites and do not reveal that you are a Sunni lest a disaster befall you. Enjoy their country and scholars and learn their customs and traditions, for this will benefit you tremendously in the future."[136]

When it was time for them to part ways, he provided the Shaykh with a sum of money under the pretense of charity and bought him a mule as a gift. They then secured means for communication through one of the people of Basra.[137]

Hempher confirmed in his memoirs that he received instructions not to neglect his agent. The secretary for the Ministry of Colonies told him:

> "The Shaykh is the best person we could rely on to serve the objectives of the Ministry." He asked him to openly discuss his plans with the Shaykh, because the latter had accepted all of the conditions presented by the agent of the Ministry in Isfahan. The Shaykh had agreed to the offer on the condition that he is protected from governments and scholars who will undoubtedly attack him when he begins to declare his

opinions and thinking. He also asked that he be provided with sufficient funds and weapons and that he be given an emirate, even a small one, on the outskirts of his country, Najd. The Ministry agreed to all of his requests start.[138]

Hempher made reference to a plan put together by the Ministry to be implemented by the Shaykh. The plan consisted of six main articles: the declaration of Muslims as infidels, deeming permissible their slaughter, confiscating their money and violating their honor, fighting the official caliphate center, controlling the Hijaz, destroying the Ka'bah, domes, shrines, and other holy Muslim sites, and spreading chaos and terror.[139] Hempher doubted the feasibility of such a plan but was reassured by the Ministry.

• • •

When Hempher returned to Basra, he was informed that the Shaykh had left Najd for a particular destination. Hempher followed him, and they agreed that he would pretend to be his slave purchased from Basra who had recently returned from a journey. Hempher became known as such:

> In 1143 CE, his resolve strengthened and he had gathered a significant number of supporters. He revealed his mission with vague words and abstract expressions to his closest allies. He then started to expand the circle of his mission, and I surrounded him with a group of tenacious men and provided them with money. I would strengthen their resolve any time they showed fatigue from attacks from the Shaykh's enemies. As he revealed his mission to more people, his enemies multiplied. Sometimes he wanted to retreat due to the pressure of rumors, but I would reinforce his determination… This is how we were with the enemies, attacking, and retreating. I had assigned spies to the enemies of the Shaykh and paid them off. Any time his enemies plotted to stir strife, those spies informed us and we were able to modify the plan. One time,

Chapter 3: Declaration of the Mission

> I was informed that some of his enemies wanted to assassinate him, so I took the necessary steps to foil that plan.[140]

• • •

It was mentioned by Ibn Bishar in *Unwan al-Majd Fi Tarikh Najd*; and by Ibn Ghannam in *Rawdat al-Afkar Wa al-Afham*; and later by Salah al-Deen al-Moukhtar in *Tarikh al-Mamlakah al-Arabiyah al- Saudiyah Fi Madihah Wa Haderhah*; and also by Amin Sa'id in *Al-Dawla al-Saudiyah*, that as soon as the Shaykh arrived in his presence, Uthman Ibn Muammar kissed him, welcomed him, and honored him. It is mentioned that the Shaykh married al-Jawharah, daughter of Abd Allah Ibn Muammar.

It was previously mentioned that Uthman had promised to support the Shaykh. The Shaykh had offered him the same deal he would later offer to Ibn Saud, or that religious matters would belong to Ibn Abd al-Wahhab and worldly matters would belong to Ibn Muammar.[141] Nasir al-Saeed mentioned that, based on Saudi sources, after the Shaykh returned to Uyaynah, he clashed with the governor of that town, Uthman Ibn Muammar, who then put him under strict surveillance, but the Shaykh escaped and travelled to Diriyah.[142]

This is in contradiction to what was mentioned by Amin Sa'id and other historians of the Saudi state. The author of *Lam al-Shahab* wrote that the agreement between the Shaykh and the governor was to establish an order between religion and its practice. They agreed that the only acceptable form of religion would be Ibn Abd al-Wahhab's doctrine.[143]

However, Amin al-Rayhani deduced that Ibn Muammar was not serious in implementing the Shaykh's plan.[144] As Ibn Muammar was murdered by the Shaykh's supporters, it is fair to question the motives of the various accounts of Ibn Muammar's relationship with the Shaykh. Negative portrayals of Ibn Muammar made the murder appear justifiable.

• • •

The Birth of Terrorism in Middle East

Concerning the relationship between the Shaykh and Ibn Muammar, Muhammad Faqih refers to a manuscript that was in the possession of a man from Jabal Amil who escaped from the Ottoman army during the First World War and joined the troops of al-Sharif Husayn Ibn Ali in Hijaz.[145] Faqih writes that he obtained the manuscript in 1920 CE in the town of Muan in the Transjordan emirate, though the author and its date are not made clear. This manuscript indicates that the author's father worked for Uthman Ibn Muammar and that his father was present on the day when Muhammad Ibn Abd al-Wahhab arrived in Uyaynah.[146]

The author of this manuscript said, as recounted by his father:

> It was early in the day when a tall white man in full gear and with a worried look on his face arrived in the presence of Shaykh Uthman. This man spoke in a strange tongue unfamiliar to the people of Najd. Shaykh Uthman was sitting among us and he did not recognize that man, nor had he seen his face before. The man asked Shaykh Uthman for assistance and the Shaykh inquired about his exact purpose. The stranger said that he was seeking the support and generosity of the Shaykh. When the latter asked him about his allegiance and master, the man answered that he is a follower of the judge Abd al-Wahhab, may God rest his soul, and that his master, Shaykh Muhammad, sent him to Shaykh Uthman to inquire about his interest after losing faith in his own family. He also said that if he honored him, supported him, and kept his enemies from him and his followers it would strengthen the emirate, both in arms and in trade.
>
> Shaykh Uthman then said to the stranger, "What you ask for is not out of the ordinary, for people like me help out those who ask them. Tell your master to come to us in Tamim and we will see to our duties."

The author of the manuscript continues to relate his father's account:

Chapter 3: Declaration of the Mission

Shortly after the follower of Ibn Abd al-Wahhab departed, his master arrived along with his women and children and some of his brothers, cousins, and a number of slaves who guarded and defended him. Shaykh Uthman received and honored them. After the noon prayers, Shaykh Uthman invited his guest to a private council. The servant who had come alone to Uthman Ibn Muammar earlier sat in on that conversation.

It should be noted that the servant mentioned appears to be of particular importance as he was allowed to attend this meeting to the exclusion of Ibn Abd al-Wahhab's other companions (many of whom were his own family). It appears that this servant was none other than Hempher himself who sought to gain the alliance of Uthman Ibn Muammar. Later, when it became evident that Ibn Muammar would not support the Shaykh to the end, he and Ibn Abd al-Wahhab turned to Muhammad Ibn Saud. Later in this chapter, I will return to the role he played in connecting the Shaykh and Ibn Saud.

In this manuscript, more detail is provided concerning the relationship between Ibn Abd al-Wahhab and Uthman than one finds in Saudi sources. This relationship lasted about four years, or from the time the Shaykh left Yamamah. This was about a year after he declared his mission upon his father's death in 1153 CE.[147] The Shaykh remained in Uyaynah from 1154 to 1158 CE. After that, according to Saudi historians, he sought refuge in Diriyah.

• • •

The Shaykh's public activity appears to have begun in Uyaynah, or Yamamah, since the date mentioned by Hempher coincides with the Shaykh's arrival and being received by Ibn Muammar. Uthman vowed to support the Shaykh and allow him to establish a system of governance in Uyaynah. Of course, as mentioned earlier, the two seem to have had a falling out. Below I will mention elements of the story of Ibn Abd al-Wahhab and Uthman Ibn Muammar that appear to be contradictory:

The Birth of Terrorism in Middle East

- Ibn Muammar welcomed the Shaykh and married him to his sister. He supported him in destroying shrines and uprooting trees, among other activities, but he was not dedicated to implementing this mission according to the Shaykh's vision.

- Both men were from Tamim.

- Ibn Muammar turned against the Shaykh after he received threats from the governor of al-Ahsa ordering him to remove or kill the Shaykh. This proved that Ibn Muammar was not dedicated to the Shaykh's cause.

- Saudi stories mention the absolute harmony between the two men.

- Saudi stories mention a falling out between the two men which led to the Shaykh's banishment and incitement by Ibn Muammar to kill him. It is said that he told his servant to kill the Shaykh, which served as a justification for killing Ibn Muammar.

- Saudi stories mention that the Shaykh left alone, banished and beaten.

- Saudi stories mention that the Shaykh left with some of his brothers, cousins, and servants in a manner that preserved his honor and safety.

- Saudi sources mention a quick exit towards Diriyah and seeking asylum with Ibn Suwaylim without the knowledge of Ibn Saud.

- Other Saudi accounts relate a rapturous reception for the Shaykh and his entourage by Ibn Saud and his entourage.

- Saudi stories ascertained the faith of Ibn Muammar and that his killing was to spite the Shaykh.

- These same Saudi stories noted that Muslims in Uyaynah confirmed that Ibn Muammar was an infidel and thus killed him following the Friday prayers.

• • •

Chapter 3: Declaration of the Mission

Let us consider the fact that Saudi historians noted that Ibn Muammar supported Ibn Abd al-Wahhab until the end, even when the latter abandoned him and joined Muhammad Ibn Saud. Uthman had led some of the Shaykh's armies against the "infidels" among the Arabs in Najd. So why was Uthman killed by supporters of Muhammad Ibn Abd al-Wahhab after they performed the Friday prayers with him? Moreover, why would they pray with an "infidel"? It is worth entertaining the notion that Ibn Muammar was assassinated due to the threat he posed to the authority of Ibn Saud.

• • •

Here I would like to take a glance at the importance of the Shaykh's "servants." Hempher's account indicates that they were the executive committee for the Shaykh's mission at large and that they functioned as an elite undercover group of officers and experts. And, as will be mentioned further, the relationship between Ibn Abd al-Wahhab and Ibn Saud grew by way of Ibn Suwaylim. I hope to shed some light on the personality of the latter, his identity, and his role in bringing them together.

Chapter 4: The Village of Diriyah and Al Saud

1: The Village of Diriyah: The Capital of Wahhabism

Perhaps no one would have been able to find the village of Diriyah on the map of the Arabian Peninsula today had Shaykh Muhammad Ibn Abd al-Wahhab not sought refuge in it when he escaped from his opponents in Uyaynah. The village became famous because it was the location of the alliance forged between the Shaykh and the leader of the village. In a short amount of time, this village would boast the spoils of war and become the capital of an authority that prevails to this day.

The developments in Diriyah were a natural result of the collapse of its cultural and social environments which prepared the grounds for religious extremism. And it seemed inevitable that the numerous tribes in the region would eventually pledge allegiance to one leader. Of course, the role of the Shaykh must not be understated, for had Ibn Abd al-Wahhab sought refuge elsewhere, Diriyah would not have been in such a position.

• • •

Diriyah, which was also called al-Mulaybid and Ghusaybah, is situated near Riyadh. Saud Ibn Makrin Ibn Markhan Ibn Ibrahim Ibn Musa, the

Chapter 4: The Village of Diriyah and Al Saud

great-grandfather of Al Saud, had lived there. The governmental and loyalist stories claim that it was given to him by Ali Ibn Dari', and so its name was derived from his own.[148]

During the period in question, the people of Diriyah had fallen upon hard times and were forced to turn to manual labor and commerce in order to survive[149] despite the fact that such work was considered shameful in Najdi society, which represented a Bedouin culture. Ibn Bishar attested to the poverty and lack of education in Diriyah: "I saw their hardships... The people were extremely ignorant and complacent in their prayers, charity, and other rituals of Islam."[150] Elsewhere he wrote, "I saw the town of Diriyah before the arrival of Shaykh Muhammad. Its people lived in a sad state of poverty and deprivation."[151]

The hamlet of Muhammad Ibn Saud, called Balwadi, consisted of about seventy homes.[152] This was confirmed by Hussein al-Shaykh Khazal: "Prior to the arrival of Shaykh Muhammad Ibn Abd al-Wahhab, it was a small village, with a small reputation and a population not exceeding seventy homes."[153]

Diriyah was an obscure, small village—one that did not seem likely to serve as the headquarters of a mission that would encompass all of Najd as well as the entire Peninsula. However, because it was the closest area to Uyaynah, Ibn Abd al-Wahhab perceived it as the only place in which he could take refuge and regroup.

The Shaykh was allowed to seek safe haven in Diriyah because it was obscure and unknown. Those who allowed him to escape did not expect his success. They did not believe he would be able to become established in Diriyah. They also did not think the people of Diriyah were capable of invading Najd and controlling it. Furthermore, Diriyah did not boast skilled craftsmen. Thus, the people of Uyaynah did not anticipate the military prowess the Wahhabis would later demonstrate. The Shaykh, thus, was allowed to take refuge there. And only two years later, he would begin his military campaigns.

The Birth of Terrorism in Middle East

Ibn Bishar mentioned that the first raid was in 1160 CE:

> [It occurred] two years after the arrival of Muhammad Ibn Abd al-Wahhab. That raid consisted of seven mounts (camels). Those who rode them fell to the ground because they did not know how to ride.[154]

According to Amin al-Rayhani, Diriyah:

> …was a small, weak town with few sources for sustenance and wealth. As the number of new arrivals seeking the Shaykh increased, earning a livelihood became even more difficult. So they started working their crafts during the night and learning during the day.[155]

The small, impoverished village of Diriyah was initially not capable of hosting newcomers, nor was its ruler. Some historians have written that the people of Diriyah were crude and engaged in sedition and deceit.

Abd al-Aziz Sayed al-Ahel, a Saudi sympathizer, has written:

> Had Muhammad Ibn Saud observed and understood the crudity of the Bedouins in his state—for, one who lives nomadically becomes crude—he would have guided the lost, extinguished the sedition and fought deception and hatred.[156]

The author of *Lam al-Shahab* writes:

> Muhammad Ibn Saud's people bore hatred and were deceitful. Their intentions were never pure in regard to their neighbors, and their crude souls were the reason he had to use money to buy their allegiance.[157]

In *Al-Hukum al-Saudi*, Khalifah Fahed writes:

> The opponents of Wahhabism had expected that Diriyah would be a tomb for Ibn Abd al-Wahhab and his ideas. They

Chapter 4: The Village of Diriyah and Al Saud

assumed that they had secured themselves, their honor and their interests when the Shaykh secluded himself in that unknown village. Therefore, they did not concern themselves with the village or the Shaykh at that point. They believed that, regardless of the Shaykh's level of activity and ambition, his mission would not expand beyond the perimeter of the village and its inhabitants, and it would not affect their own affairs. Therefore, they overlooked the situation and they assumed that would be the end of it.[158]

According to this view, the opponents of Wahhabism failed to recognize that the Shaykh had chosen a perfect environment for the advancement of his mission. He would not have found such success in Uyaynah, even though it was his birthplace and where his family and clan still lived. The people of Uyaynah were not as inclined towards embarking on such a mission and upending their daily lives, as their town enjoyed a certain level of affluence.

2: The Saud Family: Rulers of the Wahhabi State

Perhaps today the family of King Abd al-Aziz Ibn Abd al-Rahman Al Saud could populate an entire city on its own. In other words, their numbers are approximately two hundred times what the population of Diriyah was when the Shaykh arrived. The other branches of this family certainly constitute a much larger number, making its presence in the Saudi society very prominent. Their sheer size confirms the absolute power for Al Abd al-Aziz and his clan over Najd, Hijaz, and al-Ahsa. The family members continue to struggle to maintain control and defend their authority after the bitter conflict in which they engaged in obtaining it in the first place.

Regardless of the reasons that led King Abd al-Aziz to increase his progeny,[159] research today indicates a great change in their numbers. Before the onset of the Wahhabi mission, their hometown of Diriyah was impoverished and relatively unknown, with a small population and little influence. Since that time, they have established a large hereditary kingdom.

One's origin can be of utmost importance in a Bedouin culture. Thus, as the Saud family found itself at the helm of a government with power over millions of people, they began to care more about their origins. This exceptional interest in their family tree began after the establishment of the kingdom.[160]

Of course, it is usually not feasible to trace such a large family tree back to its beginnings with a great deal of accuracy. Certainly, some of the branches mentioned by the authors of the family tree were not as distinguished as they were presented to be. Some names were likely even fabricated. However, hereditary rule propelled later generations of the Saud family to locate themselves in a larger tradition.

With a certain degree of confidence we can verify the accuracy of the branch that began with Markhan Ibn Ibrahim Ibn Musa.[161] But rigorous scrutiny must be applied across the course of a period extending for more than fifteen centuries. This is, as mentioned earlier, essentially an impossible task.

3: Muhammad Ibn Saud

He was born Muhammad Ibn Saud Ibn Muhammad Ibn Makrin Ibn Markhan Ibn Ibrahim Ibn Musa, and he was the prince of the Wahhabi Saudi state and the first ally of the Shaykh. Neither Muhammad Ibn Saud, who died in 1765 CE, nor his ancestors before him could be referred to as "princes" or prominent scholars in Najd prior to the Wahhabi movement. Despite the doubt concerning the origins of his family, it can be said that his family was relatively impoverished and obscure with little influence among the large and established tribes. According to government authors and historians, the family did not even own any land until Ali Ibn Dar gave them the land that eventually became their town. In other words, they did not inherit land from their ancestors.

Chapter 4: The Village of Diriyah and Al Saud

As mentioned earlier, Diriyah was a small village of about seventy houses, and its inhabitants depended on agriculture and simple crafts for their livelihood. This, according to the Bedouin norms and values, made them second-class citizens in the eyes of others. They were aware of that classification but knew that they had no other option.

It should not come as a surprise, then, that their prince, or Shaykh, did not possess a great amount of wealth. His source of income came from what he received from the impoverished people of Diriyah at the time of harvest. He was very attached to this allowance and, in fact, made the continuation of this allowance one of his two main conditions when he agreed to a pact with Ibn Abd al-Wahhab. He would not have insisted upon such a condition except for his urgent need for this meager sum of money received from his impoverished subjects.[162]

Al Saud did not carry weight politically, militarily, socially, or economically outside of his village. Muhammad Saeed Al-Muslim writes, "Al Saud had no significance before adopting the Wahhabi mission."[163] And Muhammad Jalal Keshek has written, "Al Saud would not have any mention in history beyond that of Dahham Ibn Dawas, governor of Riyadh, had it not been for the Wahhabi movement."[164] Elsewhere Keshek writes, "We do not have any information about this family prior to Muhammad Ibn Saud."[165]

However, this same author (Keshek) also refers to the Saudis as an established royal family that well-versed in matters of leadership and governance:

> …But we can say that this family had unique characteristics, not only in its ambitions and amazing ability to persevere, renew itself and exercise leadership without relying on notable senior tribal support but also in its special council that attends to the affairs of the emirate.[166]

Keshek's statement lacks any sort of historical evidence as we know very little about the Saudis before Wahhabism. Furthermore, an impoverished village of seventy homes would be unlikely to boast the special council of which he writes.

• • •

Just as the virtues of Ibn Abd al-Wahhab are related in *Lam al-Shahab*, similarly, Muhammad Ibn Saud is presented as a man of outstanding merit. The author writes:

> Our trustworthy sources tell us that Muhammad Ibn Saud was a man with many good deeds who worshipped frequently. His father Saud and his grandfather Muhammad were rulers in Diriyah[167] with high status. Muhammad himself had a very generous nature and he possessed numerous plots of land, palms and other crops, as well as cattle.[168] It was said that he was so generous that if a man came to him seeking his help in fulfilling a debt, he would oblige him, after confirming his need, even if the debt was significant.
>
> It was said in a story that he gave a man whom he did not know four thousand gold dinars to pay off his debts. When his children, except Abd al-Aziz who was similarly generous, reproached him, he answered them that life was made to honor the sons of Adam; if the best among them, the honorable one, became lower in status, he should be helped so that the he is not looked down upon by the lowly. It was also said that Muhammad was in the habit of helping poor men get married, and he would ready them from his own money because he was such a good-natured man who wanted harmony, well being and prosperity for his people through marriage and helping one another.
>
> He liked being alone, and it was said that when he came home, he would sit alone and would not want any of his children or wives to disturb him. He would stay in that state for

Chapter 4: The Village of Diriyah and Al Saud

seven successive days or more. He did not want to fight wars with anyone, even those who attacked him first. He always ordered his people to extinguish sedition. However, his people had plenty of hatred and deceit in their hearts for those in neighboring towns. If it were not for him, no one would have traded with them due to their crude souls.[169]

However, the high praise given Ibn Saud in *Lam al-Shahab* is contradicted by the testimonies of other historians, most of whom wrote for the Saudi government.

• • •

One of those other historians (Ibn Bishar) provided an indisputable piece of evidence that Muhammad Ibn Saud lived in a state of poverty: his dependence on the proceeds from his impoverished subjects. According to Ibn Bishar, when negotiating the terms of his alliance with the Shaykh, Ibn Saud insisted on receiving his shares from the peasants at harvest time, saying:

> I rule over Diriyah and they pay me duties at the time of harvest and I worry that you will tell me not to take anything from them…[170]

The account given in *Lam al-Shahab*, then, seems implausible, for, how could Ibn Saud have bestowed large sums of money and performed so many acts of charity and provided such vast relief when he is careful about protecting his small share from his impoverished subjects?

Another question one might ask is if Muhammad Ibn Saud was as gentle as he is portrayed to be in *Lam al-Shahab*, why was Muhammad Ibn Suwaylim (the man who first hosted Ibn Abd al-Wahhab) afraid of him? Ibn Bishar writes:

> When the Shaykh [Ibn Abd al-Wahhab] entered his house, he [Ibn Suwaylim] feared for himself from Ibn Saud so the Shaykh admonished him and calmed him down, saying to him, "God will provide you and us with relief and a

way out." He then left his house for another. Some people of Diriyah learned of the Shaykh's arrival, so they secretly visited him. They wanted to inform Muhammad Ibn Saud about the Shaykh and ask for his support, but they were afraid of Ibn Saud.[171]

Later, Ibn Suwaylim's wife convinced Ibn Suwaylim to tell Ibn Saud about Ibn Abd al-Wahhab by pointing out that he may be of benefit:

> This man came to you and there is benefit in him guided to you by God. So welcome and honor him and benefit from supporting him.[172]

Ibn Saud was reportedly convinced by his wife's words. However, the question remains, how could a man of such great generosity (as per the account given in *Lam al-Shahab*) strike such fear in his subjects?

• • •

The observant reader will recognize the disparities in accounts given concerning the temperament and origins of Muhammad Ibn Saud. It is only natural that after Ibn Saud and his family had reached a position of authority, exaggerated accounts would be given in praise of him. This is a matter of significance, for examining the origins of this family can help us understand the current Saudi regime.

Chapter 5: The Third Journey to Diriyah

THE ALLIANCE BETWEEN THE SHAYKH OF THE VILLAGE AND THE SHAYKH OF RELIGION

In seeking mutual benefit, the two Shaykhs[173] formed an alliance and combined politics with Wahhabi beliefs. This was a tribal emirate, founded on the basis of religion. The members of this new coalition, who came from various tribes, made themselves loyal subjects to the prince of this tribe, Muhammad Ibn Saud. They vowed to remain loyal as long as he himself was faithful to the guidance of their religious leader, Muhammad Ibn Abd al-Wahhab.

The Wahhabi cause was critical to the success of Ibn Saud's government, as it provided a call to purify Islam of contamination in the form of polytheism and infidelity. It was agreed that its spiritual father and founder, Shaykh Muhammad Ibn Abd al-Wahhab, along with his children and grandchildren after him, would always remain at the forefront. They would bless and support its continuation as a legitimate state. Ibn Abd al-Wahhab's children and grandchildren did, in fact, remain faithful to this agreement, serving, of course, their own best interests.

In a diverse Islamic environment, the newly formed Wahhabi state had to establish a foothold, stability, and consistency. Wahhabis and Saudis gained leadership at the expense of their neighbors and by way of gaining the support of influential social leaders (such as local authors, missionaries, scholars, politicians, and poets). In recent times, Wahhabis and Saudis have been able to continue to establish influence due to the wealth they have gained by way of the oil industry. Prominent authors were hired by the Saudi state with the task of portraying the Saudi family and revered Wahhabi figured in a positive light. Furthermore, such authors were to conceal political corruption perpetrated by Saudi leaders.

• • •

The Saudi-Wahhabi coalition was not established on a legitimate or a familiar Islamic basis, nor was it established by way of a council or any sort of election. Rather, it was established based on a particular interpretation of religion and tribal politics. This is significant as this coalition would become the basis for the establishment of a form of government that would later be regarded as a part of the region's heritage and almost sacred in nature.

• • •

As mentioned above, Shaykh Muhammad Ibn Abd al-Wahhab escaped from the city of Uyaynah, his birthplace, after being exiled from Huraymalah. The precedents of his expulsion and fleeing can be found in his encounters in Basra and Damascus. The author *Lam al-Shahab* recounted that the Shaykh was exiled from every land to which he traveled.

The Shaykh was forced to migrate to Diriyah. There he hoped to find students and devotees who would partake in his classes. His hasty and abrupt exit from Uyaynah did not leave him a choice in determining a safe location where he could find stability, nor did it leave him a chance for any prior coordination with the Shaykh from Diriyah, Muhammad Ibn Saud, any of his brothers or any of his followers. The Shaykh had not previously met the Shaykh from Diriyah, even though it was said that he had met two of his brothers who frequented Uyaynah, Thanian, and Mushari.

Chapter 5: The Third Journey to Diriyah

I would now like to review the terms of the Shaykh's alliance with Ibn Saud and the extent to which it is influenced by Islamic law. I will also examine the psychological and political conditions of the Shaykh's new allies.

THE MEETING OF THE ALLIES: A MEETING WITH NO PRIOR NOTICE

The meeting occurred without prior agreement in Diriyah, the small village of Muhammad Ibn Saud. Saudi sympathizers report the unexpected entry of the Shaykh into the outskirts of the town where he stayed at the home of one of his former acquaintances, Abd Allah Ibn Suwaylim. The latter was not comfortable providing Ibn Abd al-Wahhab with hospitality and, rather, agreed only out of modesty and decency. He had expressed that he was afraid that Muhammad Ibn Saud would learn that the Shaykh was staying at his house. And even though the Shaykh tried to assure him, he saw no alternative but to move out of his house the next day to the home of another host.

Ibn Bishar, a Saudi historian, writes:

> As to the Shaykh, he walked toward Diriyah, arriving at its highest point around mid-afternoon and he directed himself towards the house of Muhammad Ibn Suwaylim al-Arini. When the Shaykh entered his house, he feared for himself from Ibn Saud, so the Shaykh admonished him and calmed him down saying to him, "God will provide you and us with relief and a way out." Some people of Diriyah learned of the Shaykh's presence and secretly visited him. He shared with them his understanding of monotheism and it settled in their hearts. They wanted to inform Muhammad Ibn Saud about the Shaykh and advise him to support him, but they were afraid of him.[174]

The Birth of Terrorism in Middle East

Some sources indicated that:

> The next day, the Shaykh moved to the house of his student, Shaykh Ahmad Ibn Suwaylim, perhaps the brother of Abd Allah Ibn Suwaylim, who flooded his home with the Shaykh's supporters and devotees.[175] Among those were Thunyan and Mushari, Muhammad Ibn Saud's two brothers, who tried to convince their brother to meet the Shaykh. At first, he was hesitant, but the two brothers consulted with his wife, Mudy, the daughter of Abu Watban from the family of Kathir, who was an intelligent woman. They told her of the Shaykh's message. God implanted a love for the Shaykh in her heart and she was relieved with his news. She then found the right time to speak of this matter to her husband saying, "God guided this man to you and there is benefit in him, so make use of the benefit that God has offered you."
>
> The prince[176] was convinced by his wife's words, and he called on his brother Mushari to invite the Shaykh in order to meet him. However, Mushari pleaded with his brother, the prince, to seek to meet the Shaykh himself saying, "Walk to this man yourself and show him glorification and reverence so that he may be delivered from harm by others." So the prince went to the Shaykh and welcomed him in the house of Ahmad Ibn Suwaylim saying, "Rejoice in a town more charitable than your own and rejoice in glory and strength."
>
> The Shaykh then said, "I predict for you glory and empowerment. These are due to the words, 'There is no god but God.' And whoever commits to [these words] and supports them shall rule through them both the country and its people. This is the word of monotheism and the first thing called for by the Messengers, from the first one to the last."[177]

Chapter 5: The Third Journey to Diriyah

• • •

It becomes clear to us from reading these texts and stories related to the Shaykh's exile at the hands of the people of Uyaynah that:

- The Shaykh went directly from Uyaynah to Diriyah, arriving either on the same day he left or the following day. Thus, it can be determined that his small convoy, which included his wives, children, and servants, moved rapidly out of fear of his rivals and opponents catching up to them. His enemies did not bother pursuing him in Diriyah for their belief that his mission would die there and that his supporters in that town did not carry much weight, even if they included the entire population of that village.

- No one among the people of Diriyah knew beforehand of the sudden arrival of the Shaykh, including the village chief and his brothers. The Shaykh arrived at the highest point in Diriyah and went to the house of Abd Allah Ibn Suwaylim, sometimes called "Muhammad Ibn Suwaylim." He was surprised by the Shaykh's arrival and feared Muhammad Ibn Saud in case the latter learned of the Shaykh's presence at his house. Muhammad Ibn Saud also did not know of the Shaykh's arrival to his own village. There were no prior arrangements between the two of them.[178]

- The Shaykh moved to the house of one of his students and admirers, Ahmad Ibn Suwaylim, perhaps the brother of Abd Allah or one of his relatives. It is not clear if Abd Allah Ibn Suwaylim insisted on Ibn Abd al-Wahhab leaving or not.

This story indicates that Abd Allah Ibn Suwaylim knew that Muhammad Ibn Saud was strict and intolerant in dealing with the people of his village. Abd Allah and his two brothers were afraid of telling Ibn Saud of the Shaykh's arrival and of asking him to support him. This is in contradiction to the account given by the author of *Lam al-Shahab* and others which spoke of Muhammad Ibn Saud's forgiveness, tolerance and care for his people

- One thing that is not entirely clear is the relationship between Muhammad Ibn Saud and the people of Diriyah. Did they all belong to the same tribe, or was he perceived as an outsider? Previously we mentioned that the Saudis were given plots of land by Ali Ibn Dir. Thus it is reasonable to conclude that they were not natives of Diriyah.

- The Shaykh met with some of his acquaintances at the house of Ahmad Ibn Suwaylim. Among these visitors were Muhammad Ibn Saud's two brothers, Thunyan and Mushari. However, the mention of crowds of supporters found in some history books appear to be exaggeration as the entire population of the village did not constitute a crowd.

- After a while, the two brothers, Thunyan and Mushari, tried to convince their brother to meet the Shaykh. However, he initially refused this meeting out of fear of the Shaykh's strong enemies across Najd and the Arabian Peninsula. Furthermore, Ibn Saud did not perceive any sort of significant benefit in supporting the Shaykh, especially since after he had been banished from Uyaynah and Huraymalah.

- The two brothers resorted to their brother's wife, Mudi,[179] to convince her husband to welcome the Shaykh. She is reported to have said, "God guided this man to you and there is benefit in him, so make use of the benefit that God has offered you." It was then that he reportedly realized the great opportunity the Shaykh offered.

- Despite Muhammad Ibn Saud agreeing meeting to meet the Shaykh, he did not intend to pursue him. Rather he intended to send for him. His two brothers pleaded with him to go to the Shaykh and show him respect in order to discourage the villagers from attacking him. This means that there were some who were opposed to the Shaykh and who were trying to prevent his support. The Shaykh had become a source of controversy and discord shortly after arriving in Diriyah. And so it

Chapter 5: The Third Journey to Diriyah

was, the prince personally went and welcomed the Shaykh, promising him glory and victory.

- Muhammad Ibn Saud's brothers apparently did not ask him to receive the Shaykh until after the protest by some of the Shaykh's opponents.[180] This may have been the reason he did not want to meet with him initially. It is not clear how long it took to convince Muhammad Ibn Saud to meet him.

THE TERMS OF THE ALLIANCE

Historical documents, the oldest of which is the story of Ibn Bishar, did not detail the terms of the alliance between the two Shaykhs. Rather, they offered quotes that could be counted among the familiar social courtesies. These documents detailed only two conditions that Ibn Saud proposed and to which Ibn Abd al-Wahhab agreed.

Clearly, the details of this alliance remain unknown to us.

This alliance endured, even among their children and grandchildren, safeguarding the interests and responsibilities of each side. Thus, it could not have been formed as simply as Ibn Bishar writes.

• • •

Ibn Bishar mentioned that Muhammad Ibn Saud marched to the house of Ahmad Ibn Suwaylim, the temporary residence of Muhammad Ibn Abd al-Wahhab and offered him glad tidings of glory and protection. The Shaykh then said to him:

> I offer you glad tidings of glory and empowerment. It is in the words, "There is no god but God" and whoever commits to them and supports them, shall rule through them both the country and its people. This is the word of monotheism and

the first thing called for by the Messengers, from the first one to the last.

The Shaykh then told him of the Prophet, his message and the way of his companions, may God be pleased with them, including that which they commanded and prohibited. Every innovation after them was to be considered an aberration. He also told of how God granted them glory, enriched them, and made them brothers through struggling in His way. He then told him about the state of the people of Najd today because of their violations through polytheism, innovations, differences, inequality, and injustice. When Muhammad [Ibn Saud] investigated the truth of monotheism and learned of the potential religious and worldly benefits within that concept, he said, "Dear Shaykh, this religion is the religion of God and His Prophet in whom there is no doubt. Rejoice in the upcoming victory for you and for what you preach and the struggle against all those who oppose monotheism. However, I have two conditions for you: I worry that if we support you and your struggle in the way of God, and God helps us and forges a path for you and us towards other countries, you will leave us and replace us with others. My second condition is that the people of Diriyah pay me a portion of their harvest and I worry that you will tell me not to take anything from them."

The Shaykh then told him, "As to the first condition, extend your hand; blood for blood and destruction for destruction. And as to your second condition, perhaps God will facilitate your conquests and will reward you with more generous spoils than your current portion." His prediction came true and, after a while, Ibn Saud was rewarded with great spoils. The Shaykh said to him, "This is more than your take

Chapter 5: The Third Journey to Diriyah

from your people." Ibn Saud subsequently stopped taking that portion from his people.

Moreover, Muhammad Ibn Saud extended his hand and swore allegiance to the Shaykh in regards to God, His Prophet, the struggle in the way of God, the establishment of the rules of Islam, enjoining the good and forbidding the evil. At that point, the Shaykh stood up, entered the village and settled with Ibn Saud.[181]

THE TRUE MOTIVES BEHIND THE ALLIANCE

Ibn Abd al-Wahhab and Ibn Saud had both experienced disappointment and periods of inactivity before uniting. They would see in the Wahhabi movement an opportunity to establish a government based on popular semi-military support. It would incorporate individuals from various tribes, towns, and villages in the area of Riyadh and Ared. Later on, these members, with the encouragement of the two partners, established a religious association to replace the tribal one. It became the basis for a religious state for which Shaykh Ibn Abd al-Wahhab would serve as the patron, visionary and spiritual guide. His children were to inherit his position. Meanwhile, Shaykh Ibn Saud wanted it to be the beginning of a hereditary rule confined to his children and grandchildren. It was clear that the withdrawal of either side of this alliance would lead to the collapse of the entire project. Thus, they were tied to one another.

Many circumstances made this coalition a success from the perspective of its supporters and followers. On a practical level, this coalition achieved victories over perceived enemies and then by way of force after achieving such victory. To Wahhabis, the transformation of Diriyah, the extent of their raids, and their spoils were all evidence of the credibility of their allies' mission. In addition, the Shaykh's prophecy that the village's poor Shaykh (Ibn Saud) will attain great wealth became a part of the legends that circulated concerning the

The Birth of Terrorism in Middle East

Saudi ruler. All of this helped them prove the greatness and legitimacy of their mission as well as the necessity for its permanence.

• • •

Shortly, I will discuss the secret of the keys to the Wahhabi movement and how it achieved coherence. Large groups joined it from among Bedouins who had grown accustomed to raids with large populations of young men from various tribes and areas. Some of the reasons for the establishment of the alliance and the general highlights of its first version, mentioned briefly by various accounts, are as follows:

- The motives behind the founding of this alliance were purely personal. On the one hand, the Shaykh had no choice but to go to Diriyah and look for a sponsor there after the failure of his previous alliance in Uyaynah and his expulsion from that city. On the other hand, in this impoverished village, the Shaykh [Ibn Saud]—who was not known for any exploits or achievements, nor was his family[182]—realized that the Shaykh presented a great opportunity. His wife convinced him to take advantage of that opportunity, and he realized that he did not have anything to lose if this alliance failed.[183]

- The Shaykh [Ibn Abd al-Wahhab] took advantage of the rivalry between Muhammad Ibn Saud and the chiefs of Bani Khalid (who invaded Diriyah in 133 AH and who were also behind the Shaykh's expulsion from Uyaynah). He resorted to Ibn Saud, the enemy of his enemies, to be a friend and an ally. In addition, the proximity of Diriyah to Uyaynah was likely the primary reason for the Shaykh seeking refuge in that village and forming an alliance with its chief.

- Muhammad Ibn Saud was hesitant to meet the Shaykh, let alone form an alliance with him. Perhaps he was fearful of the Shaykh's powerful enemies. Foremost among those was the chief of Bani Khalid, Sulayman Ibn Aray'er al-Khalidi. The latter could have, once again, invaded his village and destroyed him, especially since the village's

Chapter 5: The Third Journey to Diriyah

Shaykh did not have a military force strong enough to repel such an invasion. However, he knew that this possibility was not likely since his village was obscure and impoverished, and no one expected any sort of success for a movement beginning from there.

- After Ibn Saud was confident that there would be no repercussions from the Shaykh's arrival to his village and that no one was interested in chasing the Shaykh to Diriyah, he decided there was no harm in meeting him. He formed the alliance with him and encouraged him in his mission. He also allowed the new arrivals into the village to join the Shaykh and learn from him. This was a prelude to the establishment of a military force. Those new arrivals would later serve the will of the alliance. Chief among the alliance's objectives was expanding their control as well as their circle of influence. The Shaykh of the village found an opportunity in the Shaykh of religion, and he had an appetite for attracting admirers of this mission. He would use them for expansion and influence.

- It would seem that Muhammad Ibn Saud, after being advised by his two brothers and his wife to embrace the Shaykh as an opportunity, resolved to finally meet the Shaykh. He promised glory and immunity in his financially and militarily weak village, which could not, on its own, achieve such heights. He decided to assuage his fears and invite the Shaykh to stay with him as an ally and a partner.

- The Shaykh played up to the wishes of Muhammad Ibn Saud about expansion and power. He foretold of his control over the entire area of Najd if he were to raise the Shaykh's religious banner. As mentioned earlier, he said, "There is no god but God and whoever commits to [these words] and supports them, rules through them the country and its people." He also explained to him the struggle of the Prophet's companions and how God held them dear, made them wealthy, and made them brothers. He then drew Ibn Saud's attention towards the state of the people of Najd "in terms of violations through polytheism, innovations, differences, inequality and injustice." He provided legitimate reasons for raiding and expansion under the pretense of turning Najd into a Muslim society. He gave Ibn Saud the green light to prepare for that expansion by presenting his doctrine as a legitimate cover for his future activities.

According to Ibn Bishar, Muhammad Ibn Saud closely considered the concept of monotheism as presented by the Shaykh and recognized its potential religious and worldly benefits. Thus, he was reportedly convinced of the plan presented by the Shaykh for expansion and achieving gains and worldly interests. Dr. Madeehah Ahmad Darwish writes:

> Prince Muhammad Ibn Saud was honest with himself and with Shaykh Muhammad Ibn Abd al-Wahhab. He did not want to embark on supporting this mission without knowing the end results for his emirate.[184]

Keshek, a Saudi state employee, wrote:

> The Saudi family council had no doubt about the consequences of promoting the Shaykh... This is obvious from the hesitation of the prince in meeting the Shaykh as not to implicate the emirate. It is also evident from his wife's words, "there is benefit in this man."[185]

We also notice that Keshek uses the terms "family council," "prince," and "emirate," even though the village was too small to qualify as an emirate like Riyadh or Uyaynah. Hence, the two agreed to "struggle" and raise the banner of war.[186]

- Muhammad Ibn Saud knew that the legitimacy of his raids and expansion were based on the edicts issued by Shaykh Muhammad Ibn Abd al-Wahhab. He also recognized that he stood to benefit from the volunteers who were motivated by religious struggle as understood in the Wahhabi doctrine. Ibn Saud knew that losing the Shaykh's support

Chapter 5: The Third Journey to Diriyah

would be a disaster for such volunteers would abandon him. Therefore, he placed a condition on the Shaykh that he remain with him and not leave him to join any other power.[187]

- Muhammad Ibn Saud's two conditions were clear to the Shaykh. He had no choice in accepting these conditions since rejecting them meant banishment from Diriyah and the end of his mission. This is the reason the Shaykh accepted those conditions and stayed in Diriyah, even though he tried to deny the second condition which pertained to the collection of money from the people in an illegitimate manner. (He told Ibn Saud that God will compensate him for this law with what he will receive in legitimate money from conquests.) This form of oppression is contrary to the narrations of some historians about Ibn Saud's worship, asceticism, and generosity.[188]

- The original historical sources, such Ibn Bishar and Ibn Ghannam, did not mention any additional conditions included in the agreement regarding leadership in religious or state matters as they pertained to the two Shaykhs' descendants. Only *Lam al-Shahab* mentioned the Saud family heir. (These sources also post-dated these events.) This is in spite of the fact that the situation called for the two families to perpetuate their shared power such that the family of Ibn Abd al-Wahhab would provide a legitimate justification for the future invasions and policies of the Saud family.

The Saudi state, like *Lam al-Shahab*, presented the alliance as a strategic one that allowed the Saud family permanent governance. The family of Ibn Abd al-Wahhab was accorded only the formality of supervision in order to guarantee the continuation of practice according to the Shaykh's vision. Over time, the Shaykh's family's power became a formality, and their influence diminished. The influence remained in the hands of the Saud family. However, they employed the Shaykh's family, as well as other religious scholars, in order to legitimize their actions.[189]

The Birth of Terrorism in Middle East

• • •

It is possible to say that the general articles of the agreement between the two Shaykhs were established and that other oaths, guarantees, and promises were also made, though not documented. This alliance used, as its precedent, the religious and hereditary kingship of the Umayyad state and the states that came after it. Hereditary succession contradicted the very earliest Islamic governments. The precedents laid out by the Umayyads, then, were not legitimate according to the standards of Islamic political practice. The Saudi-Wahhabi school defended this royal hereditary line founded by the Umayyads and has dismissed any criticism of its legitimacy or the behavior of Umayyad caliphates for if the Saudi Wahhabi school allowed for the questioning of the legitimacy of the Umayyad line, which was considered its legal precedent, it would have also be obliged to allow for the question of the legitimacy of its own hereditary Saudi rule.

DIRIYAH BEFORE AND AFTER THE ALLIANCE

A year into the alliance, Diriyah had become a place of great activity in Najd with two major developments that enjoyed an unrivaled degree of enthusiasm. The first development was that the Shaykh took it upon himself to teach his doctrine of dismissing Muslims as disbelievers, or, *takfir*.[190] He spread his own monotheistic message and interpretation of Islam. The majority of the village's people (starting with its chief, then his family, and lastly with immigrants drawn by his new ideas) became the Shaykh's students.

The second development was population growth. The village's resources were insufficient for absorbing the population increase. Thus, more forms of employment were needed. Eventually, raids, wars and their abundant spoils resulted in the establishment of a market and booming trade.

Of course, the Shaykh himself was the focal point of the spirited movement in the village. He carried and defended his plan throughout his life, refusing

Chapter 5: The Third Journey to Diriyah

to listen to other Muslim scholars. This included those who belonged to the Hanbali school of thought to which he had once adhered.

• • •

The author of *Lam al-Shahab* mentioned that the two Shaykhs agreed that governing and *imamah* ("leadership") were to belong to the family of Muhammad Ibn Saud and to be passed down to his sons and grandsons. Meanwhile, the succession of religious leadership would belong to the family of Muhammad Ibn Abd al-Wahhab. Perhaps this was the first time that a Shaykh of the religion made it a requirement that succession belonged to his children and grandchildren. Normally, the role of religious leader is not inherited as the most qualified scholars usually rise to the forefront. The Shaykh, though, had an understanding of religion that contradicted much of Islamic precedent. He was therefore meticulous in ensuring that his children and grandchildren continued his particular understanding of religion so that they remained qualified to succeed him according to his own dictates. This alone would make them worthy of the partnership he created.

• • •

A careful reading of *Lam al-Shahab* confirms that the administration of public matters such as dispatching soldiers, launching invasions, and dispersing the spoils of war and finances were, like religious matters, under the control of Muhammad Ibn Abd al-Wahhab. He was the ultimate chief and no one, including Muhammad Ibn Saud and his son Abd al-Aziz, would act without his permission and direction. It then appears that the Shaykh enjoyed a great deal of power, supported by his followers from the people of Diriyah and its immigrants. Those supporters formed militias under the control of the Shaykh's doctrine. Their loyalty to Muhammad Ibn Saud was merely due to the fact that he had adopted the mission of Ibn Abd al-Wahhab and implemented it.

• • •

It can be said that Muhammad Ibn Abd al-Wahhab became the primary power in Diriyah and that he was the effective decision maker. The details of his daily schedule indicate that he was both effective and eager. He intervened directly in the management of his edicts, even basic ones. His personal disposition, usually harsh and definitive, was evident in the behavior of his followers. They adopted an openly hostile approach against those who challenged them.

The Puzzle of Ibn Suwaylim

There are numerous missing links in the story of Muhammad Ibn Abd al-Wahhab as presented by Saudi State sympathizers, such as Ibn Bishar, Ibn Ghannam, and the author of *Lam al-Shahab*. This could be because they did not expect their works to be published. Earlier I mentioned some of the inconsistent stories from *Lam al-Shahab*. The accounts given by Hempher provided some clarity in confusing matters. They allowed us to deduce the names and identities of some of those who helped the two Shaykhs in their plans to establish their state in Diriyah. I alluded in the previous two chapters to the possible roles carried out by Hempher as he developed Shaykh Muhammad Ibn Abd al-Wahhab and eventually connected him with Shaykh Muhammad Ibn Saud.

Hempher and the author of *Lam al-Shahab* both mentioned in their writings that Muhammad Ibn Abd al-Wahhab owned seven slaves. The author of *Lam al-Shahab* wrote that when Ibn Abd al-Wahhab left Yamamah, he had either seven or eight slaves with him, all of whom were armed warriors. Hempher wrote that he himself was one of those slaves. He had agreed with the Shaykh to pretend to be a slave purchased from Basra. The Ministry of Colonies also sent eleven spies who were among the finest officers and trained in Arabic and desert warfare. Those spies also presented themselves as slaves belonging to Ibn Abd al-Wahhab.[191]

These slaves were to support the Shaykh, assist him in implementing his mission, provide him with assurance, and supply him with money and combat

Chapter 5: The Third Journey to Diriyah

experience when the time would come to resort to military action. Despite such support, the Shaykh was forced out of Yamamah. As we clarified in a previous chapter, Ibn Muammar was hesitant in fully responding to this mission despite the promises of the British spy and despite the gathering of some supporters around the Shaykh in Uyaynah. He considered his continued support of the Shaykh a risky venture.

The Shaykh and his supporters realized that Ibn Muammar could not be counted on, so they turned their sights to the nearby village of Diriyah. It is possible that they were banished. It is also possible that they were driven out by the people of Uyaynah. It is after the migration to Diriyah that early accounts vary. Here, we mention the account given by Ibn Bishar which differs from previous accounts including that given by the author of *Lam al-Shahab*. Ibn Bishar writes:

> Sulayman Ibn Muhammad Ibn Ghurayr al-Hamidi, the leader of al-Ahsa, al-Qatif, and their surrounding areas, threatened Uthman Ibn Muammar and told him that he must banish the Shaykh from his town. Uthman did not express his displeasure at this request. He did not know the value of monotheism nor did he know its advocates who sought empowerment and splendor in this life and paradise in the hereafter. He sent a message to the Shaykh saying, "We have received a letter from Sulayman, the leader of al-Ahsa, and we do not have the power to fight him." The Shaykh [Ibn Abd al-Wahhab] responded, "This is what I have done and what I call for and it is in keeping with the statement 'There is no god but God,' the foundations of Islam, enjoining the good and prohibiting the evil. If you hold onto these and support them God will aid you to victory over your enemies. Then let not Sulayman bother you or scare you. I anticipate that you shall see such victory, empowerment, and dominance as to rule his country and beyond." This embarrassed Uthman and

The Birth of Terrorism in Middle East

he left the Shaykh alone. Subsequently, the issue of the leader of al-Ahsa grew in Uthman's eyes, and he sacrificed the long term for the short one.

This is because God Almighty, who knows the hidden secrets, raises whomever He wishes and humiliates whomever He wishes. In His hand is all goodness, and He is capable of anything. The prevalence of this religion, its emergence, dominance, and empowerment would be at the hands of someone else and not at the hands of Uthman.

Uthman sent another message to the Shaykh saying, "Sulayman ordered us to kill you, and we cannot afford his anger because we do not have the power to fight him. It is neither appropriate nor of noble character to kill you in our country; therefore, you are left to your own affair. Leave our country."

Uthman then ordered one of his knights, called al-Farid, to go with other riders, among them Tuwalat al-Hamarani. He told him, "Ride your horse with this man to wherever he wishes." The Shaykh indicated that he wanted to go to Diriyah. So the knight rode his horse and the Shaykh walked on foot in front of him, with only a fan to shield him from the elements and this was during a very hot time in the middle of the summer. Ibn Muammar had told his knight, "If you come upon his brother Jacob, then kill him there." Jacob was a righteous man who was unjustly killed between Diriyah and Uyaynah and his body was left in a cave by the road. The Shaykh was referred to as his brother because of his righteousness.

The knight rode and the Shaykh walked in front of him, without turning, saying the Quranic verse, "Whoever fears God, He will provide him with an outlet and provide for him

Chapter 5: The Third Journey to Diriyah

from where he does not expect," and "Praise God, thank God, there is no god but God, and God is great," all the while, and the knight did not speak to him. When the knight was the on verge of killing the Shaykh, God protected him, foiled his plot, and planted terror in his heart until he was no longer able to walk forward. So he turned his horse towards Uyaynah and said to Uthman, "I was struck by a great horror and it made me fear for myself..."[192]

This story contradicts other accounts that related that the Shaykh left Uyaynah with his slaves, family, and possessions in a state of dignity. Also, it is not clear where the horsemen who were with al-Farid and Tuwalat al-Hamarani went. Furthermore, the reception of the Shaykh by Muhammad Ibn Saud is not mentioned.

The Shaykh's exit from Uyaynah resembled his first exit from Basra, meaning it was during the heat of the summer season. Also, in this account he was saved by divine power due to the recitation of verses from the Quran. And, whereas previously we observed that the muleteer Abu Humaydan had saved him, here we find that Ibn Suwaylim saved him. After the Shaykh arrived at the center of Diriyah mid-afternoon, he went to the house of Muhammad Ibn Suwaylim al-Arini.

It is worth investigating the figure Muhammad Ibn Suwaylim. The account given portrays him simply as one who provided the Shaykh shelter. But it is also worth entertaining the possibility that he was one of the Shaykh's aides who facilitated the connection with Muhammad Ibn Saud. He may have even been associated with the spies dispatched by the Ministry of Colonies.

Ibn Bishar records that when the Shaykh entered into the house of Ibn Suwaylim:

> ...He felt as if his house was closing in on him and he feared for himself from Muhammad Ibn Saud. The Shaykh

admonished him and calmed him down, saying, "God will provide you and us with a way out."[193]

According to a second account, the Shaykh moved to the house of Ahmad Ibn Suwaylim. And according to a third account, which we discussed earlier in this chapter, Shaykh Muhammad Ibn Saud was the one who received the Shaykh.

• • •

Hussein Ibn Ghannam was reportedly a contemporary of the Shaykh. He was close to him and wrote about him at his behest. Even though Ibn Ghannam confirmed the reported exile of the Shaykh by Ibn Muammar, he did not mention that which Ibn Bishar related concerning the fear that struck the knight who was charged with accompanying the Shaykh and killing him. However, he did confirm that killing Ibn Muammar was at the behest of the Shaykh.[194]

Ibn Ghannam also recorded that the Shaykh left Uyaynah for Diriyah in 1157 CE, that he spent his first night at the house of Abd Allah Ibn Suwaylim, and that the next day he went to the home of his student, Ahmad Ibn Suwaylim.[195] It appears that Ahmad Ibn Suwaylim had been a student of the Shaykh prior to his arrival in Diriyah. And according to Ibn Ghannam, his house was on the outskirts of the village. This is understood from Ibn Ghannam's account concerning the meeting with Ibn Saud and the agreement reached at Ahmad's house. After this incident, Ibn Ghannam reports that "The Shaykh entered the village with him and settled at his house."[196]

It is not clear whether Ahmad Ibn Suwaylim was originally from Diriyah or simply one who had taken residence there (a possibility mentioned by Amin Sa'id).[197] Ibn Ghannam mentioned that Ahmad Ibn Suwaylim was among the most famous of the Shaykh's supporters, including Muhammad Ibn Saud's brothers, his ministers, and his associates from among the people of Diriyah (again, it is difficult to imagine that such a small village boasted ministers).[198] Who, then, was this Ahmad Ibn Suwaylim, a significant figure that the Saudi historians say housed the Shaykh and whose house was the site of the agreement

Chapter 5: The Third Journey to Diriyah

reached between the Shaykh of religion and the Shaykh of the village? It is worth noting that he is not mentioned again in Saudi historical literature.

Some historians indicate that Ahmad Ibn Suwaylim's full name was Ahmad Ibn Suwaylim al-Awni, indicating he was originally from Uyaynah and not indicative of a tribe or branch of a known Arab tribe. Thus, his name was not distinctive in any way leaving his origins up to interpretation. It is possible that he was the same individual who connected Ibn Abd al-Wahhab with Ibn Muammar.

Here we must closely examine the memoirs of the British spy who wrote of his own role and the role of those who posed as slaves in directing the two Shaykhs in Diriyah and then sponsoring them.[199] Ibn Bishar and Ibn Ghannam indicate that Muhammad Ibn Suwaylim[200] contacted Muhammad Ibn Saud's wife, informed her of the presence of Muhammad Ibn Abd al-Wahhab at his house and that Ibn Abd al-Wahhab had a mission that would potentially transform Diriyah into a prosperous emirate.

It is worth entertaining the possibility of the following: Ibn Suwaylim al-Awni was a resident of the outskirts of Diriyah, though originally from Uyaynah, and not from a well-known tribe or family. He was one of the Shaykh's men before he came to Diriyah. Furthermore, it is quite possible that the Shaykh did not come to Ibn Suwaylim's house by chance. Rather this appears to have been pre-arranged. Shaykh Ibn Abd al-Wahhab apparently interceded for him before Uthman Ibn Muammar in order to gain his forgiveness for lack of obedience:

> [Ibn Suwaylim] abstained from [Ibn Muammar] and left with his family, including his wife from Uyaynah who was married to him by Shaykh Muhammad al-Tamimi. He escaped towards Diriyah and enlisted in serving Muhammad Ibn Saud and his brothers for a period of time prior to the arrival of Ibn Abd al-Wahhab in Uyaynah and after disagreement occurred between the two Shaykhs, Ibn Muammar and Ibn Abd al-Wahhab.[201]

Thus, it cannot be denied that the alliances between Ibn Muammar and Ibn Abd al-Wahhab and between Ibn Saud and Ibn Abd al-Wahhab were not, as Saudi sources maintain, motivated purely by religion.

OTHER MYSTERIES IN THE LIFE OF IBN ABD AL-WAHHAB

Ibn Ghannam writes:

> The Shaykh, may God have mercy on his soul, remained in Diriyah for two years, advising people and guiding them to the right path. During that time, his followers in Uyaynah escaped and joined him, including Abd Allah Ibn Muhsin, his brothers, Zayd and Sultan, al-Muammarah (the family of Muammar), Abd Allah Ibn Ghannam,[202] and his brother Musa. Many others from the heads of the Muammar family who were opposed to Uthman Ibn Muammar in Uyaynah emigrated with these followers along with people from their own circles when they learned that the Shaykh had left to work on his own in Diriyah and was now established.[203]

This was also mentioned by Ibn Bishar.[204] And Ibn Bishar added that Shaykh Muhammad Ibn Abd al-Wahhab, after the establishment of the alliance, entered the village with Shaykh Muhammad Ibn Saud and settled in with him.[205] However, Salah al-Deen al-Moukhtar is reported to have said that Ibn Abd al-Wahhab spent some time hiding in Ibn Suwaylim's house: "He was teaching a group of the town's people the principles and rules of the true religion."[206]

It is worth investigating the role played by Ibn Suwaylim in these meetings that took place in his home and, subsequently, in the house of Muhammad Ibn Saud. Muhammad Ibn Saud was apparently intrigued by that which Muhammad Ibn Abd al-Wahhab offered him.

Chapter 5: The Third Journey to Diriyah

Amin al-Rayhani indicates that Muhammad Ibn Saud was aware of the presence of Muhammad Ibn Abd al-Wahhab:

> He was a guest at the house of his student, Ahmad Ibn Suwaylim, and his supporters thronged to visit and excessively honor him. However, Muhammad Ibn Saud, the prince of Diriyah, was hesitant in meeting him. His two brothers, Thunyan and Mushari, insisted that he should meet him, but he remained hesitant. They turned to his wife who said to her husband, "God guided this man to you and there is benefit in him, so make use of the benefit that God has put before you." The prince accepted her words and God put the love of the Shaykh's mission in his heart creating in him the desire to meet him. His brother Mushari told him, "Go to this man yourself and show him glorification and reverence so that he may be delivered from harm by others." So Muhammad Ibn Saud went to Ibn Suwaylim's house and welcomed Ibn Abd al-Wahhab.[207]

It's worth asking why Muhammad Ibn Saud hesitated in meeting Ibn Abd al-Wahhab. The Shaykh's supporters thronged to see him and Muhammad Ibn Saud's brothers begged him to receive him, but still he hesitated.

Also, what did Ibn Saud's wife tell him about the Shaykh being a benefit guided to him by God?

Where did Ibn Suwaylim get the audacity to host the Shaykh and his disciples without Ibn Saud's consent?

Were the words of the Shaykh enough to assure him, even though he knew of Ibn Saud's ill temperedness and treacherous nature?

If we rely on the story in *Lam al-Shahab*, the role of Ibn Suwaylim in bringing together the two Shaykhs was completed before Ibn Abd al-Wahhab even arrived in Diriyah. According to *Lam al-Shahab*, Ibn Saud welcomed Ibn Abd al-Wahhab by walking out to meet and honor him, along with Ibn Saud's son Abd al-Aziz and many of his family and his village's people. It was a distance of a half hour's walk, and he subsequently accorded him the highest honors by vacating his own home for the Shaykh.[208]

On that basis, the Shaykh must have been an influential person who either brought wealth or promises that satisfied the ambitions of the relatively weak Shaykh of the village. He was not just another follower and resident.

It is important to note that Amin Sa'id reported that Muhammad Ibn Suwaylim, and not Ahmad, visited Mushari and Thunyan, Muhammad Ibn Saud's two brothers, and recounted Ibn Abd al-Wahhab's stories to them and that Ibn Suwaylim told them that the Shaykh was staying at his house and that he wanted protection for him.[209]

Amin Sa'id did not mention what the previous historians did, and he did not mention the length of time that Ibn Abd al-Wahhab spent in his home. He also did not mention meeting with his disciples or giving them lessons, nor Ibn Suwaylim's position that allowed him to undertake such a request for protection.

By contemplating these texts, it is hoped that we can shed some light on the personality of Muhammad, or Ahmad, or Ibn Suwaylim and the role he played in bringing the two Shaykhs closer in Diriyah.[210]

THE INTERESTS AT STAKE FOR THE TWO SHAYKHS

A careful review of the declared terms of the agreement between the two Shaykhs indicates that the primary goal was to achieve personal interests, especially for the Shaykh of the village, Muhammad Ibn Saud. He reaffirmed in the first article that Shaykh Ibn Abd al-Wahhab must remain in Diriyah as a permanent ally and that he may not form an alliance with any other. The second article guaranteed the continuation of Ibn Saud's financial royalties which

Chapter 5: The Third Journey to Diriyah

he was accustomed to receiving from the poor in his village, even though the Shaykh promised him bigger gains if they joined hands.

The subsequent events, along with accompanying invasions and raids, have shown that financial gains were a primary goal of the two allies.

These raids, which Shaykh Ibn Abd al-Wahhab presented as being religiously motivated, brought in fantastic revenues, such that Saudi state historians would later describe them proudly.

Ibn Bishar compared the state of Diriyah before and after the wave of these raids as such:

> Those who immigrated to and settled in Diriyah were in a state of destitute and were afflicted by severe trials. At night, they would accept payment for manual labor and then during the day, they would sit with the Shaykh to study. At that time, the people of Diriyah were very weak and of limited means.
>
> When I saw Diriyah later on… I saw the wealth its people now have along with an increased number of men and weapons that are decorated with gold and silver, the like of which does not exist. I saw fine thoroughbred Omani horses and fine clothing along with other luxuries that the tongue cannot describe and the fingers and hearts tire at enumerating. So, one day, I observed from a high location known as the Batin, situated between its western houses, an area known as al-Tarif where the Saud family lived and its eastern houses known as al-Bajiri where the sons of the Shaykh lived. I saw a group of men on one side and a group of women on another and a crop of meat on a third side. Between them, I saw gold, silver, weaponry, camels, and sheep. I saw buying and selling, giving, and taking and other such actions as far as the eye can see. It all sounded like the loud buzzing of bees and the sounds of, "I bought" and, "I sold." The shops were on both eastern

and western sides and they had in them clothes, weapons, and material that cannot be described. Glory be to He whose kingdom never perishes.[211]

The nomadic culture considers raids necessary to sustain life and its spoils a primary source of legal gains. The Bedouins would generally respect warriors and disapprove of manual laborers and artisans.

In order to understand the behavior of the two Shaykhs and their supporters, we must first understand the Bedouin mentality of that time. These tribes struggled to survive and regularly fought each other just as they fought the forces of nature to remain alive. And they strove to obtain financial gains even at the expense of killing others.[212]

THE SHAYKH: A TOTALITARIAN LEADER AND EXPERT IN WEAPON MANUFACTURING AND THE AFFAIRS OF WAR

The unknown author of *Lam al-Shahab*[213] told us, based on the accounts from a man from Diriyah whose name he did not mention that after each of the two Shaykhs placed his conditions for the alliance:

> They sealed the matter with oaths, covenants, and promises, and they had witnesses to all of that. And the matter between them was cleared up both openly and secretly. The great imamate (leadership) of religion would belong to Muhammad Ibn Abd al-Wahhab, along with its associated interests in worldly matters, such as planning for wars, treaties, hostilities, and all else that is associated with the war machine. This all made Muhammad Ibn Abd al-Wahhab knowledgeable in many sciences. Among the actions that showed his knowledge in warfare was that he had ordered the people of Diriyah to learn how to fire rifles [with bullets], and it was he who had acquired those rifles. Previously in Najd, they had used more

Chapter 5: The Third Journey to Diriyah

primitive rifles, the kind that had to be stuffed with gunpowder, similar to those used by the people of Yemen.

Eventually, all matters were under the control of Muhammad Ibn Abd al-Wahhab so that Muhammad Ibn Saud and his children deferred to Muhammad Abd al-Wahhab in all matters. If he favored a matter, so did they, and if he did not favor a matter, they did the same without argument. The ongoing practice was that Muhammad Ibn Saud, along with his son, Abd al-Aziz, and the rest of his children, would visit the Shaykh twice a day, once in the morning and another time in the evening. They would sit obediently and silently, without uttering a word unless the Shaykh talked to them first. They would study under his tutelage his version of monotheism and he would also provide them special lessons separately.

Muhammad Ibn Abd al-Wahhab became a very strong force and the people of Diriyah were all under his control, along with the people from neighboring villages.[214]

• • •

This material should be considered carefully because it raises many questions for the reader.

How did it come to be that the fugitive refugee controlled all of the people of Diriyah, including its chief, who went so far in veneration that he would sit silently in his presence, along with his children, without uttering a word unless he spoke to him first?

How did he become the sole commander? And where did the pride of the "prince" go after he was accustomed to being in charge, especially when he was known to disregard all conscience and religion?[215]

How did the prince overcome his hesitation in receiving the Shaykh, let alone embracing him and putting him in charge?

The Birth of Terrorism in Middle East

And how did the people of Diriyah accept this new situation without objection or argument when they were known in Najd as hateful and viciously tricky and deceptive?[216]

Did the religious motives change everyone from one state to another so that they are at the beck and call of the Shaykh? Or did Shaykh Muhammad Ibn Abd al-Wahhab come to these people with enticing projects and rewards that made the Shaykh of Diriyah and its people hand him the reins of command?

Were the private meetings between the two Shaykhs really focused on teaching the prince the foundations of monotheism?

Where did Shaykh Ibn Abd al-Wahhab acquire his vast experience in all sciences?

This may tempt the reader to believe the story by Hempher, the agent of the Ministry of British Colonies, who recounted that he and a group of other officers from the Ministry accompanied the Shaykh to Najd. It is possible that these individuals were specialists in different fields unknown in the limited Najdi environment, including expertise in military manufacturing and weapons development.

The above makes less surprising the story told by the author of *Lam al-Shahab* about the Shaykh teaching the people of Diriyah how to use a new kind of rifle with bullets and how to use cannons, which we will discuss shortly. There is no doubt that, in the eyes of his followers, the Shaykh's knowledge of theology was superior. However, regardless of how superior he seemed in these aspects, even though this was a source of doubt for many, no one could explain his strange abilities in the manufacturing and development of weapons or the breadth of his military education.

Did his genius suddenly erupt in all specialties so that the Shaykh was able to know and excel in all of these fields?

Or did the working team accompanying him support him in these matters?

Chapter 5: The Third Journey to Diriyah

• • •

I believe that, after examining the circumstances of Shaykh Ibn Abd al-Wahhab's arrival to Diriyah and his alliance with its Shaykh, along with learning about a part of Hempher's memoirs and the author of *Lam al-Shahab* and others, one can gain a better understanding of the Shaykh's rise to power.

Chapter 6: The Strategic Objectives of the Allies

THE STRATEGIC GOALS AND METHODS OF THE ALLIES

The two allies had one single option and that was to remain a coherent unit in the face of the many challenges they encountered. They had to ensure that no one noticed any disagreement among them, as both sides depended on this alliance.

This alliance has been praised for its perceived sincerity and the virtuous nature of the Saudi-Wahhabi cause.[217] This was necessary for public perception. However, like most political alliances, the agreement between the two Shaykhs was based on personal interest, even if there existed a degree of integrity. Even in the early days of Islam, when the most elite society of the religion was supposedly emerging (since it was doing so simultaneously with the Prophet and was influenced by his upbringing), one observes alliances with the enemies of the religion and conflicts that resulted in bloodshed. Later on, this led to Muslims falling under the control of families with utmost hatred and animosity to the religion. These families did not embrace the new religion except after its victory and after the Umayyad family, which had previously fought bitterly against Muslims, became established in a position of authority. This family achieved great success in acquiring these fortunes and gaining substantially under a false

Chapter 6: The Strategic Objectives of the Allies

legitimacy after it bought and swayed tens of companions and scholars and terrorized a large number of Muslims.

• • •

The Saudi-Wahhabi alliance was successful in terms of both political and personal interest. It survived for a long time, and the involved parties were deeply committed to it. It was intended for this alliance to remain in accordance with these standards permanently, as long as it continued to achieve such large profits for its parties in this world and the hereafter.

This alliance was achieved during a state of decline in consciousness and culture in a region that would later welcome Salafi concepts. It would seem that the Salafi-Wahhabi mission took advantage of the Najdi Bedouin young men's purposelessness and ignorance at first and then that of young men across the Arabian Peninsula. Those young men were the front lines of the Wahhabi invasions, arriving before the army into different villages, towns, and regions. In fact, one can argue that they were the fifth column that paved the way for the Saudi Wahhabi invasions.

Many factors prompted the two allies to persevere in their relationship, and they could not have been attributed to true Islamic values. We will refer in this chapter to some of the means to which the two allies resorted to tighten their control and to the motives driving them to do so.

- The two allies, and their children and grandchildren after them, realized that the legitimacy that each partner gave to the other and to their roles as they were agreed upon by the alliance, ensured the establishment of a strong entity that could last for the long term, perhaps even forever, as is usually imagined by those who design hereditary kingdoms. They relied on the terms of their alliance to achieve their common interests. They strengthened their relationship with marital ties between the two families in order to enhance their solidarity and cohesion. Abd al-Aziz Ibn Muhammad Ibn Saud married one of Muhammad Abd al-Wahhab's daughters and they had a son whom they named Saud who was later known as al-Kabir and as the Imam. Muhammad Ibn Abd al-Wahhab loved Abd al-Aziz dearly and would often praise him, both because he hoped he would govern after his father one day,[218] and also because he wanted to strengthen his ties with the Saudi family.

- Muhammad Ibn Saud was an obscure prince with little wealth before the arrival of Muhammad Ibn Abd al-Wahhab, so he was tenacious in hanging on to this partner who seemed to be a gift from God who would guarantee him wealth and affluence. Perhaps he perceived Muhammad Ibn Abd al-Wahhab as being obsessed with his abnormal religious doctrine, but he did not view him as one who would challenge his chiefdom of the village or the anticipated emirate. Muhammad Ibn Abd al-Wahhab's ambitions were focused on spreading his ideals. Such an ally did not pose any danger to his future. Rather, his presence was a rare opportunity to expand his influence and achieve his own ambitions. In addition, Muhammad Ibn Abd al-Wahhab expressed his willingness to go the distance with Ibn Saud and saw the latter as his final chance after the failure of his previous alliance with Ibn Muammar in Uyaynah, and after other failures and defeats.

- The disintegration of the tribes of Najd, along with the competition among its chiefs and elders, helped draw the attention away from the new alliance between the two Shaykhs. In fact, the others may not have taken such an alliance seriously or expected the two allies to gain such power in the future. This allowed the two allies to take their time (about two years) to attract enough young men who were admirers of the Shaykh's ideas before launching limited raids on some of their neighbors under the pretense of spreading Islam and saving them from a state of infidelity and polytheism.

Diriyah became a hub for the followers of the Wahhabi mission. Since it was a neglected, impoverished, and sparsely populated village, no

Chapter 6: The Strategic Objectives of the Allies

one anticipated its danger or its possibility of transforming into an important center for the forceful spreading of the Wahhabi mission.

- The alliance between the two Shaykhs, and their children and grandchildren after them, continued after they tasted the vast financial benefits resulting from their raids. These raids transformed the poor Shaykhs of Diriyah into princes with power and wealth, and they allowed the Shaykhs to enjoy financial and moral authority as well as vast fortunes. The two Shaykhs reportedly believed that their achievements were a result of the nobility of their cause and the authenticity of their faith. They now clearly had a lot invested in the Wahhabi cause, especially since the wealth they had accumulated exceeded the budget of an average nation in those days. Earlier I mentioned Ibn Bishar's testimony about the prosperity that Diriyah enjoyed after the success of these invasions.

- The two allies resorted to a policy of causing division between other allies and their enemies and luring some of them to their own side. They also created opposing movements within a tribe or single chiefdom,[219] resorting to false promises, secret correspondences, and declarations of interim concessions until strengthening their foothold. I will mention evidence of such tactics in subsequent chapters.

- Muhammad Ibn Abd al-Wahhab's religious mission had a luster that attracted young Bedouin men arriving to Diriyah and others. They perceived it a call to the true Islam that they had not previously known thanks to their young age and the isolated environment in which they lived.

The two Shaykhs adopted their roles brilliantly as the strongest defenders of Islamic principles after the influx of volunteers lured to fight wars and invasions that would reward them in this life and the hereafter. The two Shaykhs drew these men by using strategic tactics. And thus, any sign of disagreement or dispute between the two Shaykhs would have been a de-stabilizing factor for the confidence of these followers. These early Wahhabis were an ideological army that the two Shaykhs used to carry out their mission. They were used to fight holy wars against those they deemed polytheists and infidels. For certain, Muhammad Ibn Saud did not previously have his own army nor was he experienced in warfare. He would not have been able to accomplish successful raids with Diriyah's approximately seventy families. Therefore, the two Shaykhs' only choice was to remain united in front of their followers and others since they held steadfast to principles that could only be realized through holy wars.

Muhammad Ibn Saud realized the necessity of Ibn Abd al-Wahhab's cause. That was why he had placed the condition on the Shaykh about staying with him, preventing him from leaving if they found success in the early stages. He had high hopes for this partnership, especially since those participating in later conquests were volunteers drawn in by the Shaykh's doctrine. Later on, the situation evolved as recruitment became compulsory for tribes of their followers.[220]

- The two Shaykhs took advantage of a Bedouin culture in which invasion and theft had become common place. However, they provided a religious twist, claiming that this was a godly cause and one that would be rewarded with gains in this life and virgins in the afterlife. They legitimized invasions as a promised victory from God with lavish rewards available only to the faithful servants who understand the truth of monotheism. In their opinion, the success of a few raids and acquiring the associated generous spoils were proof of the authenticity of their mission and the soundness of its direction. Otherwise their mission would have failed and been beaten by its many enemies,[221] and its supporters would have remained impoverished.

- They adopted the method of spying on their opponents and enemies as well as the people living with them. They recruited many of their followers for this task on the premise that it was a legitimate method

Chapter 6: The Strategic Objectives of the Allies

to guarantee their safety, expand their influence, keep them aware of happenings in their environment, and secure the people's loyalty and obedience to them.[222] This method of control intimidated ordinary people and their enemies.

- Muhammad Ibn Abd al-Wahhab was exceptionally talented in war tactics, including strategies like attacks and retreats, reconciliation when in a weaker position, strategically increasing force, forging alliances, and having innovative weaponry. This is despite the fact that his two partners, Muhammad Ibn Saud and his son Abd al-Aziz, did not have such knowledge. But they trusted the Shaykh and followed his direction. The Shaykh seemed to be the primary decision maker in the affairs of Diriyah and had the final word in all matters, religious or otherwise, until he focused on his private religious affairs after turning eighty, according to his biographers.[223]

- They adopted the method of bribery, which was uncontrolled and unrestricted, in order to buy influence and convince others to avoid harm to themselves and their close followers. This was in contradiction to the theoretical strictness of Muhammad Ibn Abd al-Wahhab as he perceived such matters to be a violation to sound faithfulness.[224] Ibn Saud ordered Ibn Abd al-Wahhab to give bribes, saying, "If you find people's hearts are turning away from you, bring them back by giving [bribes] for nothing is more effective in establishing relationships."[225]

- They resorted to the use of extreme force against their opponents and competitors in Uyaynah and elsewhere.[226] Their harshness became known across the entire Peninsula. The people had not seen the likes of it before, and it reached legendary status beyond imagination. Terrorism and violence were both common in the days of the two Shaykhs. This bloody, terroristic approach continued in later periods in the propagation of the Wahhabi mission. The Saudis saw this as a necessary means by which they could establish their exclusive authority in the region.[227] This led to the Wahhabi military becoming famous for terror and violence throughout all of Najd and Hijaz. The heinous precedents from Uyaynah and elsewhere created terror in the region.

Perhaps they had wanted their actions in Uyaynah to serve as a message for others to avoid future confrontations with them.

The author of *Lam al-Shahab Fi Sirat Muhammad Ibn Abd al-Wahhab* (p. 126) wrote about a raid by Abd al-Aziz Ibn Muhammad Ibn Saud I on the people of Washim who "fought him and he suffered heavy losses so he returned broken to Diriyah. There he fortified his forces then carried out a surprise attack on some forts. He forcibly entered the town and killed all of its people, including the children and elderly. He was then told, 'this is an act that does not please God. Do you kill those who do not fight?' He remained silent and did not answer at the time because he feared revenge could lead to sedition. When he conquered the entire area of Washim and appointed a prince over it on his behalf, he wrote to Muhammad Ibn Abd al-Wahhab telling him of all of his measures and informing him that some of his soldiers denounced him in killing some of the people. Muhammad Ibn Abd al-Wahhab wrote him two letters. The first one was in secret to caution him not to hasten against those who opposed him and that he should take with him so-and-so from their houses from the people of Washim and that he must bring them with him to Diriyah. He also wrote an overt letter ordering him to read it to all of his soldiers. In it, he expressed his wish that they spread this religion and he praised them and promised them victory and great rewards."

Those who joined the army of Abd al-Aziz I apparently believed that they were promoting true Islamic values. But they objected to him. Perhaps their arguments were compelling to him because he was forced into silence. Yet he still harbored revenge against those protesters even though he feared them. Ibn Abd al-Wahhab did not criticize him for killing children and the elderly when Abd al-Aziz I wrote to him informing him of those events. His only action was to advise him

Chapter 6: The Strategic Objectives of the Allies

not to hasten into killing his opposition. Ibn Abd al-Wahhab encouraged him to be repressive when he ordered him to imprison some of the eminent individuals and forcibly bring them to Diriyah. He issued one of his statements praising his army of warriors and promised them victory and great rewards in this world and the hereafter.

It seemed clear to the army and to everyone that Muhammad Ibn Abd al-Wahhab was encouraging such an approach to terrorize his opponents and intimidate them so they (along with anyone watching) would not think of resisting him. It was widely known that the early Wahhabis cut down palm trees, burned crops, and demolished homes in Uyaynah, Manfuha, Jalajil, Kharij, and elsewhere. This sent a clear message to others to surrender to them or face the same fate.

Muhammad Ibn Abd al-Wahhab's plan was to spread terror strategically. This had many successful precedents in some chapters in Islamic history filled with conflict and disputes. The defeat of Ibn Dawass, the ruler of Riyadh, proved the effectiveness of the terrorist methods that were used in Diriyah. The harsh methods that caused people to flee were recounted by Ibn Bishar, the historian and the follower of the Saud family:

> In the middle of Rabi al-Thani in 1187 AH, Abd al-Aziz readied himself along with his armies to invade Riyadh. He left Diriyah, and when he approached the town of Araqa, a messenger came from Riyadh telling him that Ibn Dawass had fled from that city. He hastened his march to it and arrived by the afternoon. He found it empty of its people, save for a few. The people of Riyadh fled, each for himself, running into the desert, just seeking a way out. This was in the middle of the summer, and many of them perished from hunger and thirst. They left Riyadh empty-handed, with food and meat in their pots, the doors to their homes not closed, and the town bursting with more money than could be counted. When Abd

al-Aziz entered Riyadh, he found it empty of its people, save for a few, so they tracked them down, killed them, and pillaged the town.

This was repeated in many cities, and it became clear that the invading Wahhabi forces were willing to cause destruction. They killed indiscriminately, burned crops, and cut down palm trees. These resources would have been beneficial for them later on, but they destroyed them anyway. They wanted to create for themselves a legendary reputation in terrorism and intimidation. Based on accounts by Ibn Bishar about the events in al-Kharij, where approximately 2,000 palm trees were cut down, and in Dalm, Fari, Natiqua, Najan, Yamama, Tadik, Houwayta, Rafia, and al-Ahsa where they killed thousands of innocent people. This all proved that resorting to such tactics was intentional. It was the basis of their strategy in winning battles without suffering much loss on their side.

There is no doubt that the spoils of war and Ibn Abd al-Wahhab's principles blinded the terrorists as to their own despicable acts. This horrible reputation would pave the way for invading Taif, Mecca, Jeddah, Medina, and other towns in Hijaz, as well as parts of Syria and Iraq.

Recently, a supporter of the Saudi rule talked about "the terror that the fighters implanted into the souls of the weakened people and that will remain attached to the reputation of these fighters in the Saudi army to be an essential factor for victory."[228]

This was to justify the unlawful violence used by the Wahhabis in establishing the kingdom of the Saud family on the dead bodies of innocent people. It is no surprise that, when such logic comes from this kind of prejudiced group, they only see what they want to see.

- They resorted to arbitrary methods in dealing with people and issuing sentences. The lack of discipline among those responsible for governing created great fear. In this way, Wahhabi policies contradicted Islamic principles. I will briefly mention some examples in order to prove

Chapter 6: The Strategic Objectives of the Allies

that the young Wahhabi state was more concerned with preserving its own interests and control than it was with applying proper Islamic teachings.

Abd al-Aziz Ibn Muhammad Ibn Saud led a large offensive against Uyaynah and, on orders from Muhammad Ibn Abd al-Wahhab, forcibly entered it. He killed many of its people, forced others to flee, destroyed its walls and houses, ruined its orchards, and cut down its palm trees. Many of the areas neighboring the emerging Wahhabi emirate submitted to its rule:

> When the people experienced the brunt of Abd al-Aziz Ibn Muhammad Ibn Saud's force and realized that he was set in his ways with Muhammad Ibn Abd al-Wahhab and that the two of them were strong and mighty, they submitted to their rule, accepting that religion. Some of them willingly accepted this religion after they evaluated it and found enough reason to accept it saying, "If this were not right, it would not have lasted and triumphed." Some others accepted this religion only as a result of persuasion, doing so out of fear. This led to careful examination amongst their ranks so that those who accepted this religion both inwardly and outwardly were brought closer, rewarded, given enough to satisfy them, and their words were accepted. Those who entered this religion out of fear and obedience were guaranteed safety, but they were regarded with caution.[229]

There were indications of pressure brought on by excessive cruelty. It led to declining morale among the people and their acceptance of the status quo. The people reluctantly and fearfully accepted this religion brought about by Muhammad Ibn Abd al-Wahhab.

One can conclude from this text that the people were carefully watched by the leaders of this emerging state. This was evident in their encouragement of their supporters and the closer associates who were given distinctions. On the other hand, they dealt with caution those who were not reassuring in their loyalty, observing them and trying to bribe and buy the consciences of some of them.

Here I would like to mention some of their orders and abusive practices.

- They ordered each prince on his way to perform the pilgrimage to pass back and forth through Diriyah, regardless of his point of origin, in order to "show their allegiance to the religion." One purpose of this order was to enhance the reputation of their ability to command obedience. Another reason was to publicize their religion to the people of all regions and arouse interest in it by making it known that they host the pilgrims.[230] In fact, they captured one convoy that did not pass through Diriyah and prevented its members from the pilgrimage. They were charged with disobedience.

- Their policies included ensuring no peace of mind for the tribes under their control. It was feared that they might collaborate against the implementation of any of their rules. So they caused unrest within the tribes and disputes among them. This was all done surreptitiously.[231]

- Once Muhammad Ibn Abd al-Wahhab settled into Diriyah, he ordered the construction of a large mosque that would be furnished only with gravel, in a similar fashion to the Prophet's mosque. Then he scheduled lessons based on his book about monotheism that he had written at the beginning of his mission. They were held every morning and every evening of every day. He used to order women and young boys to be present at these lessons in order to learn the principles of monotheism from him.

We were told that a man from the people of the valley did not attend the lessons, so Muhammad Ibn Abd al-Wahhab ordered him brought before him. He asked him, "Why do you not attend the group lessons?" The man started giving excuses. Muhammad Ibn Abd al-Wahhab then

Chapter 6: The Strategic Objectives of the Allies

told him, "In order for your repentance to be accepted, you must either shave your beard or pay a fine of 100 gold pieces." The man was of mediocre means. However, he chose to pay the fine since shaving one's beard was among the most degrading acts according to the religion and Arabian customs.[232]

- According to *Lam al-Shahab*, "Muhammad Ibn Abd al-Wahhab made congregational prayers mandatory even though this was not a requirement from Imam Ahmad's viewpoint or that of anyone else."[233]

- He also issued an edict forbidding the smoking of tobacco, and he defined the consequences for such an act: "forty whips or less, shaving the beard, or cursing, per the judge's choice of one of those three options."[234] These provisions did not previously exist in Islamic law, even in Ahmad Ibn Hanbal's.

- "People were required to pay charity from their *batini* money (usually exempted) and trade money to the imam or the leader of Muslims. He in turn would distribute those monies to the deserving. He ordered spying on people to uncover their *batini* funds. He would then forcibly take the charity amounts. That was not the usual approach for Ahmad's doctrine. Rather, he had charity money paid on *thahiri* monies (not exempted) only and then he would redistribute them as needed to the people."[235]

- He ruled on the prohibition of eating meat slaughtered by one who says, "There is no god but God and Muhammad is the Messenger of God…"[236] Previously, only the Kharijites held this view. Many of the Shaykh's practices and edicts indicated an unconventional approach that was not to be found in Islamic sources, like the Quran or prophetic tradition. This concerned Muslim scholars for it seemed to lay the groundwork for a radical new approach in dealing with the provisions of Islam.

- They pretended to have integrity and rigor in judicial sentencing, even with the leaders of the state. They claimed humility and abhorrence

143

for tyranny, obscurity, and theft. They claimed to be on the path of the Prophet. They treated poor and rich alike, and therefore, those with money did not dare cause any trouble for anyone, even simply by cursing another person, for all of these offenses were put on trial. For example, if someone labeled another as "immoral" or a "dog" or anything of that sort, this issue would be brought before the jurist, Muhammad Ibn Abd al-Wahhab, and he would be punished. Not even the governor Muhammad Ibn Saud himself or his son Abd al-Aziz were exempt.[237] This allowed them to enhance their image in front of their followers among the people of Diriyah and others.

- With the emergence of Muhammad Ibn Abd al-Wahhab and the developing Saudi Wahhabi state, the Najdi community specifically (and the Arabian one in general) adopted a pragmatic political approach. Muhammad Ibn Abd al-Wahhab emerged, contrary to his own intent, as the exemplary statesman who was careful to build his state on the suffering of the people. He brought back memories of men from the early history of Islam such as Muawiyah, Amr Ibn al-As, Abi al-Abbas al-Saffah, and their ruthless soldiers. Their ambitions were not hampered by people's tears, pains, and suffering. These men were considered good role models, and people were forbidden from criticizing them.

  In this chapter, I will mention some evidence of this pragmatic approach, in addition to those already mentioned, in order to clarify that state's preoccupation with strengthening its authority. For instance, earlier I demonstrated how the Wahhabis placated the powerful until they were strong enough to confront them later on.[238] They also oppressed the weak and carried out sudden raids, killing women, children, and the elderly who were unable to take up arms.

- It would seem that Muhammad Ibn Abd al-Wahhab was carrying out a thoughtful cultural invasion founded on a special understanding of monotheism. This understanding included the idea that the Prophet Mohammed was an ordinary person who should be treated, just like

Chapter 6: The Strategic Objectives of the Allies

any other, devoid of the station bestowed upon him according to the Quran. Ibn Abd al-Wahhab exploited Bedouins who lacked substantial knowledge of Islam in presenting an image of Islam that suited a culture of destruction and plunder.[239] He particularly influenced young men, who spearheaded the spreading of his ideologies. The number of his followers expanded thanks to the successful raids and the vast sums of money they would acquire, especially from the Islamic holy shrines (such as the shrine of the Prophet in Medina and his grandson Husayn in Karbala).

- They presented themselves as leading a simple, humble lifestyle in front of their followers in Diriyah in order to gain legitimacy in their eyes. In reality, however, they enjoyed privileges and exceptional luxuries not available to anyone else. Later on, they abandoned those pretenses after their riches became well known and undeniable.

This matter requires some attention in that Diriyah, as mentioned earlier, was an impoverished town before the advent of the Shaykh. And its state did not change quickly, even after his arrival, because the spoils of raids did not meet the needs of all of the incoming combatants from the other villages. Those newcomers had to resort to manual labor in order to support themselves.

When someone speaks of the limited expenditures by both Shaykhs in the first stage of their relationship, it was due to the fact that they were not wealthy yet. They were also obliged to feign asceticism and abstinence in front of their followers, even though their situation was not as dire as that of their followers. Therefore, Sayed Al-Ahel said about Muhammad Ibn Abd al-Wahhab's expenditures:

> The man on the mission, his children, and his family would live conservatively or lavishly according to the inflow of money into the treasury, just as the other people with rights to that money did.[240]

The Birth of Terrorism in Middle East

Al-Ahel based his information on *Lam al-Shahab*. He failed to mention, however, how much higher the funds the Shaykhs would take at the times of abundance were than those they would take at times of hardship. This was detailed by the author of *Lam al-Shahab*,[241] who recounted some of the extravagant tendencies of the Saud and Abd al-Wahhab families:

> The Saud family accorded to the house of Muhammad Ibn Abd al-Wahhab, his children, grandchildren, servants, and entourage, approximately 50,000 gold pieces. Then they allocated to their servants and followers 200,000 gold pieces. However, when their riches increased after the conquests of Bani Khalid, Hijaz, and parts of Yemen and Oman, among other places towards the end of Abd al-Aziz's reign and the beginning of the reign of his son, Saud, the children of Muhammad Ibn Abd al-Wahhab were allocated upwards of 80,000 gold pieces. This continued throughout Abd Allah Ibn Saud's days when the families were accorded monies outside the treasury's allowance, such as gifts from the imams of Yemen, Egypt, or elsewhere. They also had properties of palms and crops which they had purchased or inherited.[242]

This all means that the man with the mission was receiving at least 50,000 gold pieces and 80,000 pieces in better times. These are vast fortunes at that time and were equivalent to the budget of an entire government. No explanation has ever been provided as to how this money was spent. There is no reason to believe that it was given to the impoverished people of Najd. The authors of the Saudi state overlooked this information and, in fact, would talk about the modesty of the two allies and their descendants:

> They would sit on the floor without cushions… They would not have anyone stand up for them, and if they learned that anyone stood up for them out of fear or just for

Chapter 6: The Strategic Objectives of the Allies

appearances, they would say, "We are just like you, other than our position of authority. So do not fear us or disturb yourself with standing up for us. If you wish to honor us, it is fine, otherwise, refrain." This went on until Abd al-Aziz was killed. At that point, they hired doormen and guards, they fortified their homes, and they built retreats. No one dared to enter into their presence without their permission, and they were surrounded by guards at night."[243]

However, they ignored pretenses of humility and modesty when they gained strength and when their authority was solidified. The author of *Lam al-Shahab* wrote:

> They hired guards during the days of Saud Ibn Abd al-Aziz, and those guards were not far removed from their lineage. Even if they totaled 1,000 in number, each guard was allocated 100 gold pieces annually.[244]

In other words, the salaries for guards alone may have exceeded 100,000 gold pieces annually, in addition to their personal expenses. Nonetheless, this author still mentions the Shaykh's modesty and humility. He also claimed that the Shaykh only left behind a piece of land he had bought earlier in his life.[245]

The author of *Lam al-Shahab* wrote of the asceticism of Abd al-Aziz, who reportedly wore wool both in winter and summer and had four wives who did not adorn themselves. He also had a wooden cup for drinking water, but he often favored eating meats. However, this author neglected to talk about the extravagance and overindulgence of Ibn Abd al-Aziz's son, Saud al-Kabir. The latter saw no reason to feign asceticism. In fact, he became known for his ruthlessness. People would fear him, which in turn would allow him to expand his power and influence.

The author of *Lam al-Shahab* wrote the following about Saud Ibn Abd al-Aziz after he became the prince following his father's death:

The Birth of Terrorism in Middle East

It was no secret that when Saud became the ruler following his father's death, he was already living under these same conditions… In other words, even before his father's death, he wore fine clothing, both dyed and not dyed, and he would often wear fine, linen, Indian shirts. He would order his clothes in matching sets from the finest material, and he would have them dyed a celestial blue or a creamy color, seldom wearing white. He would wear a finely made black cloak, made in al-Ahsa, rimmed with red silk and bits of yellow or green silk woven into it as was customary in the sewing of cloaks in that town. This kind of cloak was called *qulanyah* because it was made with a special kind of very soft wool called *qulani*.

Saud always carried his sword which was encrusted with silver, gold, and jewels and whose sheath was covered with sheets of gold, on both sides, from the top and bottom.

He had four wives and six concubines from Georgia. He had secretly sent some of his people to the outskirts of the Roman lands, and they bought these concubines for him at great expense. It was said that he purchased each of them for 3,000 riyals or more because they were extremely beautiful. He also had ten Ethiopian servants, some of whom were a gift from al-Sharif Hammud Abu Mismar from Abi Arish and Tahamat Yemen while others were given to him by al-Quwassim, the people of Rais al-Khaymih, as spoils of wars.

He changed the structure of the home of his father, Abd al-Aziz, expanding it and building additional rooms and private quarters. He appointed each of his wives, and her servants, her own place, whereby there was a dividing wall between her and the others so they would not see each other. He did the same for his Georgian concubines and his Ethiopian concubines; each had her own servants and her own house.

Chapter 6: The Strategic Objectives of the Allies

He divided his time equally between his four wives whereby he would spend one night with each. However, he would come and go, day or night, as he pleased with the concubines, taking care of his needs but not sleeping or napping with them.

His wives' clothing was among the finest and most of it was Indian silk dyed with gold in different colors such as red, yellow, green, or others. They also wore long dresses made of the finest Syrian silk and embroidered with gold. These were their customary clothes in the winter. However, their clothes in the summer were mostly long dresses imported from Constantine. Their cloaks were *qulanyah*, each embroidered with two birds made from gold. He adorned them with a great amount of jewels, and they were gold studded with precious stones such as rubies. He often enjoyed seeing them wearing turquoise stones so he would send people to the Persian king to purchase such stones for him. He also treated his concubines similarly, and perhaps he secretly gave the white ones among them extra gifts.

Saud was also extravagant with his food, just like he was with his clothes. His and his children's food often included rice and rarely included wheat. He took in people from al-Ahsa and al-Qatif to make him fine food from fried meats, stuffed birds, and sweets from sugar. He took to drinking a fine drink brought in pottery from al-Ahsa, similar to Baghdadi drinks but finer and richer.

He would accept anyone's invitation to a feast, even if the host was poor. However, after he had governed for three years, he declined to walk to feasts.[246]

• • •

The Birth of Terrorism in Middle East

This imperial luxury that Saud al-Kabir adopted did not prevent venerated writers from considering him a guide to the righteous path and pure monotheism, as Abd al-Aziz Sayed al-Ahel did. He presented him as a talented leader, dedicated to his mission of change, and did not mention his preoccupations with his Georgian harem, wives, or other luxuries. Nor did he mention his preoccupation with having lavish clothes and food:

> Due to his concern with righteousness and remaining steadfast on the right path, he sent teachers that he trusted and with whom he had personal experience. This was not done out of coercion and he was not oppressive to the Bahraini teachers.[247]

• • •

Thus, the leaders of the Saudi State were able at the outset to present a façade of asceticism meant to influence their followers, even though they were immersed in luxury thanks to the money that was pouring in to the Shaykh and his new mission. Later on, they did not see a reason to conceal their wealth because their control was stable and they had already subjected the other tribes to their rule.

- The two allies, and their children after them, adopted a policy of changing their position in terms of their enemies, even at the expense of their proclaimed principles. In addition to the bribery methods ordered by Muhammad Ibn Abd al-Wahhab, they dealt with their opponents based on the strength or weakness of those tribes and not based on the position of those tribes as permanent enemies.

The author of *Lam al-Shahab* wrote that when Saud heard that Muhammad Ali Pasha intended to challenge him, based on instructions from Muhammad Ibn Abd al-Wahhab, he proceeded to rally all of the groups:

Chapter 6: The Strategic Objectives of the Allies

He felt that some of them might be turning away from him. So he sent his son Faisal bearing many gifts for their elders. He also wrote them a letter in which he praised them and incited them to fight. He told them that they were people of the religion and other such compliments. Then he appeased them with a lot of money, after which they were content with him.

Three years prior, a partial discord had appeared from a group within their congregation. Saud personally marched and fought them. Every time they sent him messengers and money and showed penance, he did not accept those offerings, because, at that point, he was secure, not having to face external opposition. But now they were trying to change their behavior because of the changing conditions.[248]

- An iron curtain was enforced over the areas under their control, preventing people from travelling outside of those areas:

They ordered that none of the people of their towns travel towards opponents' towns without permission from them, if they are nearby, or permission from their representatives for more distant towns.[249]

They also placed some of the leaders and dignitaries under house arrest to prevent them from contacting people and influencing them. Among those placed under house arrest was the Wahhabi founder's brother, Shaykh Sulayman Ibn Abd al-Wahhab, who stood firmly against his brother's teachings that considered Muslims infidels and called for violating their sanctity and plundering their monies.

Ibn Bishar writes concerning when Saud invaded al-Ahsa, he gave its people safe passage and ordered them to leave:

The Birth of Terrorism in Middle East

They left. So he settled there for a month, killing some, banishing others and imprisoning others at will. He also took money and destroyed shops. When he wanted to leave, he captured a number of family heads, brought them with him to Diriyah, and had them live there.[250]

This strategy succeeded in isolating opponents from their audiences and preventing their opinions from spreading. It can be argued, however, that this was an abusive, tyrannical approach which was in contradiction to the principles to which they claimed to adhere.

There are several examples where they resorted to this kind of conduct to preserve their interests and properties such as when Saud arrested the Prince of al-Kawasim and detained him in Diriyah so he could confiscate the tribes' properties and reconcile with the British.[251]

- Shaykh Muhammad Ibn Abd al-Wahhab succeeded in establishing a solid organizational structure for his supporters. This included the senior leadership (assumed by himself and Ibn Saud) down to the smallest group of students. According to *Lam al-Shahab*, the armed militia members set up forts and castles and later built garrisons with rifles and cannons.[252]

The relationships among the leaders of the Saudi Wahhabi State were clearly marked in the organization, even in the relationships among the leaders, their children, and followers:

Both Muhammad Ibn Saud and his children after him did not deviate from serving the interests of Muhammad Ibn Abd al-Wahhab... When the Saud family took over a large town or region, they would build a fort in that town separate from any original fort, if it had one. They would also dig a trench around the town if the ground around it were solid. They would fortify its castle and they would install in its fort about 500 to 1,000 military men, depending on the size of the town

Chapter 6: The Strategic Objectives of the Allies

and its outlying areas, and they would call them its guardians. These guardians were either from the town's people—if they deemed them worthy—or they were from other towns, as long as they were confirmed to be on the right path in relation to their religious beliefs. They would assign them many benefits, perhaps the equivalent of two or three years' worth of savings. They would also provide the fort with rifles and gunpowder, and some even had cannons. Those soldiers had generous salaries. Some were paid three or four hundred gold coins annually as they were entrusted with protecting the town.

These soldiers did not have a commander over them beyond ten men from among them, chosen based on the property they were assigned to govern. If they agreed on the selection of these ten men, they were selected, and the soldiers obeyed them. That obedience was aligned with the decisions made and declared by the imam of the Muslims. If they did not agree, the soldiers would not obey them at all, and they would not leave the fort at all.

It was their habit to appoint a judge and a mufti in the large towns and only a judge in the small ones. They assigned those people an allowance from the treasury. They also arranged four to seven agents in each town to collect the zakat, depending on the size of the town and its revenues. These agents were in addition to the rulers since a ruler had no authority whatsoever over collecting monies.

They also appointed in each town a person to watch the people. Every aspect of their lives was spied upon including their sincerity in their religion, buying and selling, tampering with measures and weights, theft, corruption, and transgressions. They also checked if the judges or rulers accepted bribes, which was considered a sin. They appointed their own ruler in each town and removed the previous one. They also appointed a prince in each region who would have greater power than the rulers of other towns.

The prince, ruler, judge, mufti, and workers were all required to be in agreement in managing and running their affairs.

As for the people of the desert, they would acknowledge their existing princes, and they would not remove them or appoint their own people. If any of them rebelled, they would replace the prince with his brother or cousin. This is because they knew that the Bedouins were not amenable to being led except by their own elders.

They appointed to every tribe a judge or mufti or prayer imam so they could hold congregational prayers for them and teach them God's rules.

If they learned that someone among the Bedouins had dedicated himself to them and the religion, they allowed most of his people's revenues to remain with him. They would even perhaps tell him, "Your obedience is enough for us and your people's zakat is yours." If they observed disobedience from anyone, they would reprimand him by isolating or imprisoning him. If they determined that they needed to kill someone, they would do so openly when possible, and they would not kill him by assassination or deceitfully by poison.

If war, murder, or demands for money occurred among their subjects, they used the rules of Islam to come to a resolution.

One of the positions of their government was that if they wanted to deal with an infringer, they either took money from

Chapter 6: The Strategic Objectives of the Allies

him, if he had it, or they would exile him from his country to outside their own kingdom or to a remote town away from his own but under their control.

If one of their own children, the devout ascetics, or a man of war perished and he had a weak family, they appropriated sufficient funds for them and they would check up on them.

These were all arrangements set forth by Muhammad Ibn Abd al-Wahhab. During some years, they were in great debt and the treasury would not be able to fulfill that debt. They would spread the word that they are indebted and that the treasury cannot meet its obligations. Word would spread among the people and each of them would respond by contributing money to the best of his ability until the whole debt was satisfied.

It was also their policy to control all revenues separately but in one place, the treasury. They did not withdraw from it at will, but rather they had rules for withdrawal based on the usual revenues. They would increase the revenues deposited into the treasury little by little, based on the king's ability. And this was by order of Muhammad Ibn Abd al-Wahhab.[253]

• • •

These actions were not in accordance with Islamic law. Thus, the Shaykh worked endlessly to establish his particular interpretation of religion which incorporated the norms and principles of the Bedouins communities in the Arabian Peninsula.

Chapter 7: Wahhabi Terror Tactics Used to Establish the State

Wahhabi doctrine was not accepting of criticism or dialogue. The ambition of the two allies, Shaykh Muhammad Ibn Abd al-Wahhab and Muhammad Ibn Saud, to establish their Islamic state drove them to rely upon violence. The Shaykhs' heirs developed Wahhabi extremism further, which is reflected in contemporary groups like al-Qaeda, Jihad, and other Salafi movements that have spread across the Islamic world in Asia, Africa, and elsewhere.[254]

The life of Shaykh Muhammad Ibn Abd al-Wahhab, his battles, and his ascension to power with his partner Muhammad Ibn Saud, under the pretext of establishing an Islamic state, gave incentive and inspirtation to later Islamic movements.

The Wahhabi school claimed that its reading of Islam is the only correct one and that all else leads to infidelity and heresy. It also insisted that its followers alone, among all Muslims, are the saved ones who deserve paradise. Based on this understanding, the nature of its confrontational and divisive outlook with other Muslims, as well as followers of other religions, becomes clear.

From the beginning, the two Shaykhs' plan was expansionist, and they strove to achieve it in various ways which I will mention in greater detail shortly.

Chapter 7: Wahhabi Terror Tactics Used to Establish the State

Later generations of Wahhabis look with admiration and pride upon the raids and invasions that earlier Wahhabis committed, as if they were rare acts of heroism. These acts are presented in schools as great exploits that paved the way for a new, pure, Islamic life, even though they were a prelude to ages of destruction, backwardness, and rivalry that brought disaster upon the Muslim world and, later on, upon other parts of the world.

• • •

Initially, the battles between the Wahhabis and their neighbors in the Arabian Peninsula remained undecided. Their expertise and fighting capabilities developed over a few years until they became a power known for its strength and ferocity.

Saudi historians wrote of two facts about the supporters and followers of the Saudis and Wahhabis in their earliest stages:

- Muhammad Ibn Saud was not a fighter or one with any combat experience but, rather, was perceived as being weak.[255]

- The two allies did not have an army or even a battalion with concrete combat capabilities.[256]

• • •

Shaykh Muhammad Ibn Abd al-Wahhab was the leader and primary decision maker in the emerging Diriyah emirate. In essence, he was the true founder of that emirate after it was transformed from a small obscure town into a strong emirate with strong political and military weight. Thus, he can be held responsible for the invasions and acts of genocide in the Arabian Peninsula and neighboring regions that took place later. His partner, Muhammad Ibn Saud, was not nearly as involved in decision-making, as confirmed by Ibn Ghannam in The History of Najd:

> The Shaykh made all decisions regarding binding and discharging, giving, and taking, and advancing or retreating in

> his own hands. The army would not advance and Muhammad Ibn Saud and his son, Abd al-Aziz, would not express any opinions unless they were aligned with the Shaykh's words and opinions. Even Abd al-Aziz would not make any decisions or carry out plans without the Shaykh's permission…[257] (pp. 89–90)

Ibn Bishar mentioned something similar.

Abd al-Aziz Sayed al-Ahel justified Wahhabi violence by writing:

> …In the early stages of raids on tribes and towns, the face of the mission was entirely Wahhabi; however, the hand behind it was entirely Saudi. The gravity of the mission showed, and some called it violence, while those who are ignorant of the religion called it heresy. The source of this seriousness or violence was that the mission was religious in origin, and politics supported and indulged it. There was no room to appease the deviant sentiments, regardless how sacred those sentiments had become for some.[258]

• • •

The Shaykh's tendency towards violence was a trait shared by his followers throughout the generations due to their admiration of him.

Some, like Sayed al-Ahel, substantiated the Shaykh's violence and favored it over dialogue and persuasion due to a perceived deviance in the Islamic world.

• • •

It is known that Shaykh Muhammad Ibn Abd al-Wahhab found devotees in the various areas of Najd. Saudi historians wrote about those followers and their activities in Huraymalah and Uyaynah (which they controlled until its prince, Uthman Ibn Muammar, the Shaykh's first ally, broke his alliance with them).

Chapter 7: Wahhabi Terror Tactics Used to Establish the State

Ibn Abd al-Wahhab's diligent activities to spread his mission was reflected in followers that decided to support him and disseminate his ideas among their respective tribes. Many joined the Shaykh in Diriyah, as I previously mentioned. However, most remained within their own tribes. They later became the nucleus of invading military forces, or the fifth column in their own towns, as was mentioned by Dr. Abd al-Raheem al-Rahman.[259] Even though this author suggested that the primary influence was Saudi from the start and that Muhammad Ibn Abd al-Wahhab was only a secondary partner for Muhammad Ibn Saud, the facts were quite to the contrary. Abd al-Rahman wrote that one of the reasons for the Wahhabi (or Saudi) victory was:

> ...the presence of elements that agreed with Salafi principles in most of the country of Najd and its towns before the arrival of the Saudi influence. These elements became military vanguards, or a fifth column, in those towns for the Saud family, who were working to disseminate the principles of the Wahhabi doctrine. In addition, there were some who had migrated from their own countries to Diriyah, and their presence in that town was the best means to uncover the weaknesses of these other competing towns. It was instrumental in the eradication of the heads of the resistance against the Saudi influence.

The presence of these elements explained an important fact: the spread of the principles of the Wahhabi mission always preceded submission to the Saudis, and, in most cases, it paved the way for its success and proliferation.[260] Abd al-Rahman also mentioned that "Wahhabism always arrived first to the regions that the Saud family targeted, and, as such, it played a big role in their victory over those regions."[261]

• • •

Abd al-Rahman confirms that the Wahhabi mission pursued a path of war and violence and that its leaders, headed by Shaykh Muhammad Ibn Abd al-Wahhab, tried to subjugate the people by force:

The Birth of Terrorism in Middle East

...It always caught my attention when I read the original sources of this history, that I can hardly find a day in the history of this country free from a raid or an invasion launched by the Saud family and their followers on regions in the Arabian Peninsula or one of its tribes or on the outskirts of the Arab states, which belonged to the Ottoman Empire, Iraq, or Syria.[262]

Thus, it is possible to regard the history of the Wahhabi movement as one of wars, invasions, and battles. Its supporters used the cruel and fierce methods in their quest to force into submission all who were not convinced of this mission. Ibn Abd al-Wahhab's followers believed he would fulfill their ambitions through conquest and that he would let them receive their fair share in this world in addition to guaranteeing their good fortune in the hereafter. The Shaykh's promises of victory in both worlds looked to be true after his first few victories.

• • •

Wahhabis demonstrated cruelty in dealing with their opponents and, thus, did not adhere to Islamic instructions for the treatment of the wounded, prisoners, the vulnerable (such as the elderly and the children), and property. As a result, they instilled terror in their enemies and became legendary for violations of sanctity as well as murder and intimidation. Wahhabi terror became a matter of great concern for their neighbors in the Arabian Peninsula, Iraq, and Syria. There are dozens of incidents of terror and excessive cruelty chronicled in history books authored by Saudis and others. Some Saudis overlooked these acts and some, like King Abd al-Aziz, embraced them in the face of criticism.[263]

Meanwhile, some historians produced romanticized accounts of the Shaykh's peaceful attempts at spreading his mission through speaking and good counsel. They tell how he exerted strenuous efforts towards that end despite the slow response to his mission. They claim that in the end, he had no choice but

Chapter 7: Wahhabi Terror Tactics Used to Establish the State

to use the sword for his mission, so he authorized a holy war and incited his followers into that war by using Prophet Muhammad as his role model.

A reading of the relevant texts makes clear that the Shaykh was behind the decision to resort to invasions and violence against those who did not answer his call. It should also be noted that he resorted to forcing people to attend the lessons he organized to teach the principles of his mission. He also punished those who did not attend his lessons despite the absence of any legal or historical precedent for such penalties:

> He established a lesson on monotheism at the mosque in the morning and evening of every day. He ordered women and children to attend those lessons so they could hear the principles of monotheism from him. It is said that a man from the people of the valley did not attend the lessons, so Muhammad Ibn Abd al-Wahhab ordered him brought before him. He asked him, "Why do you not attend the group lesson?"
>
> The man started giving excuses so Muhammad Ibn Abd al-Wahhab said, "You must either shave your beard or be fined 100 gold coins for your repentance to be accepted." The man was of mediocre means. However, he chose to pay the fine, since shaving his beard would be worse legally according to Arabian customs.[264]

• • •

Shaykh Muhammad Ibn Abd al-Wahhab was the foremost military officer, and he furnished the armies, dispatched companies, and corresponded with people of other countries. Delegates and guests sought him, and all comings and goings were to and from his place.[265]

Almost all early Saudi books relate that he was the top man, while some later ones deny that claim, even though they implicitly recognized his responsibility for all wars and invasions.

The Birth of Terrorism in Middle East

According to those who belonged to Diriyah, establishing an emirate in Diriyah under an Islamic pretext required financial and military strength which it lacked in initially. It was also a town that was incapable of absorbing a population increase.

However, Ibn Abd al-Wahhab would soon sweep through al-Taif, Uyaynah, and even Karbala. Soon enough, Diriyah boasted gold and silver. The Shaykh's followers took that as proof of the success of the mission. Thus, he was able to rally supporters. In addition, the ambition of the secondary partners among the Saud family to expand their influence and their role in the partnership (as well as to become real princes and not just local tribal elders) moved Abd al-Aziz Ibn Muhammad Ibn Saud and his son to sign off on using violence and barbarism against opponents and potential competition.

• • •

Here I would like to emphasize the difficulty involved in managing the affairs of a developing emirate with inexperienced officials. The highest official, Shaykh Muhammad Ibn Abd al-Wahhab, possessed surprising skill and experience for one who had previously lived the life of a religious scholar. Earlier I mentioned that Ibn Abd al-Wahhab worked on developing combat rifles and cannons, building forts and castles, waging psychological wars, arming his fighters with his ideologies, sending spies, causing rife among adversaries, bribing some of the elders, restricting travel for some, placing some others under house arrest, balancing the emirate's and the war's budgets, planning in advance for future military operations, as well as organizing and equipping the armies. These skills were not obtainable in the isolated, impoverished environment of Uyaynah or other parts of Najd. They were typical of an established country, and not of small, underdeveloped emirates.

And the Saud family's role was secondary to that of Ibn Abd al-Wahhab, even if Saudi historians inflated the family of Saud's roles, portraying them as princes with vast wealth and great influence. The Sauds were among the Shaykh's followers until he abdicated his power to them in his last days. This

Chapter 7: Wahhabi Terror Tactics Used to Establish the State

was only done after he determined that they would carry out his plans, that their convictions were in support of his mission, and that their journey with him was cemented and beyond the point of return. Ibn Bishar writes, "In 1202 AH, he, God rest his soul, ordered the people of Najd and others to pledge allegiance to Saud Ibn Abd al-Aziz and to make him the crown prince after his father."[266]

Saud al-Kabir was famous for his cruelty, a distinctive characteristic for the Saudi Wahhabi leadership, and that cruelty was rivaled only by that of his father, Abd al-Aziz, and his maternal grandfather, Shaykh Muhammad Ibn Abd al-Wahhab. The latter saw in his grandson a worthy heir who was qualified to forcibly subjugate those who did not answer his call.

The images of atrocities, including the beheading of opponents, were intentionally displayed as a warning for future opposition. The Wahhabis considered these atrocities justified, for the objective was to strengthen their state, defend their interests and privileges, and deter and terrorize their rivals and opponents.

Hafiz Wihbah, advisor to King Abd al-Aziz, founder of the third Saudi state, said in his book, *Jazirat al-Arab Fi al-Qarn al-Ishrin*:

> Saud al-Kabir was famous for his cruelty towards criminals and opponents. I repeatedly heard from his highness the King that he once imprisoned some shaykhs from Matir. Some of their elders came to mediate on their behalf. He felt they were too proud, so he ordered the beheading of the prisoners. He then had their heads brought to the table during a meal provided to their cousins who came to mediate on their behalf. He then ordered them to eat from that meal. This story was told by his highness King Abd al-Aziz to shaykhs from Matir who had come to mediate on behalf of Faisal al-Dawish and he repeated the incident:
>
> In Jamadi al-Awwal 1331 AH (April 13, 1913 CE), King Abd al-Aziz invaded al-Ahsa with the help of supporters. On

the same day, the King hosted a feast to which he invited some of the people, led by some of the figures that hid his soldiers the day of the invasion, and a number of the elders of the desert. He beheaded some of them and placed their heads on the table beside the food. He ordered the rest of his guests to eat, welcoming and greeting them. They hesitated and refrained from eating so he unsheathed his sword and said, "I swear to God if any of you does not eat, I will cut his head off his shoulders…" And so they ate… His intent was to terrorize, as he said to them.[267]

Ibn Bishar says about Saud's influence and his use of terrorism as a means to subdue his opponents:

…His objectives were clear. I do not know of a defeat where his banner was raised. He enjoyed an endless victory of terror. All of his days were fair, all of his raids were spoils. God threw fear in the hearts of his enemies. If they heard he was marching on them, each of them ran and left behind his brother, father, money, and his other possessions.[268]

After completing the morning prayers, he would lead the Muslims, their voices echoing with praise for God, and they would raid. The sky and earth would darken from their dust and their loud praise for God, making stupefying the intellect and providing the Muslims with certainty of victory. God would make the targeted people despair, and the sword was lifted towards all except for the young, women, and elderly. All the monies would be taken, and then they would leave with all those spoils.[269]

Ibn Bishar mentions in numerous parts of his work the Saudi-Wahhabi acts of horror with admiration. He considered them glorious deeds and acts of heroism against infidels and idolaters.

Chapter 7: Wahhabi Terror Tactics Used to Establish the State

The only justification for Saudi-Wahhabi violence was that it helped them acquire and then guard vast fortunes.[270] I also mentioned the vast amounts of money allocated by the Shaykh for himself and his Saudi partners, which continuously increased until reaching hundreds of thousands of gold dinars.[271]

• • •

I will not review the entire series of Wahhabi raids identified by historians loyal to the emirate. Rather I will mention the motivation behind these raids which seemed justified to them in the absence of religious or global civil oversight and due to the fact that, in their estimation, the entire population of the Arabian Peninsula had become infidels and heretics. The Shaykh's edicts inspired the invaders. They then set off enthusiastically to establish a Wahhabi emirate for their Shaykh.

• • •

The violations committed by Abd al-Aziz Ibn Muhammad Ibn Saud in Uyaynah were no less than those he committed in al-Washim:

> …[A city] he forcibly entered and slaughtered all, even the children and elderly. He was told that, "This act does not please God, do you kill those who do not fight?" He did not answer and remained silent because, at the time, he feared that revenge could lead to sedition.[272]

In other words, he did not seek revenge from his opponents for fear of uprise. But, when he became firmly established, he did not give others the opportunity to criticize him.

The author of *Lam al-Shahab* and others justified the violence of the leadership of the new emirate using logic that is neither in accordance with Islamic teachings nor humanitarianism.[273]

The Birth of Terrorism in Middle East

The oppression to which Muhammad Ibn Abd al-Wahhab and his followers subjected the heads of Najd made people of lesser status fear the rising Wahhabi force greatly.

One can draw a parallel to the caliphate of Yazid Ibn Muawiyah. Under Yazid, the Umayyads killed and beheaded the Prophet's grandson, Husayn, along with his companions. They would continue to use terrorism in the holy cities of Medina and Mecca. This was all done in order to intimidate and secure power.

• • •

Saudi history tells of Wahhabi atrocities throughout their history and during three stages of their state. The Wahhabi culture of invasions and violence, which were legitimized by the gains and spoils it obtained, remains prominent among Wahhabis today.

We find some of their historians compare the state of Diriyah before and after the invasions, deeming the financial gains from these activities a divine gift. Because they had supported Shaykh Ibn Abd al-Wahhab, persisted alongside him, and persevered during difficult times, they were rewarded by God.[274]

Chapter 8: Wahhabism: A System of Violence and Estrangement

1: Impressions and Conclusions

Many accounts were published by the Saudi regime in order to present their history in a favorable light. Sayed al-Ahel writes:

> The two allies were successful, and the village of Diriyah was portrayed by loyalist authors as a virtuous city where everyone cooperated in a pure and angelic fashion. They also wrote of pure souls, soaring in an atmosphere of goodness and selflessness, and a community dominated by justice and the greater good. There the rulers were said to be equal to their subjects, and the people were dedicated to loving one another. Their only worry was to uphold the religion of God and the word of monotheism.
>
> Diriyah was portrayed as a beehive where only the hard workers had a place. It was described as a new house for migrants, similar to Yathrib, or Medina, after the migration of the Prophet from Mecca. There was also talk between the

migrants from the neighboring villages of the brotherhood and its supporters among the people of Diriyah. The reader knows a lot about the people of Diriyah who were miraculously transformed from poverty and hatred into people of tolerance, sacrifice, and love of others.

The above was all accomplished thanks to the two Shaykhs and their innocence and sincerity in monotheism.[275] Since Muhammad Ibn Abd al-Wahhab did not aspire for a position of leadership, he focused his efforts on helping people arrive at pure monotheistic beliefs. He expanded all of his energy on this mission through his speeches, his writings, his planning, and the use of the sword. He did not interfere in anything save for Islamic laws, which give order to life. He was faithful, as were his sons and grandsons, to the alliance that he had formed with Muhammad Ibn Saud at the beginning. He attended to the religious mission and Muhammad Ibn Saud attended to the affairs of the state and enforcement of laws.[276]

I will not comment on this idealistic portrayal of the early Wahhabis given by al-Ahel. Instead, I will suffice with highlighting the accounts given by historians about Ibn Abd al-Wahhab's control over all aspects of life in Diriyah and his intervention in even trivial matters. It will become clear that he was the acting ruler of the new kingdom. I will also highlight the extravagant earnings he and his family received as well as all that he owned from orchards, houses, servants, and slaves.

2: THE LOGIC OF SELF-INTEREST

Why would Sayed al-Ahel and others overlook the conditions stipulated by Muhammad Ibn Abd al-Wahhab to his partner Muhammad Ibn Saud before

Chapter 8: Wahhabism: A System of Violence and Estrangement

giving allegiance to Ibn Saud? This is a matter of significance as these conditions demonstrate Ibn Abd al-Wahhab's desire to promote his own interests.[277]

Ahmad Darwish wrote openly about the motives of Ibn Saud for forging an alliance with Muhammad Ibn Abd al-Wahhab:

> Prince Muhammad Ibn Saud was honest with himself and with Shaykh Muhammad Ibn Abd al-Wahhab, for he did not want to join a mission if he did not know the end-results of the affairs in his emirate.[278]

Furthermore, Ibn Saud did not agree to the alliance until he was sure that his gains would at least remain the same or perhaps even increase. Khalifah Fahed asks:

> Would Muhammad Ibn Saud have supported the Shaykh had it not been for the incentives and potential improvements, as well as considerations for his victories, spoils, and financial gains? This leads us to question the idea that the Wahhabi mission and its champion are fortunes granted by God Almighty to Muhammad Ibn Saud. Perhaps Mudi's advice to her husband was not even remotely a display of a prudent opinion or intelligence, and the whole situation was no more than an act towards great gains, both in terms of expansion and worldly possessions.[279]

The two Shaykhs remained loyal to each other as long as their interests required such loyalty and as long as the spoils of war were continuously increasing and their own portions guaranteed.

Muhammad Jalal Keshek acknowledged the above when he wrote of the guaranteed results for the house of Saud from this alliance:

> …The Saudi family council was aware of the results of embracing the Shaykh. This is evident from the hesitation of the prince in meeting with the Shaykh so as to not implicate

his emirate, as well as from the advice of his wife about this man being a benefit…²⁸⁰

The logic of self-interest was ever present, and both families benefitted from the gains of wars with legendary sums that I discussed in the previous chapter. Of course, Muhammad Ibn Abd al-Wahhab legitimized for himself the taking of tens of thousands of gold dinars. Others did not receive such great benefits.

The presence of a religious jihad and an enthusiastic leader such as Ibn Abd al-Wahhab was bound to guarantee great wealth.

3: Unjust Punishments

The historians loyal to the Saudi state acknowledge some aberrant and unjust practices. However, these were presented in a positive light.

Previously, I touched upon the account given by the author of *Lam al-Shahab* in which the Shaykh reportedly wanted to shave the beard of a man who had not attended his classes. The man would accept a fine of 100 dinars in lieu of shaving his beard. That author also told us of the Shaykh's spying on people to uncover their private monies and obtain the taxes he forcibly levied. He also talked about how the two allies and their supporters punished some people with exorbitant fines or expulsion from their own homes:

> Their minds were not at ease concerning the tribes under their control for fear that they would join hands and oppose one of their sentences. So they caused strife and discord among the tribes but did so secretly…²⁸¹

One might argue that they were forced to carry out such policies in a hostile tribal environment. However, there is no Islamic justification for such practices.

• • •

Chapter 8: Wahhabism: A System of Violence and Estrangement

Such abusive practices were the result of a lifetime of fighting by a Shaykh who wanted to demolish towns under the pretense of returning to a proper and pure Islam based upon his own understanding. With its heavy influence, large numbers, and strong financial status, the Shaykh's school has become the foundation for radical Islamic movements.

4: False Likening Unto Authentic Prophetic Knowledge

Muhammad Ibn Abd al-Wahhab did not emerge suddenly. Rather, he was the product of a turbulent period in time. He was raised in a hostile environment that regularly witnessed rebellion, wars, and pillage. While Ibn Abd al-Wahhab's message was presented as a message of authentic prophetic knowledge, it was indeed far from the pure form of Islam it claimed to be. This is because it lacked in compassion and enlightenment and discouraged dialogue and the pursuit of deep understanding of the Quran.[282]

The Shaykh remains the most prominent and influential person among the radical and jihadi "Salafi" line.[283] The Salafi Wahhabi religious establishment in Saudi Arabia, in all its forms, has devoted its efforts to spreading his writings on monotheism, polytheism, and other topics. In addition, many books have been written about his life, battles, and raids, portraying him as essentially an invincible warrior and commander supported by a special divine power. In Saudi sources, Ibn Abd al-Wahhab is depicted as the example of a sincere reformer who saves Muslims from their backwardness and restores Islam to its original clarity, after ridding Muslims of impure polytheistic tendencies. The obsessions of infidelity and polytheistic accusations shifted to all of his followers, and they persevere in fighting others who do not follow the Shaykh's doctrine and teachings.

5: A Tendency Towards Heresy and Estrangement

Researchers and non-Muslim theologians may not detect the inflammatory nature and aggressive method of the Wahhabi movement as much as anti-Wahhabi Muslim scholars. For instance, Wahhabis claim to be the only group that will achieve salvation. They base this on a prophetic tradition to the effect that Muslims will be divided into seventy-three groups. All of them will be in hell, save for one. They also claimed a commitment to a testament, allegedly from the Prophet that reads, "You are responsible for my sunnah, and the sunnah of the guided caliphs after me."

They argue that there are two sunnahs: that of the Prophet and that of the caliphs. And they argue that the Prophet instructed the people to follow his companions (just as he encouraged his companions to be among the group that achieves salvation) when he said, "the one that I and my companions are following today."

These narratives have been challenged by Muslim scholars. This is because they raise questions like how can there be two sunnahs, one for the Prophet and one for the caliphs, when the religion and the path are one? The Salafis answer this question by claiming that the whole generation was benevolent and immaculate, destined to produce other immaculate generations. In response, it is argued that this cannot realistically be achieved. It is not conceivable for an entire generation to be immaculate. Furthermore, historical information concerning that generation indicates that they were not different from any other. In fact, it can be argued that some Muslims from subsequent generations were better than some of those who lived during the time of the Prophet.

6: Polishing the Reputation of Ibn Abd al-Wahhab to Confirm the Legitimacy of the State

The image of Ibn Abd al-Wahhab has been one of the biggest concerns of the Saudi Salafi religious establishment since the time of the early Wahhabis.

Chapter 8: Wahhabism: A System of Violence and Estrangement

This is because the Shaykh's image is the primary pillar for the legitimacy of an entire system of governance. Therefore, it is incumbent to continue the attempts to portray him as exemplary and to enhance the public's confidence in his mission.[284]

The Shaykh's seven leaflets,[285] whose content is based on a superficial reading of the Quran and prophetic traditions, have been compiled under the name of *Majmu'at Mu'allafat al-Imam Muhammad Ibn Abd al-Wahhab* ("The Collections of the Works of Imam Muhammad Ibn Abd al-Wahhab"). Universities, religious organizations, and ministries (such as those of education, civics, and religious affairs) have sponsored documenting, publishing, clarifying, and distributing these books across the globe.

For example, the Shaykh's small booklet *Al-Usul al-Thalathah* ("The Three Principles"), which does not exceed ten pages in length, was explained at great length by ten of the senior Wahhabi scholars. Those explanations filled massive volumes, numbering nearly a thousand pages.[286]

Since the outcome of his struggles ultimately resulted in a rich nation, Ibn Abd al-Wahhab has come to represent personal gain through religious endeavors. Thus, we see that many of the members of the Salafi Wahhabi line who seek religious knowledge, along with the educational and governmental institutions, view allegiance to the Shaykh as the key to acquiring prestige and wealth.

The governing body and its associated religious establishment recognized the value of immortalizing the Shaykh. This was done so that the state itself would be perceived as the heir and sponsor of his plan and so that its core would also be considered religiously legitimate. Thus, it would be forbidden to harm and criticize its direction or the behavior of its leaders. Clear lines were drawn to establish the forbidden areas therein.

The Shaykh is, then, for Wahhabis, beyond reproach and is perceived as being the legitimate heir of the righteous ancestors, or, *salaf*. He revived their traditions and restored their Sunna. Even the Shaykh's descendants are not to be criticized. That is despite what has become known about the moral depravity of many of them and the fact that they have resorted to brutal violence in harming their adversaries and in pursuit of personal gains and authority.

7: Criticizing Early Muslims is Forbidden

The Muslims of the first three centuries were to be considered beyond reproach. Thus, their narratives about prophetic traditions could not be questioned for that would mean questioning the prophetic traditions themselves. This idea was perpetuated to enforce the idea that all of the Prophet's companions were upright individuals, even though history proves otherwise.

Salafi governors promoted this concept in order to prevent people from criticizing the actions of some of the previous rulers in those centuries as well as to prove the legitimacy of their rule and of their monopoly over power. The justifications for the presence of the successors are the same as those for the presence of the predecessors. Therefore, criticism of the predecessors demolishes the successors and paves the way for their demise and is, therefore, prohibited.

The Salafi, or Wahhabi, mission recruited its followers and embraced the defense of Saudi Arabia. That state in return embraced the defense of the Wahhabi mission. This is the reason behind the merging of the two entities, the Salafi/Wahhabi religious identity and the ruling royal Saudi identity, over a period of two centuries. It is this merging that was praised by the Wahhabi literature of the government and of the clerics.

8: Using Polytheism as a Pretext to Dispose of Others

The rules and teachings of Islam do not permit Muslims to violate the blood and sanctity of each other under any pretext. Furthermore, they have

Chapter 8: Wahhabism: A System of Violence and Estrangement

clear guidelines for dealing with non-Muslims and maintaining their fortunes and lives.

Given that clear and open polytheism is the only thing that cannot be forgiven by God and is the only thing that ousts Muslims from their religion, an accusation of polytheism is a tactic used to attack others. For the Wahhabis, this required expanding the scope of the idea of polytheism in order to include the greatest number of opponents.

In reality, Muslims are not polytheists. They bear witness that there is only one God in their daily prayers. However, Wahhabis applied their own interpretation of traditions taken out of context in order to depict the Muslim masses as polytheists. This tactic continues to provide them the ability to attack others and prevail over them and to extend the Wahhabi influence within the Arabian Peninsula and Saudi Arabia using violence. And this was a source of pride for the group on many occasions as previously mentioned. Wahhabis believe that eradicating polytheism among Muslims is their duty as they are defending the true faith as set forth by the thinking of their Shaykh Ibn Abd al-Wahhab.

9: A Flawed Understanding of Islam

Believers in God Almighty, regardless of their particular creed, are known for their faith in God's wisdom, superior ability, and his creation of the heavens, earth, and creatures with His brilliant precision.[287] Many believe that God wanted His wisdom and message to be presented through certain people who are endowed with special divine care such as the messengers, prophets, and saints.[288] And the Quran speaks of the characteristics of such messengers who convey to the people some of the aspects of divine wisdom.[289]

Oftentimes, the followers of such messengers believed they were, in fact, supported in a similar manner and that they had a superior understanding of the great message that they carried.[290] However, some who come from peripheral nomadic communities that are isolated, with limited educational opportunities, cannot properly convey the message as was done by the messengers of God, nor do they possess their understanding, perception, and true sense of responsibility, let alone their ability to carry out their duties. In addition, someone who presents himself as an agent of God and a speaker on His behalf cannot fully grasp the reality of the religion merely through his own vision without understanding the loving relationship between the Creator and the creatures and his care for them, as was revealed by those messengers.

The Shaykh's understanding did not rival that of the prophet's, or even that of prominent scholars'. This is evident in his booklets (which were desired to be secret leaflets for his fighters who were organized based on a culture of invasions). Rather, these writings were based on a personal and incomplete perusal of the overall message of Islam.

• • •

In this text, I will not cover the qualifications necessary for properly conveying Islam. However, it is clear that the Shaykh was not qualified to reform Islam, even though his followers see him as the last reformer who inherited the Islamic experience and corrected its path and present him as a personality that rivaled that of the Prophet and an infallible person above criticism and condemnation.

10: Using Islamic Pretexts to Subjugate Others

In order to establish authoritarian rule, it is necessary to provide a proper justification for systematic violence. In a number of totalitarian societies governed by an elite group that subjugates society to their desires and who seek to establish hereditary rule, efforts are made to make law seem divine. Religion is used as a tool of repression to silence the people, to warn them and scare them instead of using it as a means of establishing social justice.

Chapter 8: Wahhabism: A System of Violence and Estrangement

In a theocratic and oppressive system like that of the Saudis, religious theorists and scholars are often funded by that authority, which provides them with great potential, salaries, and donations. This provides legitimacy to projects and fortifies totalitarian regimes, like those that came before the Wahhabi empire.

And submission to such authoritarian regimes has been justified by traditions falsely attributed to the Prophet. For instance, Ibadah Ibn al-Samit reports that the Prophet said to him, "You must listen and obey in good times and bad times, in things that satisfy you and things you detest. And do not contest people in their own affairs." Abu Hurayrah reports this hadith as well. He also reports that the Prophet said, "You might have princes over you that your hearts abhor and who make your skin shiver." A man then reportedly asked the Prophet, "O Messenger of God, should we fight them?" The Prophet then allegedly said, "No, so long as they establish prayers."

Another fabricated hadith reads, "Whoever obeys me, obeys God; and whoever disobeys me, disobeys God. And whoever obeys my prince, obeys me, and whoever disobeys my prince, disobeys me."

This is in spite of the traditions that confirm his saying, "There is no obedience to any creature in disobedience to God."[291]

It is worth mentioning that the Saudi Ministry of Education established a competition for students awarding a prize for those who memorized one hundred traditions that urge obedience to rulers and guardians, even when they are unjust.

Needless to say, these traditions clearly contradict firmly established Islamic concepts of justice and the establishment of virtues and elimination of vices.

11: Wahhabi Violence and the Motives for Raids

The Saudi Wahhabi ruling establishment, in the days of Ibn Abd al-Wahhab, made efforts to appear to be doing a great service to those it subjugated by saving them from polytheism and bringing them back to Islam. The Wahhabis' belief that they were doing the work of God motivated them in their flagrant violations and in the establishment of an authoritarian and hereditary system of government.

• • •

Wahhabi violence was not the first example of oppressive rule in Islamic history. Previous kingdoms and empires established under religious pretenses and based on an alleged divine right similarly resorted to harsh and violent means with victims numbering in the hundreds of thousands.

Islamic history contains numerous incidents of violence, wars, and genocide such that it might be said that the number of Muslims killed by other Muslim exceeds by tenfold those who were killed at the hands of non-Muslims.[292] This is because religion was used as a tool in the hands of expansionist leaders, kings, and emperors, from the caliphs and "commanders of the faithful," who drafted Muslims and non-Muslims in order to attack, exploit, and establish control.

To this day, one finds those who reminisce about that era of conquests. They regard it as a time that had achieved the greatest financial gains for Muslims and one of the most prosperous. We also find some who maintain (and they may be doing so truthfully as a result of their fascination with the legendary wealth and clout of the caliphs) that those achievements were to serve an Islam that was spread by the justice of the conquerors, not by the sword. However, this latter group may not be aware that those conquerors did not strive to bring people to Islam as much as they sought their own financial and material gain.

12: The Manufacture of Extremism

The strict Salafi line acknowledges and embraces the Wahhabi history of violence. It is seen as a history of virtue and sacrifice first embodied by Ibn Abd al-Wahhab.

Chapter 8: Wahhabism: A System of Violence and Estrangement

It can be said that the violence of the sword in the subsequent history of Muslims for over the last two and a half centuries has been spawned from the Najdi Shaykh and that the victims of that sword amount to the hundreds of thousands (if not millions) of people in the Arabian Peninsula and elsewhere. It can also be said that the implications of his theories on terrorism, conquests, and estrangement are still a price that is paid today through bloodbaths in Iraq, Afghanistan, Pakistan, and other eastern and western countries in the Arab world as well as Europe and the Americas.

Associations, committees, and organizations, both public and private, in the wealthiest countries of the Eastern world and especially in the Gulf, are working on spreading the Shaykh's ideas along with his books and their commentaries. They print new and appealing editions of such writings, distributing them to universities, schools, mosques, libraries, community centers, cultural organizations, public and official organizations, and other such places.

Wahhabis are aware of the existence of extremism and terrorism in their thinking. However, these ideas have become acceptable to them, and they present them as though they are on a sustainable jihadi mission continuing against all infidels in the world, or, those who do not follow their doctrine and their path.

Non-Muslim powers resort to the traditional means of protection. However, despite recruiting tens of thousands of people to fight this fierce battle, as well as taking precautionary measures at airports, and providing vital installations and research and security centers, they have yet to identify the true source of the Wahhabi destructive danger. The official organizations sponsoring Wahhabism, represented by Saudi Arabia and others, are supporters and allies of the West, which has adopted this fight against terrorism.

Western parties in the United States and Europe lead this campaign and, yet, are not entirely informed as to the nature of the Wahhabi movement and its danger. This is in contradiction to the Muslim enemies of Wahhabism who have suffered at the Wahhabis' hands since the Shaykh began his campaigns to implement his expansionist mission with the aid of his ambitious partner, Muhammad Ibn Saud, and his children.

Based on the above, the existing institutions for fighting terrorism have put their fates in the hands of the most radical Wahhabi organizations; those would be the hands that are sponsoring the growing and popular Wahhabi ideas, who commit genocide in the name of Islam. As such, the war on terrorism will remain futile as long as the Shaykh's ideals continue to find enormous proliferation in the world and sponsorship by the Saudi State and its affiliated Wahhabi institutions and organizations.

13: Ibn Abd al-Wahhab at the Forefront of the Salafis

There seems to be little hope that the Wahhabi Saudi religious institutions, operating under the direction of the Saudi state, will back down from their commitment to the Shaykh's ideas and his religious doctrine, which conflict with other Islamic religious lines. Wahhabis believe that Ibn Abd al-Wahhab represents, or at least identifies with these other lines, that he represents the Sunnis, that he is the vanguard of the "saved sect" and that he reflects the true interpretation of Islam.

Wahhabis across the globe ignore the real reason for the prosperity of the Saudi-Wahhabi movement and the real cause for the transformation from a society of invasion into one that enjoys all of the advancements of modern society, the divine gift of oil.[293]

Dozens of television channels, websites, religious podiums, research centers, schools, universities, and libraries have been, directly or indirectly, recruited to spread the Wahhabi Shaykh's ideas, which are fraught with hatred, estrangement, and incitement to carry out wars and suicide missions in the various areas of the world.[294]

Chapter 8: Wahhabism: A System of Violence and Estrangement

14: Declarations of Infidelity

The Shaykh's biggest obsession was declaring Muslims infidels and using that claim to invade and plunder. This was done, as previously mentioned, by distorting historic precedents of some of the companions of the Prophet. He then based his rulings on such distortions, legalizing horrific crimes committed against others. However, the motives for these behaviors were political and based on personal gain and not religious goals. They were related to solidifying the existing systems and removing opponents.[295]

• • •

The Salafi-Wahhabi religious establishment is centered around the Shaykh's own understanding of Quranic texts and prophetic traditions. This understanding is reflected in his limited booklets on monotheism.

The Shaykh's grandchildren and their allies of the ruling Saud family continued to present Ibn Abd al-Wahhab's understanding of Islam ideal. They were also keen on rallying people around his doctrine and mobilizing them to follow him as the true reformer. However, history demonstrates that it was a stroke of luck that created that territory's wealth of "black gold," making it one of the most influential Islamic countries decades after the Shaykh's death.

• • •

The Shaykh was capable of persuading those who lacked proper religious training by way of his strategic language concerning the Quran. He was able to gain a following by way of presenting his unorthodox concepts of monotheism. This resulted in creating a divide between Wahhabis and the rest of Muslims by claiming the latter had polytheistic tendencies and, thus, were open enemies.[296]

Historical sources demonstrate that the Shaykh had no interest in establishing dialogue and advocacy, both of which Islam demands. Rather, he split Muslims into two rival groups.

15: Between Severity for the Committed and Tolerance of the Deviant

The Wahhabis claim to be representatives of the divine on earth. Thus, by way of murder and plunder, they believed they were to provide people with punishment in this world so as to avoid punishment in the hereafter. Therefore, they assumed the majority of Muslims were deserving of punishment and they took it upon themselves to carry out the duties of the keepers of hell by tormenting those who opposed them.

This has resulted in people resenting religion and fleeing from it, rather than seeking it as an oasis of security, peace, and love. They manipulated the Quran to provide justification.

The Shaykh and his followers justified the crimes of previous oppressive governments in the history of Islam, like that of the Umayyads. And aligning oneself with the Umayyad establishment in particular requires that one obscures their opponents, which included the family of the Prophet, distorting their images and the images of their allies, and prohibiting all forms of loyalty to them, such as visiting them or paying tribute to them. The intent of preventing visits to their graves, under the guise that such visits indicate worshipping those graves, was to obscure the authority of the family of the Prophet and to make people forget about them and the crimes committed against them over time.

If the tombs of these esteemed personalities, starting with the Prophet's tomb, were obliterated, then people would become unaware of their standing in society. Meanwhile, one will not find the Wahhabis criticizing deviant interpretations of monotheism perpetuated by the Umayyad and Abbasid caliphs nor their immoral and decadent lifestyles.

The Wahhabi understanding of religion does not encourage the progress of Muslim societies. In fact, the realities of Wahhabism have proven that this movement has not accommodated modern life and its changes. While this attitude may be attributed to a form of dogmatic religious belief, in fact, this is

Chapter 8: Wahhabism: A System of Violence and Estrangement

due to the fact that ambitious Saudi rulers aimed at the expansion of their influence in the Peninsula and the surrounding areas as well as the suppression of dissension.

16: The Manufacture of Terrorist Sleeper Cells

Imam Ali ibn Abi Talib is reported to have said that military methods and discipline by the sword were not to be used against the Kharijites[297] after his time. The Imam reportedly said that these methods alone would not work with that group nor would they eliminate them, and that they would return even if their enemies thought they had wiped them out.

Imam Ali benefitted from a thorough understanding of the reality of the Kharijites and their bigotry as well as the nature of their relationships with one another. He realized that if a small number of them remained, they would be able to enlist a larger number of followers. This was due to their ability to affect those who lacked a proper Islamic education.

• • •

The approach that applied to the Kharijites also applies to the Wahhabis since their doctrine promotes a similar approach to the study of the Quran. Thus, they are a great threat to the world and a source of alienation, conflict, and war.

It is not such that eliminating them in the bloody wars of Afghanistan will eliminate the Wahhabis entirely. The environments that embrace the ideas of Shaykh Muhammad Ibn Abd al-Wahhab will, in the future, produce large numbers of these people who are no less enthusiastic or motivated than the extremist generations the world has already seen.

Therefore, an ideological confrontation is the only effective means of combating this violent mission rooted in the Shaykh's writings, ideas, and positions.

No effort to prevent the sleeper cells from coming back in the future will be effective unless there is a comprehensive ideological agenda to confront Wahhabi ideas that continue to be spread in the midst of large groups of Muslims in the Arabian Peninsula, Africa, Asia, and even the Americas and Europe.

Unfortunately, a lack of understanding from the responsible parties of the nature of the Wahhabi mission (which opposes any conciliatory tendencies), has precluded an effective solution to Wahhabism thus far.

17: The Link Between Wahhabism and al-Qaeda, the Taliban, and Other Radical Extremist Movements

Various groups have adopted the ideas of the Wahhabi school which has its basis in Shaykh Muhammad Abd al-Wahhab's understanding of Islam. These groups include al-Qaeda, Osama Ibn Laden and his associates and admirers who are to be found among Takfiri parties, deadly sleeper cells, some religious schools, some Islamic groups, some speakers, and large swaths of Islamic communities.

Muhammad Ibrahim Mabrouk, an Islamic writer who calls for the return of the caliphate, confirms that Islamic movements need to emulate the great imams of Islamic history, especially those who were close to the original sources of the religion, such as Ibn Taymiyyah, Ibn al-Qayyim al-Jawziyyah, Imam Muhammad Ibn Abd al-Wahhab, Imam al-Maududi, and Imam al-Banna.[298]

Ibn al-Qayyim was the direct student of Ibn Taymiyyah and it was he who kept Ibn Taymiyyah's legacy and books in the public eye. He was clearly dedicated to transferring Ibn Taymiyyah's legacy to others.

Centuries later, Muhammad Ibn Abd al-Wahhab would study the works of both Ibn Taymiyyah and Ibn al-Qayyim. Muhammad Ibrahim Mabrouk believed that Ibn Abd al-Wahhab's appearance was a shock to the Islamic world,

Chapter 8: Wahhabism: A System of Violence and Estrangement

leading to disturbances in the prevailing beliefs, concepts, innovations, and myths, as well as the eradication of many of these from the hearts and minds of Muslims.[299]

Ibn Abd al-Wahhab's life, battles, and ascent to power (with his ally Muhammad Ibn Saud), under the pretext of establishing an Islamic state similar to the one in Medina at the beginning of Islam, provided the incentive for later Muslims to repeat his experiment. However, their mission ended with abject failure from a religious perspective at the hands of his partners who monopolized governance and made it authoritarian and hereditary.

The Wahhabi school claims that its understanding of Islam is the only correct one and that all else leads to infidelity and heresy. It insists that its followers are the only saved ones who will attain salvation from among all Muslims. Based on that understanding, we can discern the nature of its confrontational and divisive perception of the followers of other religions and sects.

Today, the Wahhabi school is more prosperous than ever. Its followers are growing at an alarming rate in underdeveloped and densely populated parts of the world. These areas include Pakistan, Egypt, Afghanistan, Saudi Arabia, the Gulf Emirates, Syria, Jordan, and Somalia. In addition, there is less noticeable growth in Europe and the United States. Gradually, Wahhabis are also finding support in Indonesia and India. And Wahhabism receives secret support from governments who claim to be acting in the name of religion.

Wahhabi supporters strive to propagate their interpretation of Islam through providing free meals while distributing thousands of tons of publications. They also rely upon other means, including radio, television, the Internet, audio recordings, mosques, schools, cultural and recreational camps and religious charitable organizations.[300] And there is no sign that support for Wahhabism is waning.

Wahhabis present their cause to others as a purely religious movement unrelated to violence and terrorism. In fact, they claim that they contribute to the fight against terror by killing or arresting some of their opponents in their own country.

In addition to repairing their own image, this tactic is used to oppress other sects of Islam. This is done on the pretext that Wahhabis are peaceful and the other sects are violent, when the opposite is clearly the case. This sort of persecution is most prevalent within the borders of Saudi Arabia. Governments (such as Saudi Arabia and some of the Gulf countries) that provide a safe haven for the Wahhabi doctrine, or are lenient towards it, secretly accommodate and provide support for extremist groups. They continue to do so as long as such groups are not in conflict with the country's internal security. They allow those groups to infiltrate other countries and carry out terrorist attacks in those places as long as their own interests are achieved.

18: Legitimizing Terrorism in Wahhabi Discourse

Radical extremists, Salafis who claim to advocate tolerance and moderation, and members of violent Islamic movements all embrace concepts that can be attributed to Wahhabism.

At first glance, it may seem that some Wahhabis or Salafis are characterized by tolerance or even indifference to the beliefs of others. Some may even seem to hate extremism. Thus, to non-Muslim researchers, the Wahhabi doctrine may appear to have nothing to do with extremism. Furthermore, Wahhabism may seem to be but another school among the many schools of Islam with its own reading of sacred texts. However, there is a great difference between Wahhabis and other forms of reform, or, claims to the earliest generations of Muslims (the *salaf*).

Wahhabi rhetoric continues to echo the language of the first two founders of the Diriyah emirate that was founded on invasions, coercion, looting, repression, and violence. Many studies of the emergence of the emirate of Diriyah have shown that Shaykh Muhammad Ibn Abd al-Wahhab achieved his ambitions for religious influence by exploiting the political ambitions of Muhammad Ibn Saud, the latter having justified his support of the Shaykh with the pretense of reforming Islam and Muslims. Thus, Muhammad Ibn Abd al-Wahhab provided the ideal religious support for Muhammad Ibn Saud's political expansion plan.

Chapter 8: Wahhabism: A System of Violence and Estrangement

It should be noted that oftentimes Wahhabis defend, and perhaps even deny, their tyrannical tendencies to accuse others of infidelity. They do this despite clear documentation to the contrary throughout all stages of their existence, as well as their political and religious actions whenever they faced objections, condemnation, or were under attack.

19: Addendum: Ahmad Ibn Abd al-Halim Ibn Taymiyyah (1262–1328 CE)

Ahmad Ibn Abd al-Halim Ibn Taymiyyah was a controversial Hanbali jurist and the founder and patron of the "Salafi" movement. He was reportedly distinguished by a powerful memory and remarkable intelligence, but he also became famous for his temper and prejudice against his dissenters.

He exhausted his energies in sharp theological battles that fueled discord among the various Islamic sects. He lived most of his life in Damascus in a historical and social background inclined towards the Umayyad family empire which was known for its tendencies towards expansion and tyranny. The Umayyad family ascended to power under controversial circumstances. It then proceeded to resort to implanting a huge amount of fabricated traditions (allegedly from Prophet Muhammad) in order to strengthen its control. In later centuries, these fabricated traditions would become sacred religious heritage and would be relied upon by scholars of the authorities who sought to legitimize their actions.

Ibn Taymiyyah is considered the representative of the first accusations of infidelity and violence in Damascus, the first sponsor of extremism, and the nucleus of its opposition to tolerant Islam. He employed vague and misleading language when arguing the validity of his views, like repeating phrases such as: "the agreement of people of knowledge," "consensus of the predecessors," "the predecessors said," and "the predecessors believed," etc. He also repeated similar phrases to prove the invalidity of his opponents' views, including: "this tradition was not recorded in any of the books by the people of traditions," "none of the predecessors acted according to this tradition, neither did the scholars, majority, or our companions," etc. He would use these phrases in an attempt to prove that he was relying on a broad base of trustworthy scholars, whose names he curiously omitted, in order to gain influence and followers. He committed numerous errors in an effort to promote his opinion and doctrine.

He attracted a large segment of those who lacked proper religious training and admired his speaking ability, reasoning, and his hostile stance toward philosophy, logic, and rational arguments.

His articles, books, particular understanding of Islam, and methodological approach caused theological battles, some of which resulted in a bloody pattern of anger and hatred from his admirers and supporters against others. Thus, Ibn Taymiyyah is the most prominent cause of discord, division, and sectarian battles whose repercussions continue to rock not only the Islamic world but the world as a whole. The world also continues to live with the repercussions of his unorthodox interpretation of Hanbali jurisprudence.

Ibn Taymiyyah's ideas would not have survived even among the followers of the Hanbali doctrine within the limits of Najd. Muhammad Ibn Abd al-Wahhab is largely responsible for the survival of Ibn Taymiyyah's ideas as he adopted, disseminated, and reinforced them in the Saudi emirate by way of force.

In particular, the followers of the Salafi Wahhabi doctrine still perceive him as a reviver of religion and towering figure, calling him "Shaykh al-Islam." The Saudi royal ruling establishment, with all of its sectors and its cultural and governmental movements, strives to spread aesthetically appealing editions of his books. These books are then taught in schools, universities, mosques, and cultural institutions throughout the Saudi kingdom, as well as some schools in other parts of the world, including Europe and the United States. His students and admirers are, thus now to be found outside the traditional, sectarian geographical boundaries of Wahhabism.

References

- Abd al-Hameed, Sa'eb, *Ibn Taymiyyah, Hayatahou, Aqaidahou*. Beirut: Markaz al-Ghadeer Lel-Deerassat al-Islameeyah. 1st ed. 1994 CE.

- Abd al-Majeed, Muhammad, *Al-Tamyiz al-Ta'ifi Fi al-Saudiyah*.

- Abd al-Wahhab, Shaykh Abd Allah Ibn al-Shaykh Muhammad Ibn and others, *Rasa'el Fi al-Tawheed Wa al-Iman*. Beirut: Dar al-Qualam. 1st ed. 1406 AH / 1986 CE.

- Abd al-Wahhab, Shaykh Abd Allah Ibn al-Shaykh Muhammad Ibn and others, *Al-Moukafirat al-Waquee'a*. Explained and presented by Dr. Mahmoud Matrajee.

- Abd al-Wahhab, Shaykh Sulayman Ibn al-Shaykh, *Al-sawa'iq al-ilahiyah fi al-radd 'ala al-Wahhabiyah*. Beirut: 1st ed. 1419 AH / 1998 CE.

- Abd al-Wahhab, Shaykh Muhammad Ibn, *Ketab Al Tawheed, Hak Allah Ala al-Abeed*. Beirut: Dar al-Koutob al-Elmeeyah. 5th ed. 1409 AH / 1989 CE.

- Abd al-Wahhab, Shaykh Muhammad Ibn, *Ketab Kashef al-Shoubouhat Fi al-Tawheed*. Explained and presented by Doctor Mahmoud Matrajee. Followed by the addendum Tese' Rassa'el. Beirut: Dar al-Qualam. 1st ed. 1406 AH / 1986 CE.

- Abd al-Wahhab, Shaykh Muhammad Ibn, *Al-Wassa'el*. An Addendum to Tarikh Ibn Ghannam, previously mentioned.

The Birth of Terrorism in Middle East

- Abd al-Wahhab, Shaykh Muhammad Ibn, *Al-Kaba'er*. Review and comments by Shaykh Abd Allah Ibn Abd al-Lateef Al al-Shaykh. Riyadh: Maktabat al-Ma'aref. Year of publication unknown.

- Abd al-Wahhab, Shaykh Muhammad Ibn, *Jame' Shourouh Al-Usul al-Thalathah*. Explained by ten of the greatest Wahhabi jurists. Alexandria: Dar al-Quomma and Dar al-Iman, 2004 CE.

- Abd al-Wahhab, Shaykh Muhammad Ibn, *Moukhtassarat Seerat al-Rassoul*. Egypt: al-Matba'a al-Salafiyah.

- Abu Zahra, Dr. Muhammad, *Ibn Taymiyyah, Hayatahou Wa Asrahou, Araahou al-Feqheeyah*. Cairo: 1958 CE.

- Al-Akkad, Dr. Salah, *Da'wat Harakat al-Islah al-Salafi*, al-Majjalla al-Tareekheeyah al-Massreeyah 7 (1958 CE).

- Al-Alusi, Mahmoud Shekri, *Tarikh Najd*. Review and comments by Muhammad Bahjat al-Atharee. Cairo. 2nd 2d. 1347 AH.

- Al-Amin, al-Allama Sayed Muhsin al-Hussaini al-Amili, *Kashef al-Erteyab Fi Ma'rifat Muhammad Ibn Abd al-Wahhab*. Beirut: 1411 AH / 1991 CE.

- Al-Bassam, Abd Allah Ibn Muhammad, *Touhfat al-Shareq Fi Akhbar Najd Wa al-Hijaz Wa al-Iraq*. Reviewed by Ibrahim al-Khaledee. Kuwait: 1st ed. 2000 CE.

- Al-Bassam, Shaykh Abd Allah, *Ulama Najd Fi Khilal Sittat Qurun*, Mecca: al-Nahda al-Hadeetha, 1395 AH.

- Al-Batrik, Dr. Abd al-Hamid, *Al-Wahhabyah Deen Wa Dawlah* Majallat Kollyat al-Banat, University of Ayn Shames.

- Al Hanbali, Sulayman Ibn Samhan al-Najdi, *Tanbih Dhawi al-Albab al-Salimah Ann al-Wouquou Fi al-Alfaz al-Moubtada al-Wakheemah* and *Tabriat al-Shaykhayn al-Imamayn Min Tazweer Ahel-al-Kazeb Wa al-Mayn*. Riyadh: Dar al-Aseemah. 2nd ed. 1410 AH.

References

- Al-Haydari, Ibrahim Fasih Ibn al-Sayed Sibghat Allah, *Unwan al-Majd Fi Bayan Ahwal Baghdad Wa al-Basrah Wa Najd*. London: Dar al-Hikmah, 1998.

- Al-Houssari, Sate, *Al-Bilad al-Arabiyah Wa al-Dawla al-Othmaniyah*. Beirut: 1960 CE.

- Al Ibn Ali, Judge Ahmad Ibn Hajar Al Butami, *Shaykh Muhammad Ibn Abd al-Wahhab, Aqidatuhu al-Salafiyah Wa Dawatuhu al-Islahiyah*. Reviewed and presented by Shaykh Abd al-Aziz Ibn Abd Allah Ibn Bazz. 12th ed. Qatar: 1992.

- Al-Kahtan, Shaykh Ahmad and Muhammad al-Zayn, *Imam al-Tawhid: Shaykh Muhammad Ibn Abd al-Wahhab*. Kuwait: Maktabat al-Sundus, 1986.

- Al-Karakoukli, Rassoul, *Dawhat al-Wouzara Fi Tarikh Baghdad al-Zawra*. Trans. By Moussa Kazem Nowress. Beirut: Dar al-Keetab al-Arabee 1385 AH / 1965 CE.

- Al-Katheri, Sayed Muhammad, *Al-Salafiyah Bayn Ahel al-Sunna Wa al-Imamiyah*. Beirut: Dar al-Ghadeer, 1st ed. 1418 AH / 1997 CE.

- Al-Moukhtar, Salah al-Deen, *Tarikh al-Mamlakah al-Arabiyah al- Saudiyah Fi Madihah Wa Haderhah*. Beirut: Maktabat Dar al-Hayat, 1957 CE.

- Al-Muslim, Muhammad Saeed, *Sahel al-Zahab al-Aswad*. Beirut: Dar Maktabat al-Hayat, 1382 AH / 1962 CE.

- Al-Rahman, Dr. Abd al-Raheem, *Al-Dawlah al-Saudiyah al-Ula*. Cairo: Dar al-Ketab al-Jame'ee. 6th ed. 1418 AH / 1997 CE.

- Al-Rawdawi, Sayed Murtada. *Safha Ann Al Saud al-Wahhabieen Wa Ara' Ulama' al-Sunna Fi al-Wahhabiyah*. Date and place of publication unknown.

- Al-Rayhani, Amin, *Tarikh Najd al-Hadith*. Beirut: Tab' Dar al-Jil, 1988.

- Al-Rouwaished, Abd Allah Ibn Sa'ed, *Al-Imam al-Shaykh Muhammad Ibn Abd al-Wahhab Fi al-Tarikh*. Egypt: Maktabat Issa al-Babee al-Halabi Wa Shourakah, 1392 AH / 1972 CE.

The Birth of Terrorism in Middle East

- Al-Sabhani, al-Allama Shaykh Jaafar, *Ma' al-Wahhabiyah Fi Khoutatihem Wa Aqaidihim.* Tehran: 1406 AH.

- Al-Saeed, Nasir, *Tarikh Al Saud, Manshourat Iteehad Sha'eb al-Jazeera al-Arabiyah.* Date and place of publication unknown.

- Al-Shayal, Dr. Jamal al-Deen, *Al-Harakat al-Islaheeyah Wa Marakez al-Thakafa Fi al-Shareq al-Islamee al-Hadith.* Cairo: 1975 CE.

- Al-Yamani, Haythem, *Al Saud.* Majallat al-Wehdah al-Islamiyah, vol. 60, August 1987 CE.

- Al-Yasini, Ayman, *Al-Din Wa al-Dawlah Fi al-Mamlakah al-Arabiyah al-Saudiyah.* Trans. Doctor Kamal al-Yazjee. London: Dar al-Saki, 1987.

- Darwish, Dr. Madeehah Ahmad, *Tarikh al-Dawla al-Saudiyah Hatta al-Roubo' al-Awal Min al-Quarn al-Eshrin.*

- Faqih, Muhammad, *Takawon al-Tabaiyah al-Saudiyah.* Beirut. 1st ed. 1412 AH / 1991 CE.

- Fasilif, *Tarikh al-Arabiyah al-Saudiyah,* Trans. Jalal al-Deen al-Masheetah and Khayree al-Damen. Moscow: 1986 CE.

- Ghourabiyah, Dr. Abd al-Karim, *Moukademat Tarikh al-Arab al-Hadith.* Damascus: 1380 AH / 1960 CE.

- Hempher, *Memoirs.* Trans. D. G. K. 1937 CE. Place of publication unknown.

- Ibn Bishar al-Najdi, Uthman, *Unwan al-Majd Fi Tarikh Najd,* Riyadh: Maktabat al-Riyadh al-Hadeethah. Year of publication unknown.

- Ibn Ghannam, Shaykh Hussein, *Tarikh Najd* also known as *Rawdat al-Afkar Wa al-Afham Li Mourtad Hal al-Imam Wa Ta'dad Ghazawat Zawee al-Islam.* Edited and reviewed by Dr. Nasser al-Deen al-Assad. Beirut - Cairo: Dar al-Shourouk. 4th ed. 1415 AH / 1994 CE.

References

- Ibn Taymiyyah, Taki al-Deen Ahmad (Shaykh al-Islam), *Al-Ouboudeyah Fi al-Islam*. Cairo: al-Matba'a al-Salafiyah. 4th ed. 1400 AH.

- Ibn Taymiyyah, Taki al-Deen Ahmad (Shaykh al-Islam), *Al-Jawab al-Baher Fi Zouwar al-Makaber*. Explained and presented by Doctor Mahmoud Matrajee. Beirut: Dar al-Qualam. 1st ed. 1406 AH / 1986 CE.

- Ibn Taymiyyah, Taki al-Deen Ahmad (Shaykh al-Islam), *Amrad al-Kouloub Wa Sheefa'eha, al-Tuhfah al-Iraqiyah Fee al-A'mal al-Kalbeeyah*. Explained and presented by Doctor Mahmoud Matrajee. Beirut: Dar al-Qualam. 1st ed. 1406 AH / 1986 CE.

- Ibn Taymiyyah, Taki al-Deen Ahmad (Shaykh al-Islam), *Qaeda Fi al-Waseelah*. Riyadh: Dar al-Aseemah. 1st ed. 1420 AH / 1999 CE.

- Jameeyat Ehya al-Turath al-Islamee Fee al-Kuwait. Daleel al-Masharee' al-Islameeyah. 9th ed. 2006 CE.

- Kahala, Omar Reda, *Goghrafiyat Shebeh al-Jazeera al-Arabiyah*. Damascus.

- Keshek, Muhammad Jalal, *Al-Saudiyeen Wa al-Hal al-Islami*. Cairo: al-Matba'a al-Fanneeyah. 4th ed. 1984 CE.

- Khalifah, Fahed, *Al-Hukum al-Saudi,* London: Dar al-Saffa. 1st ed. 1991 CE.

- Khazal, Hussein al-Shaykh, *Tarikh al-Jazeera al-Arabiyah Fi Aser al-Shaykh Muhammad Ibn Abd al-Wahhab*. Beirut: Maktabat al-Hilal, 1968 CE.

- Mabrouk, Muhammad Ibrahim, *Mouwajahat al-Mouwajaha*. Cairo: Dar Thabet, 1994 CE.

- Miltebron, *Al-Ghoghrafiyah al- Umamiyah*. Trans. Refa'at al-Tahtawi. Egypt: 1916 CE.

- Mustafa, Fareed, *Al Saud Fi al-Tarikh*. Damascus: 1949 CE.

- Sa'id, Amin, *Tarikh al-Mamlakah al-Arabiyah al-Saudiyah*. Beirut: 1964.

The Birth of Terrorism in Middle East

- Saleem, Omar Ibn Abd al-Moun'em, *Al-Manhaj al-Salafi End al-Shaykh Nasser al-Deen al-Albani,* Cairo: Dar al-Deeya'.

- Sayed al-Ahel, Abd al-Aziz, Daeeyat al-Tawheed, Muhammad Ibn Abd al-Wahhab. Beirut: Dar al-Elem Lel-Malayeen. 2nd ed. 1978 CE.

- Taha, Dr. Mahmoud, *Goghrafiyat Shebeh al-Jazeera al-Arab, al-Mamlakha al-Arabiyah al-Saudiyah.* Cairo: 1965 CE.

- Unknown author, *Lam al-Shahab Fi Sirat Muhammad Ibn Abd al-Wahhab.* Reviewed by Dr. Ahmad Mustafa Abu Hakimah. Beirut: 1967 CE. Addendum: *Muhammad Ibn Abd al-Wahhab* by Aziz al-Azamah. Beirut: Dar Riyadh al-Rayss Lel Koutob Wa al-Nasher. 1st ed. 2000 CE.

- Vassiliev, Alexei, *Tarikh al-Arabiya al-Saudiyah*, translated by Jalal al-Mashitah and Khayri al-Damin, Moscow: Dar al-Takadum, 1986.

- Wahbeh, Hafez, *Jazeerat al-Arab Fi al-Karn al-Eshreen.* Cairo: 1946.

References

[1] Historically, Najd is known to be a place of false prophets. Najd was also a source of reversion and separation.

[2] Details concerning his life will ensue.

[3] The four caliphs who succeeded the Prophet.

[4] Husayn Ibn Ali Ibn Abi Talib is the son of Fatimah, daughter of Prophet Muhammad. He was born in the third year after Hijrah, and was martyred on the tenth day of Muharram in 61 AH along with seventeen members of his household and approximately seventy companions on the grounds of Karbala. They fought valiantly but were ultimately slaughtered. Their decapitated heads were circulated on the tips of spears in numerous towns situated between Kufa and Damascus on orders of the Umayyad Caliph Yazid Ibn Muawiyah and executed by his governor in Kufa, 'Ubayd Allah Ibn Ziyad.

[5] The Wahhabis invaded Karbala on April 20, 1802 CE with an army of 12,000. They vandalized the burial site of Imam Husayn and slaughtered most of the city's inhabitants, even the women and children, resulting in the massacre of over 4,000 victims and shaking the conscience of the world. They pillaged the shrine and the city and carried their spoils on the backs of 4,000 camels. This incident was proudly referenced and praised by Uthman Ibn Bishar al-Najdi in his book *Unwan al-Majd Fi Tarikh Najd*, vol. 1, p. 121.

The Birth of Terrorism in Middle East

⁶ A number of Wahhabi edicts, speeches, and lectures attack some Islamic sects and call for jihad against them. Some of these include:

- A letter by the general director of Idarat al-Buhuth al-Islamiyyah Wa al-Ifta' Wa al-Da'wah Wa al-Irshad, number 2/145, dated January 19, 1409 AH concerning the prohibition of butchers from working in slaughterhouses unless one can prove he/she is "a proper believing Muslim who denounces the myths of worshipping shrines and denounces all blasphemous beliefs and fabrications such as those of the Qadianis and the Rafidis, among others." This was signed by the minister of affairs for towns and villages, Ibrahim Ibn Abd Allah, on February 14, 1409 AH.

- An edict by the permanent committee of al-Buhuth al-'Ilmiyyah Wa al-Ifta' published in the Ifta' newspaper on January 25, 1408 AH, issue 208: "It is not permissible for a Muslim to follow the Imami Shiite, nor the Zaydiyyah Shiite, doctrines, nor any other such doctrine from the people of fabrications."

- Edict number 7308 published by the permanent committee of al-Buhuth and signed by the president, Abd al-Aziz Ibn Abd Allah Ibn Bazz, and his vice president, Abd al-Razzaq Afifi, and two members of the committee declaring "anyone praying to Ali, Hasan, Husayn, or their likes to be infidels and polytheists, outside the bounds of the Islamic community and it is not permissible to let them marry Muslim women and it is not permissible to marry from among their women and it is not permissible to eat from their slaughtered animals."

- Edict number 1661, signed by the same members of the committee under the leadership of Abd al-Aziz Ibn Abd Allah Ibn Bazz claiming that the "Ja'faris are polytheists who have abandoned Islam and it is not permissible to eat from their slaughtered animals since those would be considered forbidden dead animals, even if the name of God was invoked over them."

References

- An edict signed by Shaykh Abd Allah Ibn Jabarin on March 22, 1412 AH: "Slaughter of animals by the Rafidi is not legitimate, nor is it legitimate to eat from their slaughtered animals because the Rafidis are most often polytheists and insincerity to them is a tenet of faith, may God quell their evil."

- The wave of these edicts grew and they were signed by jurists, missionaries, and lecturers from the government ranks who considered non-Wahhabis to be "infidels who should be fought and exterminated." Among these edicts is the declaration by Shaykh Adel al-Kalbani, the imam of the Mecca shrine, on the BBC television channel when he said, "I do not deem all Shiite infidels since there are some among them who are ignorant." However when asked about the Shiite scholars, he answered, "I see all of their scholars, with no exception, as infidels." It is known that the Wahhabi ruling on the Shiites and others is that they are unbelievers and liars who have abandoned Islam, and, as such, they are to be killed.

[7] His full name is Osama Ibn Muhammad Ibn Awad Ibn Laden. He was born in Riyadh in the Saudi kingdom to a wealthy father whose estate was estimated at $900,000,000. He had a strong relationship with the Saud family. He organized al-Qaeda, an armed Salafi jihadi organization, established in Afghanistan in 1988 CE. Al-Qaeda attacked military and civilian targets across the world. Osama declared war on the United States and later claimed his organization was responsible for the World Trade Center attacks in New York that took place on September 11th, 2001 and claimed 2,997 civilian lives. Osama was not known to have been an accomplished scholar, although he found support and backing from major Sunni scholars, such as the Saudi Arabian Mufti Shaykh Muhammad Ibn Othaymyn who met with him, praised him and his jihad, and prayed to God to bless him. He was also praised by Shaykh Ibn Jebrin, one of the most prominent Saudi scholars.

[8] Ayman al-Zawahiri was born in 1951 CE in the Beheira Governorate of Egypt. He was al-Qaeda's second in command. He studied medicine in Cairo

and joined extremist jihadi organizations. He moved to Pakistan in pursuit of a doctorate but ended up with al-Qaeda and Bin Laden.

[9] He was born Muhammad Omar Moujahed Ibn al-Moulawi Gholam Nabee Akhouned Ibn al-Moulah Muhammad Rassoul Akhouned Ibn al-Moulawi Muhammad Ayaz in 1959 CE in the suburbs of Kandahar in Afghanistan. He belongs to a Pashtun tribe. He is the spiritual father to the Afghan Taliban and was the president of Afghanistan from 1996 until 2001. His government collapsed following the United States invasion of Afghanistan that was brought on because he sheltered Osama Ibn Laden and al-Qaeda terrorists. He refused to appear on television as it was forbidden according to Salafi doctrine. In 2001, he issued an order to destroy all of Afghanistan's Buddhist statues since they were considered idols. He is currently in hiding.

[10] He was born Abu Mas'ab al-Zarkawi, or Ahmad Fadel Nazzal al-Khelaylah, in 1966 CE in the city of Zarqa', Jordan. He headed training camps in Afghanistan and went to Iraq after the collapse of the Saddam Hussein regime, becoming a leader of the Rafedeen branch of al-Qaeda. He formed armed groups that became responsible for dozens of explosions and the death of hundreds of innocent civilians. He was killed in Iraq in 2006 CE.

[11] Muhammad Rasheed Rida was born in the suburbs of Tripoli in Lebanon in 1856 AD, and he died in Egypt in 1935 CE. He is respected for his intellectual achievements. He founded the Manar magazine and has several publications, the most famous of which being an interpretation of the Quran, titled *Al-Manar*.

[12] Jouhayman Ibn Muhammad Ibn Sayef al-Hafi al-Ateebee (1936–1980 CE) was employed by the Saudi National Guard for eighteen years. He studied religious sciences in Mecca and Medina. He met Muhammad Ibn Abd Allah al-Kahtani, one of the students of Shaykh Abd al-Aziz Ibn Bazz who was the kingdom's mufti. He barricaded himself and his followers in the sanctuary of Mecca on the first of Muharram in 1400 AH (October 20, 1979) during morning prayers and asked people to pledge allegiance to his son-in-law after having

References

sealed the doors, believing he was the reformer of the next century after Hijrah. His actions came to an end when Saudi forces entered the holy mosque with the aid of French forces and were able to quell him and his followers. They were sentenced to death, and, subsequently, sixty-one men from that group were beheaded.

[13] Utopia is a philosophical term given to an ideal place where no social ills, such as poverty, oppression, disease, enmity, etc., exist. This term appeared in a book written by Thomas Moore in 1516 CE, and he may have followed Plato's example in his book *The Virtuous City*.

[14] A mountainous and isolated region in Afghanistan. Some of its caves have become the headquarters of some al-Qaeda leaders during their war with the United States.

[15] The Holy Quran mentions in many of its verses the insincerity, disbelief, or treason of some who claimed to be companions to the Prophet and who pretended to be Muslims, chief among them was Abd Allah Ibn Abi Salul. Some of these verses include:

"What, will you not fight a people who broke their oaths and aimed at the expulsion of the Messenger, and attacked you first; do you fear them? But Allah is more worthy of being feared by you, if you are believers." Al-Tawbah, verse 13

"The dwellers of the desert are very greater in unbelief and hypocrisy, and more disposed not to know the limits of what Allah has revealed to His Messenger; and Allah is Knowing, Wise." Al-Tawbah, verse 97

"And there are hypocrites from among those around you from the dwellers of the desert and from among the people of Medina [as well]; they are stubborn in hypocrisy; you do not know them. We know them. We will chastise them twice, then shall they be turned back to a grievous chastisement." Al-Tawbah, verse 101

[16] He was born Ahmad Ibn Abd al-Halim Ibn Abd al-Salam Ibn Abd Allah Taqi al-Din Abu al-Abbas al-Namiri al-Amiri, known by his followers as

The Birth of Terrorism in Middle East

"Shaykh al-Islam", in 661 CE in Harran, a town currently located in present-day Turkey on the island of Ibn Amro between the Tigris and the Euphrates rivers. He moved with his father and family to Damascus in 667 CE when the Mongols overtook the area of Harran and oppressed its people. He grew up in Damascus and learned religious sciences during that period from his father and the scholars of his time. He went to Damascus with his father when he was young. He was known for his debates and arguments with Islamic scholars from various sects. I have dedicated an addendum to discuss him further later in this book.

[17] There are many verses in the Quran on this subject, among them are:

"And whoever kills a believer intentionally, his punishment is hell; he shall abide in it, and Allah will send His wrath on him and curse him and prepare for him a painful chastisement." Al-Nisa, verse 93

"For this reason did We prescribe to the children of Israel that whoever slays a soul, unless it be for manslaughter or for mischief in the land, it is as though he slew all men; and whoever saves a soul, it is as though he saved all of mankind; and certainly Our messengers came to them with clear arguments, but after that, many of them certainly act extravagantly in the land." Al-Ma'idah, verse 32

"And do not kill any one whom Allah has forbidden, except due to a just cause. And whoever is slain unjustly, We have indeed given to his heir authority, so let him not exceed the just limits in slaying; surely he is aided." Al-Isra', verse 33

[18] This relates to a form of research called by the interpreters of the Holy Quran *'Ulum al-Quran* ("The Quranic Sciences").

[19] The Kharijites are a group of people whose origins go back to the time of the Prophet. Their numbers expanded and they rebelled against Imam Ali Ibn Abi Talib and pressured him into accepting the arbitration in the war of Siffin. They subsequently objected, demanding that he refuse that arbitration on the grounds that it was unfair and biased towards Mu'awiyah Ibn Abi Sufyan. They

References

asked him to seek repentance and to go back on his promise of accepting the arbitration. They later formed an armed movement under the leadership of Abd Allah Ibn Wahhab al-Rasibi, attacking civilians and women, even stabbing pregnant women. This led Imam Ali Ibn Abi Talib to fight them, after warning them, in the region of Nahrawan during the month of Ramadan in 37 AH. Only a few of them escaped. However, they later reemerged in the form of armed groups in support of the Umayyad state.

[20] He was born Muhammad Ibn Abd al-Wahhab Ibn Sulayman Ibn 'Ali ibn Muhammad Ibn Ahmad Ibn Rashid Ibn Barid Ibn Muhammad Ibn Barid Ibn Mushrif Ibn 'Umar Ibn Ba'dad Ibn Rayis Ibn Zakhir Ibn Muhammad Ibn Wahiyib al-Tamimi al-Najdi. This was cited by the genealogist for Shaykh Muhammad Ibn Abd al-Wahhab's family tree. He mentioned approximately seventy ancestors before connecting the family to Mudirr, Nizar, and Mu'add, the first ancestors of the Arabs. It is known that, before the Shaykh's time, the Shaykh's family was not among the distinguished families and its name was not recognized until after his mission and the founding of the Saud emirate. I do not believe that historically we can be confident in the long list of ancestors that was cited by the Riyadh librarian, Sayid Muhammad Amin al-Tamimi, in the family tree that he put together in 1943 CE. However, I am confident in the family branches of the Shaykh's children, following their partnership with the Saud family in governing the Arabian Peninsula. Prior to that period, it is not likely that records would have been kept concerning Bedouin family trees in an instable and nomadic environment, especially since literacy was not common.

Sociologists and anthropologists have expressed doubts concerning the purity of origin and race, especially among nomadic tribes and roaming Bedouins in regions unaccustomed to stability and peace such as the Arabian Peninsula and other areas where slavery, bondage, raids, and captivity were a prevailing norm until recent history and where many variations in lineage were present. In addition, it is difficult to guarantee the accuracy of lineage for all those born, over such long periods of time, in communities that carried out raids, pillaged women, desecrating them and selling them, until recent history. Moreover, there are indications of such doubts in Arabic literature and culture.

[21] Some sources indicate that he was born in 1115 AH (1703 or 1704 CE) and he died in 1207 AH (1791 CE), with some minor disagreements about the specific dates. Some sources that examined his life did not cite a birth year. Reference:

- *Tanbih Dhawi al-Albab al-Salimah* and *Tabriat al-Shaykhayn al-Imamayn*, Shaykh Sulayman Ibn Samhan al-Najdi al-Hanbali, p. 89
- *Al-Fajr al-Sadiq*, p. 16
- *Al-Dawlah al-Saudiyah al-Ula*, Dr. Abd al-Raheem al-Rahman, p. 35
- *Khulasat-ul-Kalam Fi Umaraa al-Bait al-Haraam*, Shaykh Ahmad Ibn Zayni Dahlan

[22] He was born Musaylamah Ibn Habib. He emerged during the days of Prophet Muhammad and claimed prophethood, and thus became known as *al-kadh-dhab* ("the liar").

[23] It is possible to say that the Saudi state was established in 1158 AH / 1745 CE, and lasted until 1233 AH / 1818 CE, when it fell to Ibrahim Pasha. It was reestablished a second and a third time by Abd al-Aziz Ibn Saud after less than a century, and it continues to exist today.

[24] The eponymous figure of the Wahhabi school. Some historians say that this doctrine was not named a Muhammadiyyah doctrine, in reference to the name of its founder, in order to avoid the similarity to the Prophet's name so as to avoid confusion. Muhammad Ibn Farid Wajdi, *Da'irat al-Ma'arif al-Islamiyyah*, volume 10, p. 871, as mentioned in *Al-Muktatif* magazine, volume 27, p. 892.

[25] *Al-Wahhabyah Deen Wa Dawlah*, Dr. Abd al-Hamid al-Batrik, p. 42, referencing *Al-Taj al-Mukalal*, Abu al-Tayyib Siddiq, p. 310

[26] In his book *Tanbih Dhawi al-Albab al-Salimah* and the book *Tabriat al-Shaykhayn al-Imamayn*, pp. 89–90, the author wrote on pp. 161–2:

References

The Shaykh grew up in the care of his father who raised him well and taught him himself... Since the Shaykh was often set in his own ways, deep in thoughts, reflection, and thinking and hungry for more knowledge, he decided to travel to other countries seeking knowledge. Therefore, he performed the pilgrimage and then left for Medina where he contacted the two Shaykhs, Abd Allah Ibn Ibrahim and Muhammad Hayat al-Sindi, and stayed with them for a while, after which he returned to Najd. From there, he traveled to Basra and then Baghdad. During that time, he was learning plenty about the field of monotheism, law, and other sciences. He tried to travel to Damascus and then Egypt. However, he was prevented from doing so. Thereafter, he returned to his own country with more knowledge than was possible for anyone else in his time. He then went to see his father, who at the time was in Huraymalah.

[27] *Lam al-shahab fi sirat Muhammad Ibn Abd al-Wahhab* was written by an unknown author and examined by Dr. Ahmad Mustafa Abu Hakimah. Printed in Beirut in 1967 CE. Parts of it were also printed later in the book *Muhammad Ibn Abd al-Wahhab*, by Aziz al-Azamah, pp. 112–140.

[28] *Tarikh Najd,* Hussein Ibn Ghannam, also known by the title *Rawdat al-Afkar Wa al-Afham Li Mourtad Hal al-Imam Wa Ta'dad Ghazawat Zawee al-Islam*, p. 81

[29] Ibid., p. 82

[30] Sajjah is a woman who claimed prophethood at the same time of Musaylamah al-Kadhdhab. Al-Aswad al-Anasi claimed prophethood after the return of Prophet Muhammad from his final pilgrimage and the onset of his illness. Talihah al-Asadi revealed his prophethood after the passing of Prophet Mohammed, and it is said he subsequently recanted and repented.

[31] *Kashef al-Erteyab Fi Ma'rifat Muhammad Ibn Abd al-Wahhab*, Al-Allama Sayed Muhsin al-Hussaini al-Amili al-Amin, p. 7. Taken from a summary of *Khulasat-ul-Kalam Fi Umaraa al-Bait al-Haraam,* Shaykh Ahmad Ibn Zayni Dahlan.

[32] *Safha Ann Al Saud al-Wahhabiyin,* Sayed Murtada Al-Rawdawi, based on the book *Al-Fajr al-Sadiq*, pp. 15–16

The Birth of Terrorism in Middle East

[33] *Kashef al-Erteyab Fi Ma'rifat Muhammad Ibn Abd al-Wahhab*, p. 9, about *Tarikh Najd* by Mahmoud Shekri al-Alusi

[34] This book was printed in Beirut, Lebanon, comprised of 305 pages, research and commentary by al-Sarawi. The second edition was published in 1998 under the title *Al-sawa'iq al-ilahiyah fi al-radd 'ala al-Wahhabiyah* by Shaykh Sulayman Ibn al-Shaykh Abd al-Wahhab Ibn Sulayman Ibn 'Ali Ibn Ahmad Ibn Rashid Ibn Barid Ibn Mushrif al-Najdi al-Hanbali who died in 1210 CE.

[35] *Ma' al-Wahhabiyah Fi Khoutatihem Wa Aqaidihim*, Al-Allama Shaykh Jaafar a-Sabhani, pp. 17–18, from the book *Al-Futuhat al-Makkiyyah*, second volume, p. 357

[36] Miltebron is the author of the book *Al-Ghoghrafiyah al- Umamiyah* which was printed in Egypt in 1916 CE and translated by Rifa'at al-Tahtawi, the founder of the translation school (Madrasat al-Tarjimah, founded in 1835 CE, later known as Madrasat al-Alson).

[37] *Kashef al-Erteyab Fi Ma'rifat Muhammad Ibn Abd al-Wahhab*, Al-Allama Sayed Muhsin al-Hussaini al-Amili al-Amin, p. 8

[38] Nasir al-Saeed said:

Muhammad Ibn Abd al-Wahhab comes from a Jewish family from the Jews of Dounmah in Turkey. This group infiltrated Islam with the intent of harming it and escaping the oppression of the Ottoman rulers. It is certain that Sholman, or Sulayman, the grandfather of the one who later became known by the name "Muhammad Ibn Abd al-Wahhab," came from a town called Boursa in Turkey. His name was Sholman Karkuzi, which means "watermelon" in Turkish. He was a well-known trader of watermelons in Boursa, Turkey. However, this line of work did not suit him. He decided to trade in religion, since that is more profitable than trading in watermelons for someone in the company of oppressive rulers.

And so Sholman left his town Boursa in Turkey for Damascus with his wife and he became "Sulayman." He lived in one of the suburbs of Damascus, known

References

as "Doma." He started using religion as his trade. However, the people of Syria recognized his bad intentions and refused his work. They tied his feet and beat him harshly. After ten days, he escaped and fled to Egypt. It was only a short time later that the people of Egypt banished him, so he walked to Hijaz and settled in Mecca. He started swindling the people in the name of religion. The people of Mecca also banished him, however, so he went to Medina, where he was also banished, all within the period of four years. He left for Najd and settled in a town called Uyaynah, where he found fertile grounds for his swindling. So he settled there and claimed that he was from the progeny of Rubya'ah and that his father moved to Morocco when he was younger, indicating that he was born there.

In Uyaynah, he had his son, Abd al-Wahhab Ibn Sulayman, who in turn had many children, among them Muhammad Ibn Abd al-Wahhab. And so, Muhammad Ibn Abd al-Wahhab followed in the cheating and swindling footsteps of his father, Abd al-Wahhab, and grandfather, Suleiman Karkuzi, and he was exiled from Najd… *Tarikh Al Saud*, Nasir al-Saeed, vol. 1, pp. 19–20

As I mentioned earlier, the small tightly-knit community would not have accepted a stranger in their midst until after confirming his identity. Of course, this story deserves further examination.

[39] The area of Uyaynah, prior to 1163 AH / 1746 CE and prior to its destruction at the hands of Saudi forces, was approximately 40 sq. km. It was crowded with homes such that women, on the days of weddings, holidays, and other special occasions, would exchange well-wishes, conversation, and news from their windows. These well-wishes, information, and news would quickly spread throughout the town in less than one hour due to its crowded state. *Tarikh Al Saud*, Nasir al-Saeed, p. 22. As I mentioned elsewhere, this city was later ruined at the beginning of the alliance between the Shaykh and Muhammad Ibn Saud.

[40] *Tarikh Najd al-Hadith*, Amin al-Rayhani, p. 25

[41] Ared is the area which includes the main towns and villages of Najd, such as Riyadh, Uyaynah, al-Kharij and Diriyah.

The Birth of Terrorism in Middle East

[42] *Al-Dawlah al-Saudiyah al-Ula,* Dr. Abd al-Raheem al-Rahman, vol. 1, p. 23

[43] Same as the previous source, based on *Goghrafiyat Shebeh al-Jazeera al-Arabiyah,* vol. 1, p. 144 as referenced by Dr. Mahmoud Taha. In spite of the author of *Al-Dawlah al-Saudiyah al-Ula* ascertaining the purity of lineage for the Arabic tribes in that area, he also admitted that the distribution of tribes had changed since the time before Islam due to the movement of many to outside of the Arabian Peninsula during the days of conquest. These tribes settled in Syria and Damascus. Despite the fact that many members of the tribes remained there, the length of time and the period of movement, along with the changing weather patterns and the mixing and marriage between tribes and slaves, made it difficult to maintain the ethnic purity of the people in the Arabian Peninsula.

[44] *Tarikh al-Arabiya al-Saudiyah,* Alexei Vassiliev, pp. 47–48

[45] *Al-Salafiyah Bayn Ahel al-Sunna Wa al-Imamiyah,* Sayed Muhammad Al-Katheri, p. 319

[46] Ibid., p. 48

[47] *Goghrafiyat Shebeh al-Jazeera al-Arabiyah,* Omar Reda Kahala, p. 246, based on *Al-Dawlah al-Saudiyah al-Ula*

[48] *Al-Bilad al-Arabiyah Wa al-Dawla al-Othmaniyah,* Sate Al-Houssari, p. 238

[49] *Moukademat Tarikh al-Arab al-Hadith,* Dr. Abd al-Karim Ghourabiyah, vol. 1, p. 34

[50] *Al-Dawlah al-Saudiyah al-Thaniyah,* p. 30

[51] Al-Qadriyyah is a group of Muslims who claimed that a person is able to choose doing good or bad deeds on his own. Other Muslims denied this belief on the grounds that it sets one up in opposition to God Almighty. This group stood in opposition to another group, called the al-Mujabbarah, who believed that a human being was forced to do his share of good and bad deeds. They were opposed by scholars of Islam, including Imam Ja'far al-Sadiq who is quoted to

References

have said, "There is neither compulsion nor delegation (of authority). The truth lies between the two."

[52] Al-Murji'ah ("those who postpone") is a group which claimed that believing was in the heart and mind without any accompanying deeds. In doing so, they "postponed" deeds. They saw that the case of one who commits a greater sin is turned over to God Almighty who then decides what to do about the person in the hereafter.

[53] Al-Mujassimah is a group that maintains that God has a body. They assign Him adjectives and characteristics based on their understanding of certain Quranic verses such as, "And your Lord comes and (also come) the angels in ranks," (89:22); "Surely your Lord is Allah, Who created the heavens and the earth in six periods of time, and He is firm in power; He throws the veil of night over the day, which it pursues incessantly; and (He created) the sun and the moon and the stars, made subservient by His command; surely His is the creation and the command; blessed is Allah, the Lord of the worlds." (7:54). However, the Quran has many other verses that contradict their belief such as, "there is nothing like something that bears His likeness, and He is the Hearing, the Seeing," (42:11) and "Allah is the Light of the heavens and the earth. " (24:35)

[54] Ka'ab al-Ahbar, Abd Allah Ibn Salam, and Wahb Ibn Munabih are converts from Islam to Judaism. They were famous for narratives and strange stories that they told based in Judaism, which they claimed were attributed to Islam.

[55] *Al Saud Fi al-Tarikh,* Fareed Mustafa, p. 8

[56] *Tarikh Najd also known as Rawdat al-Afkar Wa al-Afham Li Mourtad Hal al-Imam Wa Ta'dad Ghazawat Zawee al-Islam* (known as *Tarikh Najd*), Shaykh Hussein Ibn Ghannam, p. 11

[57] Ibid., p. 11

[58] This happened during the regime of Saddam Hussein in 1991, and it was called the second Gulf War because it followed the first Gulf War when Saddam Hussein attacked Iran in 1980 (a war that lasted until 1988).

59 Perhaps he meant "this sect."

60 *Unwan al-Majd Fi Tarikh Najd,* Uthman Ibn Bishar al-Najdi, vol. 1, pp. 22–23

61 *Da'wat Harakat al-Islah al-Salafi,* Dr. Salah al-Akkad, Journal of History, vol. 7, p. 87

62 *Al-Dawlah al-Saudiyah al-Ula,* p. 29

63 *Unwan al-Majd Fi Tarikh Najd,* p. 86

64 *Al-Dawlah al-Saudiyah al-Thaniyah,* p. 29

65 Well-known historical and Arabic sources, such as *Tarikh Ibn al-Athir, Al-Nujum al-Zahirah, Al-Bidayah wa al-Nihayah,* and *Tarikh Ibn Khaldun,* among others, are rife with news of fierce fighting led by followers of the Hanbali doctrine against the followers of Ahl al-Bayt and others.

66 Among these, for example, is the book *Tarikh Najd al-Hadith* by Amin al-Rayhani. This book was completed in January 1927 CE. The author was associated with King Abdul-Aziz Ibn Saud and was the recipient of Saudi grants. He relied in his accounts, as he stated, on "the men of history from among Al Saud, including King Abd al-Aziz, *Rawdat al-Afkar Wa al-Afham* by Ibn Ghannam and *Unwan al-Majd Fi Tarikh Najd* by Ibn Bishar. Al-Rayhani bore witness that Ibn Bishar had examined the details and was truthful in his account, even though almost seventy-five years separated the two. He also relied on *Tarikh Ibn 'Isa* which he described as weak "but free of concavity and assonance." Al-Rayhani similarly dismissed other historians such as Burkhart, Padilla E. Balkh, and Ali Bayk al-Abbasi. He also relied on a handwritten book titled *Muthir al-Wajd fi ma'rifat ansab muluk Najd,* Rashid Ibn Ali al-Hanbali, saying that "it helped me in confirming the lineage of Al Saud and Al Abd al-Wahhab."

It is known that confirming these lineages (which link them to Mudir, Rubya'a, Nizar, Ma'id, and 'Adnan) requires extensive research and access to documentation that has not surfaced in the Arabian Peninsula which has remained static

References

in this regard. Al-Rayhani acknowledged this, writing on page eight, "thirteen hundred years passed, and those Arabs remain unchanged, the same as they have been. Time did not change anything in their civil, or rather Bedouin, affairs. None of the factors of social evolution affected them until the arrival of Abd al-Aziz."

[67] *Unwan al-Majd Fi Tarikh Najd*, v. 1, p. 17

[68] *Rawdat al-Afkar Wa al-Afham*, Ibn Ghannam, p. 28

[69] *Al-Wahhabyah Deen Wa Dawlah*, Dr. Abd al-Hamid al-Batrik, p. 43, based on *Al-Dawlah al-Saudiyah al-Ula*, p. 38

[70] *Al-Harakat al-Islaheeyah Wa Marakez al-Thakafa Fi al-Shareq al-Islamee al-Hadith*, Dr. Jamal al-Deen al-Shayal, vol. 1, p. 56

[71] *Unwan al-Majd Fi Bayan Ahwal Baghdad Wa al-Basrah Wa Najd*, Ibrahim Fasih Ibn al-Sayed Sibghat Allah al-Haydari, pp. 230–231

[72] *Tanbih Dhawi al-Albab al-Salimah* and the book *Tabriat al-Shaykhayn al-Imamayn*, Sulayman Ibn Samhan al-Najdi al-Hanbali, pp. 89–91

[73] Perhaps the author meant clothes of poor people or ascetics.

[74] *Lam al-Shahab*, pp. 112–117

[75] Lineage is the grace and the pride that a man associates with his forefathers. Pedigree is the grace and the pride that a man associates with himself.

[76] *Lam al-Shahab*, p. 118

[77] In addition to the criticism mentioned in the second story that Ibrahim Fasih al-Haydari directed at the Shaykh, he also criticized him for his excessive prejudice saying, "The mentioned Shaykh Muhammad, in his youth, frequently read books of elucidation, traditions, and beliefs. I think his frequent readings without consulting reliable scholars and learning from them led him to the prejudice for which he was known. That is because learning independently and formulating autonomous opinions lead to falling into trouble, opposing the public, and violating norms. The Shaykh frequently showed disapproval of the

people of Najd in many things, and nobody helped him, even if some people approved of his behavior." *Unwan al-Majd*, p. 231

[78] Eedah al-Maknoun, vol. 2, p. 190 from *Al-sawa'iq al-ilahiyah fi al-radd 'ala al-Wahhabiyah*, Beirut, Lebanon, first edition 1998

[79] *Mr. Hempher's Memoirs.* We will discuss some of the details of these memoirs that are relevant to some of the events mentioned by the author of *Lam al-Shahab*, Ibn Bishar, and Ibn Ghannam.

[80] Haythem al-Yamani in an article about *Al Saud*, Majallat al-Wehdah al-Islamiyah magazine, vol. 60, August 1987. This researcher said in his article:

The British rushed towards the Arabian Peninsula to prepare themselves to reap the fruit. After they secured their friendship with some of the tribes and families on the shores, they were able to reach the inner parts of the Peninsula, with its tribes and prevailing value system. They met an ambitious man who wanted to establish a stronghold but was lacking the money and material to entice the Bedouin tribes to submit to his leadership. This man had no respect for conscience or religion for he was hungry for wars and power. He was ferocious, personifying the harshness of the desert at its utmost. This man was Muhammad Ibn Abd al-Wahhab, whose own influence did not extend beyond setting himself up as the leader of his weak family in a small town in the area of Najd, called Diriyah.

The British saw their objectives in the aspirations of this man, since his aims of political influence were not recognized by anyone and his tribal prejudice (his tribe being no more than a few decades old) was too weak to support the achievement of his ambitions. In addition to weapons and money, those ambitions needed the establishment of unifying agents for this rule of diverse allegiances. It needed to be firmly committed to strengthening Al Saud at the center and needed to have a tribal base. In other words, it needed to be on the same ideological level in order to create a new prejudice beyond the tribal affiliation. And therefore, Muhammad Ibn Saud found the right answer at the right time in the Wahhabi movement.

References

From the perspective of the author, the British fostered the alliance between Muhammad Ibn Saud and Muhammad Ibn Abd al-Wahhab after they gave up on Ibn Muammar who did not want to squander his own alliance with the mighty Bani Khaled, rulers of the eastern coast of the Peninsula. He refused, despite the enticements of Muhammad Ibn Abd al-Wahhab and his offer of replacing all of the benefits that would be withheld from him by Bani Khaled (*Lam al-Shahab*, p. 35).

Even though there are interpretations that later on claimed that Muhammad Ibn Abd al-Wahhab's offer was based on his conviction that he and Ibn Muammar would have great influence, helping them control all of the areas of the Peninsula and recouping all losses potentially experienced by Ibn Muammar, it would seem (according to the account above) that Muhammad Ibn Abd al-Wahhab's offer indicated that he was counting on a much greater strength supporting him, such as a British ally.

[81] *Memoirs of Mr. Hempher*, p. 30

[82] *Lam al-Shahab*, p.15

[83] *Lam al-Shahab*, pp.15–16

[84] *Memoirs of Mr. Hempher*, p. 35

[85] *Lam al-Shahab*, p.17

[86] *Lam al-Shahab*, p.19

[87] This was used as a justification by some with the intention of drinking alcohol. This practice was to be found among the followers of the Umayyad and Abbasid states. Gatherings with alcohol, singing, and adultery were commonplace and were elaborately discussed in works of Islamic heritage, such as the book *Kitab al-Aghani* by Abi Faraj al-Isfahani. However, this does not mean that these behaviors were normal or legal in the eyes of Islam, regardless of the justifications.

The Birth of Terrorism in Middle East

[88] He said in his advice that "we rescued Spain from the infidels, meaning 'the Muslims,' with alcohol and prostitution. We should try to restore the rest of our countries with those two great powers." Afterwards, he wrote, "Muhammad Ibn Abd al-Wahhab did not care about prayers, praying sometimes and not at other times." *Memoirs of Mr. Hempher,* pp. 38–39

[89] In this regard, Dr. Abd al-Hamid al-Batrik said in *Al-Wahhabyah Deen Wa Dawlah* that "many who followed the doctrine were Bedouins who misunderstood its principles and thus went to extremes in declaring Muslims to be infidels if they did not share their opinions and adopt their principles. As such, they made it obligatory to kill them." p. 56

Dr. Abd al-Raheem al-Rahman says, "they also worked on implementing their principles and disseminating them by force without waiting for people to be convinced. Intolerance and extremism persisted the followers of this doctrine." *Al-Dawlah al-Saudiyah al-Ula,* p. 57

Ahmad Amin said, "Many of them considered that every region among the Islamic regions, besides their own, was a region in which innovations were rampant. As such, they were not considered to be Islamic territories and they became a field of war and struggle (jihad)." *Zuama al-Islah Fi al-Asr al-Hadith,* Ahmad Amin, p. 20

[90] A large number of Iraqi Sunnis deny the al-Qaeda/Wahhabi approach as they infiltrated into the western areas of Iraq after the fall of Saddam Hussein's regime in 2003. It was denied despite the attempts of the "Body of Muslim Scholars" and their leader who adopted this doctrine to make it more palatable to the group.

[91] *Tarikh al-Mamlakah al-Arabiyah al- Saudiyah Fi Madihah Wa Haderhah,* Salah al-Deen al-Moukhtar, According to the author, this book has a more modern tone than the previously-mentioned Hussein Ibn Ghannam's book (*Rawdat al-Afkar Wa al-Afham* also known as *Tarikh Najd*).

References

[92] *Tarikh al-Mamlakah al-Arabiyah al- Saudiyah Fi Madihah Wa Haderhah*, Salah al-Deen al-Moukhtar, pp. 36–37

[93] *Memoirs of Mr. Hempher*, p. 80

[94] Ibid., p. 82

[95] Ibid., p. 84

[96] Some sources reported that the reason for Shaykh Abd al-Wahhab's move to Huraymalah was due to his isolation from the judiciary in Uyaynah by its first prince, Muhammad Ibn Abd Allah Ibn Muammar.

[97] *Rawdat al-Afkar Wa al-Afham*, p. 77. He mentioned in *Tanbih Dhawi al-Albab al-Salimah*, p. 162, "And when he found his footing at his father's, the Shaykh began fabricating myths, falsehoods, and heresies, and he rolled up his sleeves to eradicate the illusions harmful to the religion and to spread the rightful belief."

Ibrahim Fasih al-Haydari mentioned in *Unwan al-Majd*, p. 233, that Shaykh Muhammad was inseparable from his father and he studied with him again. He also showed his condemnation to the beliefs of the Najdi people which led to dispute and controversy between him and his father, Shaykh Abd al-Wahhab, as well as between him and the people for two years until his father's death.

[98] Shaykh Sulayman Ibn Abd al-Wahhab wrote a book in response to his brother, as previously noted, and he refuted all of his brother's arguments for declaring Muslims unbelievers. He incited the people of Huraymalah against him during the Saudi invasion to the Najd areas. They rebelled in 1165 CE and repulsed the Saudi forces. A year later, they attacked Diriyah, but Abd al-Aziz Ibn Muhammad Ibn Saud occupied their city in 1168 CE. Shaykh Sulayman Ibn Abd al-Wahhab was escorted to Diriyah where he spent the rest of his life under house arrest by order of his brother, Shaykh Muhammad Ibn Abd al-Wahhab.

[99] His position became known in all of the Ared countries: Uyaynah, Diriyah, and Manfouhah. The people were divided into two groups: one that loved him

and his mission and one that denied it. The former committed themselves to it and pledged allegiance to him and followed in his footsteps. *Tarikh Najd*, Ibn Ghannam, vol. 1, pp. 20–29

[100] *Al Saud Fi al-Tarikh,* Fareed Mustafa, p. 9

[101] *Al-Dawlah al-Saudiyah al-Ula,* vol. 1, p. 48

[102] There is a story by Shaykh Sulayman Ibn Sahman al-Najdi al-Hanbali about the escape of the Shaykh from Huraymalah. He said:

During the time of the Shaykh, Houraimela was a town without a prince or an emirate, but rather it was like a ball being thrown between the leaders of two tribes; the tribe of Abeed and another one. One day, it happened that the Shaykh enjoined some of the foolish people from the tribe of Abeed from committing shameful acts indicative of poor morality. They set out to humiliate him and kill him. They intended to carry out their decision. They went to him at night and sheltered themselves near a wall. While they were in that state, someone shouted from that place so those corrupt souls thought the shouting was directed at them. They fled and God spared the Shaykh from their evil. In the morning, the Shaykh went to Uyaynah where prince Osman received him with salutations, welcome, and full honors. The Shaykh proceeded to spread his monotheistic realities and prince Osman guaranteed keeping him alive and aiding him against his enemies. *Tabriat al-Shaykhayn al-Imamayn*, pp. 162–163

According to such accounts, happy coincidences repeatedly saved the Shaykh's life, such as the shouting that happened at that location and made the killers flee before they could kill him. These appear to be attempts at establishing that the Shaykh was under divine care.

[103] *Tarikh Najd al-Hadith,* Amin al-Rayhani, p. 25:

From one side of Ared is Huraymalah, then Sadous, where there is a statue for which the British paid 1,500 pounds. It protrudes out of the ground with writings on it, its visible height around two meters. Then Kharrama, Amaryah,

References

Abou Kabash, Jameela then Uyaynah, Diriyah, Araja, Riyadh, and Manfouhah, etc. *Unwan al-Majd*, p. 200

[104] *Lam al-Shahab* (Bab al-Tawasso' al-Wahhabi Fee al-Jazeera), p. 119

[105] *Tarikh Al Saud,* Nasir al-Saeed, vol. 1. p. 22

[106] *Lam al-Shahab*, p. 117

[107] In the dictionary *Qamoos al-Muheet*: Horn of Satan and its two horns are its nation and the followers of his opinion, power, propagation, and oppression.

Imam Ahmad Ibn Hanbal said in his *Musnad* (volume 2, p. 118) narrating from Ibn 'Umar that the Prophet said, "God bless Damascus for us. God bless Yemen for us." They said, "What about Najd for us?" He said, "There are earthquakes and tribulations there." Or , in another report, "That's where the horn of the devil rises."

This was also mentioned by al-Tirmidhi in *Al-Manaqib*.

Ahmad, in *Musnad Abd Allah Ibn Omar* and Muslim in his *Sahih* mentioned the saying by the Prophet as he faced east, "The head of the disbelief starts here, where the horn of the devil rises."

Al-Bukhari in the book *Al-Fitan* said about Ibn 'Umar that he stood by the podium and said, "Sedition is right here, where the horn of the devil rises" or he said the "horn of the sun."

Al-Bukhari narrated from Ibn 'Umar that he heard the Prophet say as he faced east, "However, the sedition starts here where the horn of the devil rises."

Malik, in *Al-Muwatta'*, narrated from Ibn 'Umar, "I saw the Prophet of God point to the east and say, 'The sedition starts here where the horn of the devil rises.'"

Muslim in his *Sahih* said, "The head of disbelief is from the east."

A narrative: The harshness of hearts and estrangement are in the east, and faith in the people of Hijaz. The first two accounts, that the horn of the devil rises from Najd, explain the other accounts and prove that when he said east, he meant Najd. In addition, when he said, "where the horn of the devil or the horn of the sun rises," he also meant Najd. This is because Najd was to the east of Medina. From *Kamous al-Amkeenah Wa al-Beeka*: The country of Najd is located east of Hijaz and it is in two parts, the Hijazi Najd and the Ared Najd. From there came al-Qarameetah, Mousailemah al-Kazzab, and the Wahhabis. Its capital is the city of Riyadh, population 30,000. Earthquakes, sedition, and the rise of the devil's horn, which the Prophet mentioned, point to its location being in Najd. *Kashef al-Erteyab Fi Ma'rifat Muhammad Ibn Abd al-Wahhab* pp. 100–101. Shaykh Suleiman Ibn Abd al-Wahhab, the Shaykh's brother, used these sayings as his proofs among others saying, "I bear witness that the Messenger of God is truthful. He fulfilled his trust and relayed the message." Suleiman also said, "We mention some of the evidence from this tradition:

The Prophet saying, "Islam is Yamani, and sedition comes from the east" several times to comprehend.

The Prophet prayed for Hijaz and its people many times but refused to pray for the people of the east, especially the people of Najd, because of all the sedition among them.

The first incident of sedition after the Prophet's time was in our land, or Najd, so we refer to the words of Shaykh Sulayman Ibn Abd al-Wahhab, "Our country is the first one where sedition emerged and we do not know any among the Muslim countries with more sedition, neither ancient nor recent." *Al-Sawa'iq al-Ilahiyyah fi al-radd 'ala al-Wahhabiyyah*, p. 102

And the responses by Shaykh Suleiman Ibn Abd al-Wahhab, the Shaykh's brother, should be considered and studied seriously and objectively.

[108] *Al-Sawa'iq al-Ilahiyyah fi al-radd 'ala al-Wahhabiyyah*, p. 141

[109] *Unwan al-Majd*, p. 231:

I believe reading many books without consulting with reputable scholars and learning from them led the Shaykh to his reported prejudices. Learning

References

autonomously and being independent in opinion lead to trouble, dissention among people and a breach in norms.

Ibrahim Fasih al-Haydari pointed to unbridled jurisprudence without regard to established legal and jurist standards, something in evidence today. Shaykh Muhammad Ibn Abd al-Wahhab's school produced millions of jurists who provide interpretations and pass edicts of holy wars, fighting, and accusations of infidelity. They used the Quran and traditions as grounds for these edicts and based them on the culture of the Wahhabi school which calls for such unbridled jurisprudence.

[110] One of the contemporary historians and journalists, Muhammad Jalal Keshek, justifies in his book, *Al-Saudiyeen Wa al-Hal al-Islami*, that the declaration of Muslims as infidels by the Saudi governing body and its religious corollary, Wahhabism, was the means to legitimize the spilling of their blood, violating their honor, and usurping their wealth. He writes:

If they had taught them that those besides the Brothers were also Muslims, and had they known that both the killer and the killed would be in Hell, would the army of the Brothers have risen? Would the Saudi Kingdom have been liberated or founded?

He means to ask: If the Saudi rulers had not taught the "Brothers" (most of whom were Bedouins) that others were not Muslim, would the Brothers have carried out their religiously-motivated war against them to gain conquest over their countries and spill their blood? And would the Saudi state have been established? Thus, he seems to be arguing that lies are justified in this case and declaring others as disbelievers has its political reasons.

However, these pragmatists also often praise the Saudi Islamic nation and its fairness.

[111] Sennemar: A builder from Yemen. He built the palace of Ghamdan for a king who then killed him because he knew the secrets of the palace. This is an adage used to describe someone who is ungrateful.

The Birth of Terrorism in Middle East

[112] *Lam al-Shahab Fi Sirat Muhammad Ibn Abd al-Wahhab*, pp. 122–3. Ibrahim Fasih al-Haydari noted that Shaykh Muhammad Ibn Abd al-Wahhab moved from Huraymalah to the town of Uyaynah, whose governor at the time, Uthman Ibn Hamad Ibn Muammar, welcomed and honored the Shaykh and attempted to support him. Uthman said, "I anticipate that God Almighty will support you if you in fact were upright in supporting the fact that there is no God but God Himself. In that case, you will own Najd and its Arabs. Osman helped the Shaykh who then declared his mission, enjoined the good, and prohibited transgressions and persisted in denouncing people. Some of the people of Uyaynah became his followers." *Unwan al-Majd*, p. 233

[113] Ibid.

[114] *Tanbih Dhawi al-Albab al-Salimah*, Sulayman Ibn Samhan al-Najdi al-Hanbali, p. 163

[115] *Kashef al-Erteyab Fi Ma'rifat Muhammad Ibn Abd al-Wahhab*, p. 9, from Mahmoud Shekri al-Alusi, *Tarikh Najd*

Ibrahim Fasih al-Haydari wrote in *Unwan al-Majd*:

Uthman Ibn Hamad Ibn Muammar welcomed and honored the Shaykh and attempted to support him. He then said to the named Osman, "I anticipate that God Almighty will support you if you in fact support the fact that there is no God but God Himself. In that case, you will own Najd and its Arabs. Uthman helped the Shaykh, who then declared his mission, enjoined the good, prohibited transgressions, and persisted in denouncing people. Some of the people of Uyaynah became his followers. He cut down trees that were exalted in those regions and he destroyed the dome of Zayd Ibn al-Khattab in the town of al-Jubaylah and became more prominent.

Word of this reached Sulayman Ibn Muhammad Ibn Aziz al-Hamidi, governor of Ihsa', Katif, and their subsidiaries, so he sent a letter to Uthman saying, "The conscript that you have has done what he has done and said what he has said. If

References

my letter reaches you, kill him. If you do not kill him, we will cut off your yields which we have here in Ihsa'." His yields were 2,200 pieces of gold, along with related food and clothing. When this letter reached 'Uthman, he was unable to disobey it. So he sent for Shaykh Muhammad and he told him of 'Uthman's letter saying, "We are unable to fight Sulayman."

The Shaykh then told him, "If you support me, you will own Najd."

Uthman turned away from him. He then sent for him again and said, "Sulayman has ordered us to kill you and we are unable to disobey him or fight him. However, it is not customary or honorable to kill you in our country so you are left to your own affair. Leave our country."

He then ordered one of his knights, known as Farid, to drive the Shaykh out of his country. The knight rode his horse while the Shaykh walked in front of him with only a fan with him. This was during very hot times in the summer. On the way, the knight was about to kill the Shaykh, but God prevented him from doing so which led to horror and great fear in the knight. The latter then let the Shaykh go free.

It was said that Uthman Ibn Muammar was the one who ordered the knight to kill the Shaykh at his brother's gravesite, however others denied that story. The Shaykh then walked to Diriyah.

The latter part of this story climaxes into another dramatic performance where the Shaykh escapes certain danger. This knight was on the verge of killing him but did not because of a sudden affliction of horror and great fear. This seems to be another attempt at assigning for the Shaykh a unique position near God and the role that God has prepared for him in saving this religion. We find many such situations where the Shaykh miraculously escapes with no logical explanation.

[116] *Al-Dawlah al-Saudiyah al-Ula*, Dr. Abd al-Raheem al-Rahman, pp. 233–234

[117] Dr. Abd al-Raheem al-Rahman seemed to confirm the animosity of the scholars and the princes toward the Shaykh:

The Birth of Terrorism in Middle East

They started scaring those in power from the Shaykh's doctrine. They claimed that he was filling the hearts of the ignorant with his words and that he was strengthening them in his own way so they will defy their rulers and declare their rebellion. *Tanbih Dhawi al-Albab al-Salimah,* pp. 163–164

Also review Hussein Ibn Ghannam, p. 79.

Dr. Abd al-Raheem al-Rahman seemingly accepting of the Wahhabi inclinations, did not discuss the real reasons that led that group to be afraid from this new doctrine.

[118] I will cite the two stories:

The first story: Under the chapter related to the expansion of Wahhabism in the Peninsula:

Some trusted sources who were contemporaries to the Shaykh and whom we saw when they were elders in Zubayr and Kuwait, told us:

The truth behind the innovation of Muhammad Ibn Abd al-Wahhab was that when he returned from his journey and settled in his town, it was a weak town relative to others in Najd. People were fleeing from it because of the oppression that was taking place in it and the repression by its rulers and administrators. Transgressions in that town were beyond those in others. Its people were lost and their hearts were full of hypocrisy. It was even said that many people lived in Yamamah, estimated at around 6,000 or more houses, when during the days of the Shaykh, it had 300 houses.

One of these trusted sources said: When Muhammad Ibn Abd al-Wahhab wanted to reveal his innovation, he remained in his house for eight months, isolated from people and always reading books. When that period was over, he went among the people one day with a small book in his hand and said, "Bear witness on me to God that I adopt the content of this book and that I say what is written in it is the only truth." So a man named Ali Ibn Rabee'ah, who was one of the elders of Bani Tamim from the tribe of Bani Saed, said to him, "Muhammad, you are an honorable man among your people, do not say what

References

is not true and then regret causing sedition among the people." The Shaykh then said, "Here is the book, read it. If you find any flaws in it, blame it on me."

So the man took the book and he looked through it from beginning to end, and then returned it to the Shaykh saying, "This is the truth so show us how to follow its direction and what we need to do to circulate it."

Muhammad Ibn Abd al-Wahhab said, "The way to circulate this book is through good advice and good deeds."

Ali Ibn Rabee'ah said, "What if that did not work?"

The Shaykh said, "Then with the sword."

So he replied, "Why is it allowed to kill he who does not follow it?"

He replied, "Because he would be a polytheist infidel."

He said, "Can you really say that?"

He replied, "Yes, and it is my belief."

That group dispersed and the Shaykh returned to his house. His cousin, Abd Allah Ibn Hussein, came to him and said, "Is what is being claimed you said about this doctrine true?"

He replied, "Yes."

So he said, "By God, who none other than Him we worship, if you called any of Bani Sanan to this doctrine, I will have your head."

Arguments and fighting ensued between the two of them and Abd Allah directed his sword at the Shaykh and hit him on the hand, almost cutting it off. Some of his cousins intervened to stop him, leading to dissention among the tribes of Bani Tameem in Yamamah. It was said that on that day, Hammad Ibn Rashid al-Sa'edee, Saleh Ibn Fahd al-Sanani, Joubair Ibn Nasser al-Hendi, along with seven others who were not named but were from Bani Sanan were killed.

The Birth of Terrorism in Middle East

The narrator said, "Muhammad Ibn Abd al-Wahhab stayed for a whole year in Yamamah, carrying on with his religion. The turmoil among the people continued because of him. Some people believed him and others did not until the people who were supporting were humiliated, some of them were defeated, and others were killed while others took refuge in their homes and their fortresses."

His story spread across Najd and Suleiman Ibn Shames al-Aneezee, one of the elite in his own town, heard about it. They were on the edge of Ared, so he sent to the elders of Yamamah from Tamim and others, "This is a situation occurring in your town, started by this scholar. Beware of following his instructions and do not give him a place to live or be sheltered among you in Yamamah. If news reaches me that you welcomed and protected him, I will come upon you with men and knights and I will pass you around all of Bunizah."

When word of Suleiman Ibn Shames' message reached the people of Yamamah, some of them said, "We have to obey him because the people of Ounayzah are a people of war and we are only a few, not even totaling a tenth of them, in the number of men or amount of money. Suleiman is calling us for something that is his right and we cannot take it lightly or back down from it. Muhammad Ibn Abd al-Wahhab is not dear to us like our own selves and our pride, especially since he brought to us an innovation of infidelity and he tried to declare Muslims unbelievers with that innovation."

They all agreed to force him out of his house, even his own cousins. A crier called on Friday for them to get together following the prayers to expel Muhammad Ibn Abd al-Wahhab from their town. If he refused to go, they would kill him. When his brother, Ali Ibn Abd al-Wahhab, who was not a scholar and was lowly among the group, heard about this plan, he went to his brother Muhammad Ibn Abd al-Wahhab saying, "My brother, by God, I advise you to leave Yamamah today. Go wherever you want for God's earth is vast. If what you claim is true, God will dedicate the heart of one of his creations to reveal and protect it."

The Shaykh thought well of his brother's opinion and said, "How can I leave in the middle of the day? And I would not leave my people and town without all of my family, children, and money. I also worry that one of their people might confront me and my pride prevents me from accepting that. Go to Ali Ibn Rabee'ah and Abd Allah Ibn Hussein and get their promise and word. If they give you those, we will leave then, and God help us. If you come to know about them anything to the contrary, God will aid us and we will remain in this fort of ours and it is our duty to defend against attack."

He specifically named Ali Ibn Rabee'ah and Abd Allah Ibn Hussein al-Sanani because it was those two that he feared and because they held the reins of the tribes in Yamamah, which were from the descendants of Tameem.

His brother, Ali Ibn Abd al-Wahhab, went to those two after the Friday prayers and the people had left the mosque with their weapons, intent on marching on the Shaykh's fortress, imprisoning his family, taking his money, and giving safe passage only to the Shaykh to leave immediately.

Some who told us this story said that Muhammad Ibn Abd al-Wahhab had lots of money that he had accumulated during his travels. The people of his town knew of this money. They also knew that his seven or eight slaves (which he had bought from Mecca and who were fighters) should not be taken lightly. He also had his two sons who were born prior to his journey, Nasser and Abd al-Wahhab, as well as four men who were his close cousins, the children of Hussein Ibn Muhammad and brothers to Abd Allah Ibn Hussein who we mentioned earlier. The presence of these people with him protected him from his enemies, and he was willing to fight from his fortress. When his brother, Ali Ibn Abd al-Wahhab, told Ali Ibn Rabee'ah and Abd Allah of the Shaykh's message, they agreed to it. So he went to Muhammad Ibn Abd al-Wahhab and told him, "They gave you their word." So he prepared himself, his family, and his followers to leave.

They left that day around sundown and they arrived to the valley, the town of Muhammad Ibn Saud, Diriyah, etc.

The second story: By the same unknown author of *Lam al-Shahab Fi Sirat Muhammad Ibn Abd al-Wahhab*.

The Birth of Terrorism in Middle East

We were told by a trustworthy man from Diriyah, "At first, when Muhammad Ibn Abd al-Wahhab left his people and house, he went to Oynayyah before arriving Diriyah and forming an alliance with Muhammad Ibn Saud. He sought refuge with Osman Ibn Muammar al-Tamimi, the governor of Uyaynah, and they agreed to establish this matter and religion and work honorably since knowledge without action is not beneficial. They agreed to invalidate all Muslim sects and others but this one. Many of the people of Uyaynah agreed with them, including the elite of the town and those among the close followers of Ibn Muammar. There were some people who did not agree. Perhaps some people from Najd came to him and pledged allegiance to him once they heard of him. These events took place towards the end of the year 1150 CE.

However, the elders and most prominent people in the rest of Najd did not like the spread of this religion since it invalidated laws and basic rules on which their government was founded. This is because the towns of Najd and its tribes did not have one overwhelming ruler or governor able to prevent oppression and support the oppressed. Rather, it had governors in each of its towns, cities, or villages. Each group had its own Shaykh who they sought in their affairs. Bedouins are made up of many tribes; they used the prairies for grazing and the wells and springs for drinking. Each Shaykh governs his tribe with his people's consent, and any person who shows more generosity and more courage becomes one of their elders. They also have lesser elders from the same tribe who oppose the more established elders. The Bedouins used customs and norms, and not religious laws, to obtain rulings on their issues. They accepted bribes that were used to invalidate the truth. These rulers were oppressors since they prevented the people from ruling by Islamic laws. The more developed people of Najd used Islamic laws to settle their disagreements and cases, except the people in the valley of Dawasser and the mountain of Shammer because they were more similar to nomads than to urban people. The people of Najd fought each other based on their needs and interests even though each governor had his own party and close associates. If he wanted to acquire that which did not belong to him, all of the others fought him. This was their situation for a long time. If the greed, at least outwardly, ends, there

References

can then be a treaty between the people of these countries. When liberated, the governors of Najd were all angered, except Uthman Ibn Muammar and the one from Diriyah.

When the gentry of Najd saw the actions of Muhammad Ibn Abd al-Wahhab and feared the consequences of those actions, they complained to Suleiman Muhammad al-Hamidi al-Khaleede, the governor of all of Bani Khaled, al-Ehsa, al-Qateef, and Qatar. They beseeched him to march on the governor of al-'Uyaynah and remove him from his country. They sought help from Suleiman because all of Najd at the time was not aware of Osman Ibn Muammar and that he was very strong, formidable, and had many soldiers and lots of money. This is because his city was the largest in Najd and had the greatest harvest of crops and yields, and its people were more obedient to their ruler than others.

When the news about Muhammad Ibn Abd al-Wahhab reached Suleiman, he wrote a letter to Osman Ibn Muammar ordering him to "evict that Najdi Shaykh from your country to the ends of the Arabian Peninsula or send him to me and I will look into his matter. If you do not respond to one of these two orders, I will eliminate your positions in al-Ehsa and I will surely prevent your collectors from collecting your share from the date trees therein." Ibn Muammar owned palm trees and land in al-Ehsa inherited from his elders and forefathers, and their yearly revenue reached 60,000 in riyals and gold.

He also told him, "I will prevent the merchants from your country from frequenting our areas, including al-Ehsa, Kateef, Qatar, and others. In fact, I will prevent them from travelling into any country where I can reach them."

Sulayman had a long reach in the Arab lands, especially towards Iraq following Najd and in Najd itself, as well as the outskirts of Damascus. His military was large, his country was mighty and his courage was known. His people, the "Khawalids" were very strong and numerous. He would also invade Najd if each of its rulers did not please him with some sort of tribute.

The Birth of Terrorism in Middle East

When the letter of Sulayman Ibn Muhammad al-Khaleede reached Osman Ibn Muammar al-Tamimi, he was concerned. He hated to be considered an enemy by Sulayman. He was also angry that Muhammad Ibn Abd al-Wahhab left him, but he carried out the easier choice. He apologized to Muhammad Ibn Abd al-Wahhab in secret saying to him, "Fighting this man, Suleiman Al Muhammad, would be difficult for us at the very beginning." And he confirmed his words by continuing, "Our opinion is that you march from Uyaynah with God's blessings to any country you wish from His lands and live there for a year or two until we see what God ordains after that. And then you can return to us."

Muhammad Ibn Abd al-Wahhab said, "Do not be afraid from these words. God will make you victorious. And all of the returns that have been withheld from you, I will hand over to you in their entirety every year. I pray that this matter will move ahead in spite of the one who dislikes it."

However, after Muhammad Ibn Abd al-Wahhab gave his advice to Uthman Ibn Muammar to persist in this religion and promote it, he realized that Uthman would not be able to openly continue doing so. Therefore, Muhammad Ibn Abd al-Wahhab left Uyaynah to Diriyah, where Muhammad Ibn Saud was (pp. 119–124).

[119] The scholars of Najd and Hijaz were clear in their refusal of the Shaykh's doctrine from the beginning. These scholars were later accused of being afraid of change itself, as was mentioned by the author of *Lam al-Shahab*, who wrote:

However, the elders and most prominent people in the rest of Najd did not like the spread of this religion since it invalidated laws and basic rules on which their government was founded. This is because the towns of Najd and its tribes did not have one overwhelming ruler or governor, able to prevent oppression and support the oppressed… The Bedouins used customs and norms, and not laws, to obtain rulings on their issues… The more developed people of Najd referred to Islamic law to settle their disagreements (pp. 122–123).

References

The intent was to portray the religious Shaykhs of Najd, mostly from the Hanbalis, as priests of idols that were worshipped prior to Islam, whose only worry was to acquire personal gains, and that the Shaykh came along to change this reality.

[120] According to *Lam al-Shahab*:

He was satisfied with little if he did not easily find its alternative. It was said that one day, before his travels, there was a gathering of people discussing the state of the world and gathering of money and the creative ways to earn it. A man, named Sulayman Ibn Raed al-Ounairi, who was a merchant famous for doing good deeds in the area, said to Muhammad Ibn Abd al-Wahhab, "You are a man of little money and many children." At the time Muhammad Ibn Abd al-Wahhab had three wives, two sons, and two daughters. "I am giving you such and such of my money. Take it and travel to the Roman countries, areas such as Halab and Damascus. To honor you, you can have half of my profits from trade you conduct even though I would have given any other man only a third." The others in that group signaled to the Shaykh to accept the offer and proceed in his travels but he refused saying, "If I become a trader, I will become a captive of humiliation and greed, and I will miss out on the peace of mind as I pursue learning and knowledge. Even though the Provider endows us with subsistence, I do not pursue it in a manner that distracts and tires. The intent is not to gather lots of money; otherwise he would not have changed his ways." It was his habit that if he had guests who wanted to depart, he would provide for them whatever he could afford and that was not commonplace in that town. (*Lam al-Shahab*, p. 118)

[121] When he received the letter from the governor of al-Ahsa', he was unable to oppose him. He kept his concerns to himself because he did not know the effects of monotheism, nor did he know who would support him in this world and the hereafter. Ibn Bishar, *Unwan al-Majd Fi Tarikh Najd*, p. 10

[122] *Ulama Najd Fi Khilal Sittat Qurun*, Shaykh Abd Allah al-Bassam, p. 33

[123] Even though he showed animosity towards them at the beginning, after the Shaykh moved to Diriyah and formed his alliance with Muhammad Ibn Saud,

The Birth of Terrorism in Middle East

Uthman Ibn Muammar started carrying out raids against them from Uyaynah. Prince Muhammad Ibn Saud was in such a state of weakness, and so lacking in provisions, that he was not able to face Uthman Ibn Muammar's raids. *Ulama Najd Fi Khilal Sittat Qurun*, Shaykh Abd Allah al-Bassam, pp. 37–38

[124] *Tarikh al-Jazeera al-Arabiyah Fi Aser al-Shaykh Muhammad Ibn Abd al-Wahhab,* Hussein al-Shaykh Khazal, pp. 216–219

[125] *Unwan al-Majd Fi Tarikh Najd,* Ibn Bishar, p. 10

As for Ibn Ghannam, he writes:

When the evil of Uthman Ibn Muammar grew against the people of monotheism, and both his hatred towards them and his support for the infidels became apparent, and when the truth of the stories told about him became evident to Shaykh Muhammad Ibn Abd al-Wahhab, and people from all over the country came to him and complained to him about their fear of his treachery against the Muslims, the Shaykh then said to the delegation of the Uyaynah people, 'I want you to pledge allegiance to the religion of God and his Prophet and that you will support those who support him and fight those who fight him, even if it were your own prince Osman.' They gave him the promise of that belief and swore to that allegiance. Panic filled Osman's heart and his hatred increased. The devil enticed him to kill Muslims and banish them to the furthest lands. So he sent for Ibn Souwait and Ibrahim Ibn Suleiman, the apostate head of Thermada, inviting them to come to him so he could betray Muslims. When the people of Islam confirmed these intentions, a group of them made a pact to kill him. Among those were Hamad Ibn Rashed and Ibrahim Ibn Zaid. When the Friday prayers were complete, they killed him in his place of prayers during the month of Rajab, 1163 AH (*Tarikh Najd*, p. 103)

[126] Sayed al-Ahel writes:

Muhammad Ibn Abd al-Wahhab went to Diriyah, knowing its governor's, Ibn Muammar, feeling toward him… The people of Uyaynah were aware of Ibn Muammar's following and belief in the monotheistic doctrine, so they

References

ambushed and assassinated him. By doing so, they hurt the chances for reform in his sect and among his people since Ibn Muammar was from Taymiyyah. Abd al-Aziz Sayed al-Ahel, *Daeeyat al-Tawheed, Muhammad Ibn Abd al-Wahhab*, p. 89

[127] *Tarikh Najd*, Mahmoud Shekri al-Aloussi, p. 97

[128] Ibid., p. 97

[129] *Tarikh al-Jazeera al-Arabiyah Fi Aser al-Shaykh Muhammad Ibn Abd al-Wahhab*, Hussein al-Shaykh Khazal

[130] *Lam al-Shahab*, p. 121

[131] Ibid., p. 116

[132] *Tarikh al-Mamlakah al-Arabiyah al- Saudiyah Fi Madihah Wa Haderhah*, Salah al-Deen al-Moukhtar

[133] *al-Mouzakarat*, pp. 34–35

[134] Ibid., p. 40

[135] *Lam al-Shahab*, p. 114

[136] Ibid., pp. 50–51

[137] Ibid., p. 51

[138] Ibid., pp. 81–82

[139] Ibid., pp. 82–83

[140] Ibid., pp. 84–85

[141] *Tarikh al-Mamlakah al-Arabiyah al-Saudiyah*, Amin Sa'id, vol. 1, p. 40

[142] *Tarikh Al Saud*, Nasir al-Saeed, p. 20

[143] *Lam al-Shahab*, p. 32

144 Amin al-Rayhani, *al-Amal al-Kamilah*, vol. 2. *Al- Mou'sassah al-Arabiyah Lel-Dirassat Wa al-Nasher*, p. 37

145 *Takawon al-Tabaiyah al-Saudiyah*, Muhammad Faqih , p. 77

146 The author called it *al-Makhtoutah* and the readers were promised it would be discussed in the future. We will refer to it by this name.

147 Mawsou'at al-Siyasah, *Al- Mou'sassah al-Arabiyah Lel-Dirassat Wa al-Nasher*, vol. 3, p. 182

148 The information about the reason for naming the village "Diriyah" is conflicting and includes the above-mentioned one. It would seem that more than one village was so named, including Diriyah in Umm al-Sahik near al-Qatif in the Arabian Gulf. It has been said that Markhan Ibn Ibrahim Ibn Musa was the first to inhabit that village, and then he moved to Diriyah in the area of Ared near Riyadh. The Saudi state authors did not give plausible reasons for that move. However, others have cited reasons that I will mention when I discuss the family lineage of al-Saud, about whom there are stories in need of careful examination.

In fact, the name "Diriyah" was given to the area of Mulaybid and Ghusaybah before the arrival of the Shaykh. Thus, the matter is not as Ibn Bishar claimed, who wrote, "It was named so after all of the development, the inflow of people to meet Abd al-Aziz and the increase in his power. The town's situation became comparable to a *dari'i*, which linguistically means "shirt," or "traditional war clothing." Source: *Lam al-Shahab,* a Biography of Muhammad Ibn Abd al-Wahhab, p. 121

149 *Unwan al-Majd*, Ibrahim Fasih al-Haydari, p. 236

150 *Unwan al-Majd Fi Tarikh Najd*, p. 13

151 Ibid., p. 13

152 *Lam al-Shahab*, p. 121

153 *Ulama Najd Fi Khilal Sittat Qurun*, Shaykh Abd Allah al-Bassam, p. 340

References

[154] *Unwan al-Majd Fi Tarikh Najd*, p. 11

[155] This late historian, a friend of King Abd al-Aziz, wrote that the immigrants and not the people of Diriyah worked in commerce and manual labor, even though Ibn Bishar and others had said that the people of Diriyah did the work out of poverty. *Tarikh Najd al-Hadith*, Amin al-Rayhani, p. 40.

[156] *Daeeyat al-Tawheed, Muhammad Ibn Abd al-Wahhab*, Abd al-Aziz Sayed al-Ahel

[157] *Lam al-Shahab*, p. 131

[158] *Al-Hukum al-Saudi*, Khalifah Fahed, p. 7

[159] Perhaps this included his many marriages from the daughters of various tribes, in Najd, Higaz, and others, in order to gain their cooperation. In addition, marrying slaves and captives could have been to establish an extended family at all levels of government and society to better hold the reins of the new kingdom. However, the large number of princes and princesses later became a burden on the kingdom because of competition, the emergence of rival centers of power within the ruling family over command, influence, and wealth. Many family members chose paths that were not in line with the official Wahhabi religion, and those princes, who were usually above the law, created administrative, financial, and social corruption.

This phenomenon was practiced by most of the old hereditary ruling lines to ensure the extension of power for its families and the continuation of its governance. Even today, some regimes resort to the same method of enlarging the family in an attempt to keep the inherited governance within its members, as was the case in the time of Saddam Hussein in Iraq. This does not, however, manifest itself in the same manner as it did in Saudi Arabia where it lasted for the entire twentieth century.

[160] The great effort exerted by the Saudi family in order to establish its origins is suspicious. An attempt was made in order to find dozens of ancestors for the Saud family as well as for the family of Shaykh Abd al-Wahhab and then

The Birth of Terrorism in Middle East

subsequently link all of them to the Prophet Muhammad. Thus these two families could be counted among the finest of the tribe of Quraysh, the Prophet's tribe.

[161] The largest paradox occurred in the truth of the names of these men and their origin. Some historians have referenced widely circulating information in the Arabian Peninsula indicating that the real names of these men were in fact Mordechai Ben Ibrahim Ben Moshe and they were wealthy Jewish merchants. One of their sons, Mordechai, adopted the name Markhan in order to draw closer to one of the branches of the tribe of Anza, or Goat. He claimed that his family came to Basra as a result of a feud with their cousins and he offered to go with them to Najd with his gold. They welcomed their wealthy cousin and, in fact, he went with them and subsequently moved to several places, including Umm al-Sahik in al-Qatif. He then named it Diriyah in reference to a shield that he claimed belonged to Prophet Muhammad that was taken from a martyr in the battle of Uhud (where the Muslims were defeated and betrayed by the Jews).

Mordecai had wide influence in al-Qatif due to his vast wealth; however, he was compelled to flee from Alagaman, Bani Hajer, and Bani Khalid, who razed his village and wanted to kill him after they discovered his true identity. He went to al-Moulaibed and Ghoussaybeh, near Riyadh, where he sought and received protection from its owner Abdullah Ibn Hajer. However, he responded by killing him and his family and renaming that area "Diriyah."

Another story indicates that the name Diriyah was derived from the name of Ali Ibn Dari'i who belonged to the same tribe of Markhan, or Mordechai, and that he gave his land to the latter and he hosted him generously. He also professed Islam outwardly. He lived there for some time and proceeded to marry numerous times in order to produce the largest number of children. All of his children were given local Arabic names.

One of his children who came with him from Basra, Mac Ren or Makran, had a son called Muhammad and that son had one of his own named Saud. This is the name with which the family became known. Saud had a few sons, among them

References

Mushari, Thanyan, and Muhammad. The latter is the one who met Shaykh Muhammad Ibn Abd al-Wahhab and he became known as Muhammad Ibn Saud. (*Tarikh Najd*, pp. 14–18)

Perhaps it is important to point out that the names Markhan or Musa were not repeated in the family tree from that point. No one in the family was given either of those names again.

It is appropriate to recall here what the well-known Egyptian writer, Muhammad Husayn Heikal, said with respect to the sensitivity of King Faisal Ibn Abdul Aziz to Jewish names: Among other things, the King believed that Bregenev was Jewish because of his first name Lyoned, which he believed to be a derivative of the name Lyon, also a Jewish name in his opinion. (*Kharif al-Ghadab*, Muhammad Husayn Heikal, p. 121).

On September 17, 1969, Heikal made statements (to the Washington Post, which were then reported by several Arabic newspapers, including al-Hayat in Beirut) saying, "Today we are cousins, belonging to our Semite heritage…in addition to our patriotic connections. Our country is the original source of Jews from which they then spread to all parts of the world." See Safha Ann Al Saud al-Wahhabiyin, p. 22.

[162] I will discuss this matter in detail when covering the terms of agreement between the two allies. It is known that Muhammad Ibn Saud continued to receive his portion from his peasants, as determined by himself, after his alliance with the Shaykh and until he no longer needed it thanks to the spoils of later wars.

[163] *Sahel al-Zahab al-Aswad,* Muhammad Saeed al-Muslim, p. 176

[164] *Al-Saudiyeen Wa al-Hal al-Islami,* Muhammad Jalal Keshek, p. 114

[165] Ibid., p. 42

[166] Ibid.

[167] We do not know who appointed them rulers. The Ottoman Empire did not appoint them as he confirms that they had no relationship whatsoever to the people of Diriyah. This points to the rumors about their origins.

The Birth of Terrorism in Middle East

[168] He was careful to take his portion from them because of his need as he later clarified to Shaykh Muhammad Ibn Abd al-Wahhab. He would not relinquish that portion until two years into the alliance after receiving plentiful spoils from raids.

[169] *Lam al-Shahab*, pp. 130–131. He also mentioned that the people of Diriyah were the most vicious among the people of Najd in manners of treachery and ruses, and they were the most hateful and hostile, p. 125.

[170] *Unwan al-Majd Fi Tarikh Najd*, Uthman Ibn Bishar al-Najdi, pp. 11–12

[171] Ibid, p. 12

[172] Ibid, p. 12

[173] The author of *Lam al-Shahab* said that Muhammad Ibn Saud was called the "Shaykh" prior to following Muhammad Ibn Abd al-Wahhab. He forbade people from calling him or anyone with that title or other similar titles unless they were people of knowledge.

[174] *Unwan al-Majd Fi Tarikh Najd*, p 11 and in other editions "he directed himself towards the house of Abd Allah Ibn Suweilem."

[175] Perhaps this is an exaggeration from the author of *Al-Dawlah al-Saudiyah al-Ula*, and perhaps Ibn Bishar (the source of this information) was more accurate in his account. He said that those who visited him were from the people of Diriyah and wanted to be introduced to his mission. It would seem that some of them were convinced of it.

[176] He was not a prince at that time, but rather he was a shaykh for a small tribe.

[177] *Unwan al-Majd Fi Tarikh Najd*, pp. 11–12

[178] However, there are other sources close to the Saud family that tried to crown Muhammad Ibn Saud with virtues that would make him seem like the Shaykh's true savior and that he was planning the Shaykh's welcome prior to his arrival. It was said that he received him with great hospitality right from the start and

References

implied that the Shaykh would not have otherwise come to Diriyah and his mission would have died.

Some historians tried to liken the Shaykh's going to Diriyah to the Prophet's migration to Yathreb. According to their accounts, the Shaykh was received like a conquering victor in that town by a throng of supporters and followers, with Muhammad Ibn Saud at their forefront.

Hussein al-Shaykh Khazal said about the Shaykh's followers in Diriyah that they closely followed the Shaykh's news and they were eager for it. They would wish for him to come to them. As soon as news of the Shaykh's plans to come to their town reached them, they were very happy and they planned his welcome. When the Shaykh embarked on his trip to Diriyah, they informed Muhammad Ibn Saud, the ruler of the town, who then sent a number of knights to welcome the Shaykh. When the Shaykh's convoy arrived to the outskirts of Diriyah, Muhammad Ibn Saud came out to welcome him, accompanied by his brothers, Thounyan, Moushari, and Farhan, and his son Abd al-Aziz, as well as many others from his own family and the people of the town. When the Shaykh arrived to the high point in Diriyah, he and his convoy went towards the house of Ahmad Ibn Suwaylim al-Arini which was located at the beginning of the town. The latter welcomed the Shaykh in a most appropriate manner.

When the people welcoming the Shaykh left, Shaykh Ahmad Ibn Suwaylim became worried that the Shaykh's mission may not be welcomed by the ruler of Diriyah and that the latter might hesitate in supporting it. This led to signs of worry on his face. The Shaykh noticed those signs and he calmed him down said, "Do not worry. God will provide us with relief and a way out because we only want peace, security, and the protection of this mission." Shaykh Ahmad calmed down and he was reassured. *Tarikh al-Jazeera al-Arabiyah Fi Aser al-Shaykh Muhammad Ibn Abd al-Wahhab*, Hussein al-Shaykh Khazal, pp. 158–159

The above contradicts previous historians, such as Ibn Bishar, the author of *Lam al-Shahab*, and others. Earlier, I mentioned that the Shaykh reportedly escaped from Uyaynah and suddenly arrived in Diriyah. Also, Diriyah reportedly did not have knights that Muhammad Ibn Saud could have sent to welcome the Shaykh.

The official Saudi story that is taught to students in schools supports the early historians and denied the fabricated story by Hussein al-Shaykh Khazal. The government's story says:

"The people of Diriyah knew of the Shaykh's news so they started visiting him in secret. They listened to his lectures and advice. The people of the town wanted to inform the prince about the Shaykh so he could support him, but they feared him so they contacted his wife, Mudi, who had wit and intelligence. She told her husband about the status of the Shaykh and his piety and that he is a benefit driven by God to them. She said to him, 'Welcome and honor him and take advantage of his support.' He took her advice." *Al-Kitab al-Madrasi li al-Saff al-Thani Thanawi Adabi,* p. 278

[179] One of the authors went as far as comparing her to Khadija, the Mother of the Believers, and comparing her positions to those of Sayeda Khadija when she supported the Prophet and bore a lot to help his message succeed. Amin al-Rayhani writes:

Muhammad Ibn Saud, the prince of Diriyah, was hesitant about meeting him. His two brothers Thounyan and Moushari insisted that he should but he was still hesitant. They then turned to his wife, who was among the wise intelligent women, and they told her about the Shaykh's mission and what he forbids. She was satisfied, and she promised them a good outcome. This signifies the power of the good influence of a woman, even when she is part of a harem and is concealed behind a veil, if she was wise and knowledgeable about the affairs of the state. This honorable 'Khadija' said to her prince Ibn Saud, 'God guided this man to you and there is benefit in him, so make use of that benefit that God has offered you.' He accepted her advice. God put in his heart love for this man and love for his mission… *Tarikh Najd al-Hadith,* p. 40

[180] The author of *Lam al-Shahab* wrote that the Shaykh was inciting the people of the valley in Diriyah to be persistent in their animosity to those who

References

opposed him. When a year had passed, all of the people of the valley belonged to his religion and obeyed him save for four of them. The author called them by their names: Yasir Ibn Ahmad, Sayyar Ibn Dahyan, Abdan Ibn Saleh, and Musa Ibn Hasim. They left with their families and it was hard for them to leave the religion of Muslims to which they were accustomed so they lived in the town of Quasseem, also called Tharmada. *Lam al-Shahab*, p. 132. Perhaps they were ousted from Diriyah forcibly because they were not following the Shaykh and he wanted the village to be all for him and his followers.

[181] *Unwan al-Majd Fi Tarikh Najd*, p. 12. The author of *Lam al-Shahab* recounts two stories that contradicted Ibn Bishar's.

The first story:

Muhammad Ibn Saud heard of the arrival of Muhammad Ibn Abd al-Wahhab. He had previously heard of him and heard of his new doctrine. He came to him and shook hands with him saying, "This village is your village and this place is your place. Do not fear your enemies. By God, if all of Najd was closed upon us, we will not send you away from us." The Shaykh said, "You are the greatest and most honorable among them. I want a promise from you that you will struggle for this religion and that leadership and the imamah are for you and your descendants after you and the religious leadership and caliphate are mine and my descendants' after me forever. We do not make decisions, accords, or wars unless we agree to it. If you agree to these conditions, I tell you that God will reveal to you matters not realized by the greatest kings and sultans and that the consequences of your actions with God will be rewarded because you followed and supported your religion and your position is no less than that of the companions and caliphates that supported the Prophet. What position is better than this?" Muhammad Ibn Saud said, "I agree and pledge allegiance to that." So the two of them formed their allegiance and each of them had his own conditions for his counterpart. Muhammad Ibn Saud personally vacated his own house for Muhammad Ibn Abd al-Wahhab, and he stayed at his brother's house, Omar Ibn Saud. *Lam al-Shahab*, p. 124

The Birth of Terrorism in Middle East

The second story:

Muhammad Ibn Abd al-Wahhab moved from Uyaynah to Diriyah where, at the time, Muhammad Ibn Saud was. When he was a half hour away from Diriyah, Muhammad Ibn Saud was informed of him. He went out, along with his son Abd al-Aziz and many of the people of his town, to welcome him with acceptance and generosity. He gave him the ultimate welcome when he vacated his own home for him. He also pledged allegiance to this religion and to spreading it. Then each of them had conditions for the other one, and they confirmed their allegiance with an oath, promise, and documentation. They had witnesses to this, so the matters between them were clear.

The great Imamah, that of the religion, was for Muhammad Ibn Abd al-Wahhab, along with what follows it from the worldly interests such as arranging for wars, accords, animosity, and all that belonged to the war machine and its mechanisms. This made Muhammad Ibn Abd al-Wahhab a resourceful strategist, knowledgeable and well-versed in all matters… *Lam al-Shahab*, pp. 124–125

The official Saudi stories support the account by Ibn Bishar and are not in agreement with the two stories by the author of *Lam al-Shahab*. I had mentioned in this chapter the official account that is taught in the Saudi Schools, which is aligned with Ibn Bishar's account. Review *Al-Kitab al-Madrasi li al-Saff al-Thani Thanawi Adabi*, p. 278.

The different stories agree that an alliance was formed between the two Shaykhs, but they do not mention enough details about this alliance.

Other accounts are concerned with what was written by the author of *Lam al-Shahab*. They write of the purity, loyalty, and honesty of the children and grandchildren, the princes and imams, who inherited this alliance. Abd al-Aziz Sayed al-Ahel writes:

They agreed that the religious Imamah belonged to Muhammad Ibn Abd al-Wahhab and that with this the great Imamah came the foundation for this

References

world and the interests of the believers, including acquiring money, making conquests, and forging accords. The leadership of the nation belonged to Muhammad Ibn Saud, including leadership second to the religious one! From then on, each of them had a pure heart with external and internal honesty towards his partner and the alliance they had formed. This honesty in loyalty and clear heart was also transferred to their descendants, and so they forever survive in the souls of their children and grandchildren… After the Shaykh, came Hussein, Ali, Abd al-Rahman, Abd al-Latif, and others from their descendants. Those were the guides and the imams, and they held the religion as their top priority, followed by the state and its princes. *Daeeyat al-Tawheed, Muhammad Ibn Abd al-Wahhab,* Abd al-Aziz Sayed al-Ahel, pp. 91–92

[182] "The Saud family did not have any status worth mentioning prior to adopting the mission." Abd al-Aziz Sayed al-Ahel. Muhammad Saeed Al-Muslim, p. 176.

[183] Saudi sources confirm that Diriyah was a small, impoverished village and that its Shaykh Muhammad Ibn Saud lived off portions he collected from its people during the days of harvest. Nonetheless, Saudi sympathizers write of his wealth, generosity, and unique attributes. Here is an example from Abd al-Aziz Sayed al-Ahel:

Muhammad Ibn Abd al-Wahhab set his sights and mind on this Muhammad because of his generosity and love for doing good deeds. His generosity was that he paid off the debts of some people and dowries for husbands and wives from the treasury as did Omar Ibn Abd al-Aziz. Muhammad Ibn Saud had an opinion in the politics of his people and was a man of religion. Perhaps he was able to see through his perception of the nomadic crudity of the people in his state. He would look after the lost, quell sedition, and fight treachery and hatred. As to his religious practices, he was ascetic, prayed frequently in secret, and was diligent in his worship without boasting of it visibly or audibly. *Daeeyat al-Tawheed,* pp. 90–91

[184] *Tarikh al-Dawla al-Saudiyah Hatta al-Roubo' al-Awal Min al-Quarn al-Eshrin,* p. 19

185 *Al-Saudiyeen Wa al-Hal al-Islami,* Muhammad Jalal Keshek, p. 50

186 It was said in the book *Tarikh al-Mamlakah al-Arabiyah al- Saudiyah Fi Madihah Wa Haderhah – Lee al-Saff al-Thaleth al-Moutawaset,* p. 65:

When the prince pledged his allegiance to the Shaykh in regards to God's religion and His prophet, the struggle for the sake of God, the establishment of Islamic laws, enjoining good, and prohibiting evil, the prince asked the Shaykh that he not leave them. This agreement, between the house of Saud and the Shaykh's family, remains in effect to our present day. Thus, the agreement was established between the two to struggle for the sake of God, to raise the words of monotheism, to enjoin good, and to prohibit evil. This is a logical and legitimate agreement, and it was the bases upon which the Saudi state was founded. This was the beginning of great development in the Arabian Peninsula.

187 Dr. Abd al-Raheem al-Rahman writes:

This agreement denotes prince Muhammad Ibn Saud's long term vision, for he saw that the best manner to spread his political influence across Najd and to enhance Diriyah's importance was the religious struggle to which he agreed with Shaykh Muhammad Ibn Abd al-Wahhab. This is supported by his condition to the Shaykh not to leave him and join someone else when the call for his mission expanded and its directives spread in the towns of the region. He feared that such a move would lead back to a contraction in his kingdom. When he was confident that the Shaykh agreed to this condition that was the path to his political ambitions, he agreed to the Shaykh's second condition.

This was the start of the movement for religious struggles, and it was supported by political might. It transformed Diriyah into a religious, political, and war capital, all at the same time." The magazine Deerassat al-Khaleej Wa al-Jazeera al-Arabeeyah – Keeyadat al-Dawla al-Saudeeyah Wa Athrhah Ala Moujtama' Shebeh al-Jazeera al-Arabeeyah. Volume 25, 1401 AH, p. 68

188 Ibn Bishar indicated that Muhammad Ibn Saud continued taking spoils from the people of his village even after his alliance with Muhammad Ibn Abd

References

al-Wahhab, who had predicted great gains for him. This prediction came true after one year when he was brought great spoils. Muhammad Ibn Abd al-Wahhab told him, "This exceeds the amount you take from the people of your town." He left it after that. In other words, he had continued taking spoils from the people of his village until he acquired a greater gain during one of the raids, at least a year after the formation of his alliance with the Shaykh.

[189] Dr. Al-Othaymayn supported that by saying that the sons' persistence in their positions was a result not of their agreement but of their qualifications:

Some authors pointed out that the Shaykh and the prince also agreed that the political matters would be in the hands of Muhammad Ibn Saud and his progeny while the religious matters would be for Muhammad Ibn Abd al-Wahhab and his progeny. It would seem that such an agreement did not happen. However, that idea was formulated by some to be a result of observing later occurrences. It was natural that the political leadership in Diriyah, which became the foundation of the new state, remained in the hands of the Saud family. This is because they were the princes of the town prior to that agreement. Their stance towards the Shaykh reinforced their position and strengthened the continuity of their leadership. Abd al-Aziz Ibn Muhammad was qualified to replace his father in leading the state. It was also natural for the religious matters to be in the hands of Shaykh Muhammad's children due to their proficient knowledge, especially his son Abd Allah Ibn Muhammad and due to their father's position in guiding the mission and administering the affairs of the state. Therefore, what followed was a natural result and most likely, it was not based on a prior agreement. *Tawasset al-Hokom al-Saudi,* Dr. Al-Othaymayn, p. 63

Muhammad Jalal Keshek writes:

The prince swore allegiance to the Shaykh. However, there was a clear understanding under the direction of Islamic teachings as the scholar explained them that the emirate belonged to Ibn Saud. It was wrong to call this setup a coalition or agreement. The Shaykh was not looking at the emirate and its surroundings, but rather he was looking for a prince who would pledge allegiance to him.

The Birth of Terrorism in Middle East

In addition, he was not ignorant of the meaning of imamah in Islam and its incompatibility with a plurality in the seat of power. He was only aiming to change the governance by guiding the princes. This is where one of the characteristics of the family of Saud becomes very clear for the prince refused with the utmost eloquence to be just a prince who is guided by a Shaykh who, in turn, goes around to other emirates and countries making Ibn Saud out to be just another of many princes. That was the reason he asked the Shaykh the polite question about his position in the future, and he extracted a commitment from him to remain under the banner of the Saud family, meaning this was the only family who could lead the Shaykh's mission in which the latter believed and which was adopted by the Saudi family. This openness in rejecting any prejudice against the rights of the emirate was found in all of the prominent princes who led that family, and it reached its peak with Abd al-Aziz al-Saud... The Shaykh's flexibility must raise an issue of great significance. The issue of inheriting the kingship has remained controversial in Islamic political jurisprudence. The Shaykh had agreed to keep the kingship in one family, according to the system of Wilayat al-Ahd, established in the Islamic world since the murder of Imam Ali. In other words, the current ruler determines his successor based on very flexible interpretations of the precedent set by Abu Bakr." *Al-Saudiyeen Wa al-Hal al-Islami,* Muhammad Jalal Keshek, p. 113

[190] *Takfiri* is an Arabic word meaning a doctrine that declares others disbelievers.

[191] *Memoirs of Mr. Hempher,* p. 84

[192] *Unwan al-Majd, pp.* 10–11

[193] Ibid., p. 11

[194] The account given in *Tarikh Najd [Rawdat al-Afkar Wa al-Afham]* is as follows:

When Uthman Ibn Muammar's wrath increased against the people of monotheism, and when he showed some of his hatred to them and his support of the people of falsehood, and when it became clear that the stories about the Shaykh

References

were true, and when all of the people of the town came to him complaining about their fear of his betrayal of the Muslims, the Shaykh then said to the delegation that was visiting him from the people of Uyaynah: "I want you to pledge your allegiance to the religion of God and His prophet, supporting those who support him and fighting those who fight him, even if it were your own prince Osman."

They gave him that promise and they all agreed to that allegiance. This filled Osman's heart with terror and increased his hatred. The devil embellished for him to destroy Muslims and banish them to the furthest countries. So he sent to Ibn Souwait and Ibrahim Ibn Suleiman, the apostate leader of Tharmad, asking them to come to him so he could carry out his intent of destroying the Muslims.

When the Muslims confirmed that, a group of them vowed to kill him: Hamad Ibn Rashed and Ibrahim Ibn Zaid. When the Friday prayers were completed, they killed him in the mosque's oratory during Rajab 1163 AH. *Tarikh Najd*

It should be noted that an apostate would not be allowed to lead the Friday prayer per Islamic law.

[195] *Tarikh Najd,* Hussein Ibn Ghannam, p. 86

[196] Ibid., p. 87

[197] *Tarikh al-Dawla al-Saudiyah,* Amin Sa'id, p. 38

[198] Ibid.

[199] Hempher writes:

After years of work, the Ministry was able to persuade Muhammad Ibn Saud to our side. They sent me a messenger to tell me that and to prove the necessity of cooperation between the two Muhammads. Muhammad Ibn Abd al-Wahhab had the religion and Muhammad Ibn Saud had the power and together they would capture the people's hearts and bodies. History has proven that religious governments are more resilient, more powerful, and more feared.

The Birth of Terrorism in Middle East

And so it was. Afterwards, our side became much stronger. We took Diriyah as the capital of the new rule and the new religion. The Ministry secretly provided this new government with enough money. The new government outwardly purchased a number of slaves who in reality were among the finest of the Ministry's officers, trained in the Arabic language and desert warfare. Altogether, we were 11, and we collaborated to make the necessary plans. The two Muhammads followed the plans we put together for them and we would often objectively discuss the affairs if there were no private ones from the Ministry. *Memoirs of Mr. Hempher*, pp. 85–86

[200] Or Ahmad Ibn Suwaylim or Muhammad Ibn Suwaylim al-Arini as mentioned by others.

[201] The Manuscript, pp. 66–67

Muhammad Ibn Faqih or Ahmad Ibn Suwaylim, said:

We had no information about the lineage of this Muhammad Ibn Suwaylim other than that he was known in Diriyah as Oynyee, in relationship to Uyaynah, the town from which he came. Prior to coming to Uyaynah, he was in al-Ehsa, but there was no confirmation that he was from there or from any tribe or group.

According to the author of the manuscript, he was beneficial in matters of commerce and therefore possessed vast knowledge about the harvests and products of the different towns, paths for convoys in the deserts, and had well-developed relationships with the tradesmen in the cities and ports especially those in Basra because trade with them was of utmost importance to the leaders of the tribes of Najd. Other ports in the Gulf were secondary in importance.

Regardless of this man's characteristics and attributes and the extent of his importance in trade for the ruler of Uyaynah, we can be certain that the person to whom Muhammad Ibn Abd al-Wahhab ran in Diriyah and with whom he hid for a period of time had vast knowledge and abilities for negotiating and persuading. These were necessary traits to anyone working in commerce

References

during that time. This was certain from the manner that Ibn Suwaylim followed in convincing Muhammad Ibn Saud to form an alliance with Ibn Abd al-Wahhab.

If we are able to deduce anything about the traits and characteristics of Ibn Suwaylim based on his profession, it would be that he was capable of playing an important role in the intelligence field at that time. The traits needed for a man who was the communication link between the British (who had made Basra and some of the Gulf ports centers for their activities) and Muhammad Ibn Abd al-Wahhab (their agent in southern Najd) were plentiful in this man. This is especially true when we add to the above traits ingratitude and disowning of his benefactor by disobeying Osman Ibn Muammar and resorting to the patronage of Muhammad Ibn Saud, who was rebelling at the time against the ruler of Uyaynah. This is a trait that was not in line with the norms or popular customs in the Arabian Peninsula at the time.

This reality lets us deduce with confidence that Muhammad Ibn Suwaylim had a clear connection to Ibn Abd al-Wahhab's mission. He was a tool of communication between Ibn Abd al-Wahhab and his British "slaves" covering his movements and travels under the guise of working in commerce. His reports about Muhammad Ibn Saud and his people prompted the British to select Ibn Saud as an ally. So they signaled to him to use his influence and intelligence with Muhammad Ibn Saud's wife, Mudy, since she had impact on her husband's decisions to where Salah al-Deen al-Moukhtar described her as having "intelligence and knowledge..." *Takawon al-Tabaiyah al-Saudiyah*, Muhammad Faqih, pp. 84–85

[202] Possibly related to the historian Ibn Ghannam.

[203] *Tarikh Najd* also known as *Rawdat al-Afkar Wa al-Afham*, Hussein Ibn Ghannam, p. 88

[204] "When he settled in Diriyah, his followers in Uyaynah escaped to him, along with others who belonged to the religion and were accompanied by heads of the Muammar family who were opposed to Osman Ibn Muammar in Uyaynah.

The Birth of Terrorism in Middle East

Others from neighboring towns also emigrated to Diriyah when they learned that the Shaykh was working on his own and was secure." *Unwan al-Majd Fi Tarikh Najd,* Uthman Ibn Bishar al-Najdi, p. 12

205 Ibid., p. 12

206 Salah al-Deen al-Moukhtar, *Tarikh al-Mamlakah al-Arabiyah al-Saudiyah Fi Madihah Wa Haderhah,* p. 38

207 *Tarikh Najd al-Hadith,* Amin al-Rayhani, p. 40

208 *Lam al-Shahab,* p. 35

209 *Tarikh al-Dawla al-Saudiyah,* p. 38

210 Muhammad Faqih said in his book, *Takawon al-Tabaiyah al-Saudiyah,* which is a sociological, historical take on this subject, summarizing his conclusions that were based on reading critiques by Saudi historians:

Muhammad Ibn Abd al-Wahhab sought refuge in Diriyah after he was abandoned by Osman Ibn Muammar, the ruler of Uyaynah. He hid with one of the aids of the British intelligence called Muhammad Ibn Suwaylim who covered up the presence of Muhammad Ibn Abd al-Wahhab long enough for Ibn Suwaylim to contact the British intelligence who used Basra as headquarters for their work in Najd and other towns in the Islamic regions.

Ibn Suwaylim took advantage of his profession in commerce to move to Basra and contact the foreigners. He told them of Ibn Abd al-Wahhab's situation including Ibn Muammar abandoning him. He also told them of Ibn Saud's situation in Diriyah and his wife's influence on him. The British intelligence provided him with the necessary instructions and the plan that must be followed in order to continue on the agreed-upon path with Ibn Abd al-Wahhab with some modifications. These included that Muhammad Ibn Saud was to assume the role previously assigned to Ibn Muammar with the stipulations that decisions on all matters this time around would be in Ibn Abd al-Wahhab's hands and that monetary and weaponry assistance would be to Ibn Abd al-Wahhab and not to Ibn Saud.

References

The British intelligence asked Ibn Suwaylim to work on Mudy, Ibn Saud's wife, to pressure her husband to accept the deal. It is possible that he went back to her with expensive presents to tempt her, given the impact of presents on the hearts of ambitious women, such as Mudy, who seek power and control. It is also possible that he had some of the necessary funds for Ibn Abd al-Wahhab as a price for forging an alliance with Ibn Saud.

With the return of Ibn Suwaylim to Diriyah and his ability to convince Mudy of the necessity to pressure her husband into an alliance with Ibn Abd al-Wahhab, the features of the deal between the two sides started to emerge. The new British plan, to execute the most serious and heinous political-religious project witnessed by the Islamic nation in its history, started to see the light. Regardless whether Muhammad Ibn Saud had a previous relationship with the British, we gather from the Saudi and Wahhabi narratives about the meeting between the two men and the initial interventions that took place and the role that Muhammad Ibn Suwaylim played in this subject that these two men were well aware of each other and of each other's intent as well as of the roles awaiting each of them in the British plans. In other words, Muhammad Ibn Saud was involved with this plan at least from the point when he met Ibn Abd al-Wahhab in Ibn Suwaylim's house and pledged allegiance to rectify and promote this religion. pp. 90–91

[211] *Unwan al-Majd Fi Tarikh Najd,* Uthman Ibn Bishar al-Najdi, pp. 13–14

[212] "It was their policy to control all revenues separately in the treasury. They did not use those monies whenever they pleased, but rather they had rules that allowed habitual withdrawals. This allowed their purse to increase little by little based on the ability of their king. This was by order of Muhammad Ibn Abd al-Wahhab.

They decided that Muhammad Ibn Abd al-Wahhab, his children, grandchildren, servants, and dependents would receive close to 50,000 gold pieces. Then they decided to make their own annual allowance and that of their people, servants, and other dependents close to 200,000 gold pieces.

The Birth of Terrorism in Middle East

However, when their conquests of the lands of Bani Khalid, Hijaz, and parts of Yemen and Oman increased their wealth during the last days of Abd al-Aziz's rule and the beginning of his son Saud's reign, they allocated to the children of Muhammad Ibn Abd al-Wahhab approximately 80,000 gold pieces annually. This continued until the days of Abd Allah Ibn Saud. It was known that they also received money beyond the allowance from the treasury, such as gifts they received from the Imam in Sana in Yemen or the people of Egypt or others. These gifts were brought to them by the Persian pilgrims passing through their lands. The family also owned palm trees that they had purchased or inherited." *Lam al-Shahab*, p. 134

[213] Supported and published by the Saudi government which, in turn, advertises for him and considers him one of the key sources on Muhammad Ibn Abd al-Wahhab, al-Saud, and the Wahhabi movement.

[214] *Lam al-Shahab*, pp. 124–125

[215] *Al Saud,* Haythem al-Yamani, p. 43

[216] *Lam al-Shahab*, p. 36

[217] Abd al-Aziz Sayed al-Ahel writes of what he perceives as a praiseworthy alliance between the two Shaykhs:

Since he, Shaykh Muhammad Ibn Abd al-Wahhab, was not desirous of possessions or rule, he confined his main concern to driving the people's beliefs towards pure monotheism and focused his tongue and pen to this rhetoric effort and his planning and sword to this struggle. He dealt with nothing save for the Islamic laws that organize the matters of life. He was loyal, as were his children and grandchildren, to the alliance he had formed with Muhammad Ibn Saud. Since that alliance, each of them was therefore his partner or to the alliance to which he had committed. Their hearts were pure, with both inward and outward honesty. Such honesty in loyalty and serenity was transferred to their offspring; and when they passed on, they left their mark evident in the hearts of their children and grandchildren. They had the first rank in the religion and

References

the second in the state after the princes… *Daeeyat al-Tawheed, Muhammad Ibn Abd al-Wahhab*, Abd al-Aziz Sayed al-Ahel, p. 91 et seq.

Hussein al-Shaykh Khazal said:

The objectives of these two reformers and rescuers converged and their word was unified so it seemed they became one spirit in two bodies and they never disagreed or hesitated in carrying out the principles by which they were guided. These principles were the rescue from polytheism and salvation from misguidance, injustice, and tyranny." *Tarikh al-Jazeera al-Arabiyah Fi Aser al-Shaykh Muhammad Ibn Abd al-Wahhab*, p. 43

[218] The author of *Lam al-Shahab* said, "Abd al-Aziz had dignity, reverence, and competence. His temperament was close to that of Muhammad Ibn Abd al-Wahhab and that made the latter love him excessively and he would say about him, 'This is an Imam. This is the defender of the religion,' and he would praise him." p. 126

[219] The author of *Lam al-Shahab* said:

It was their policy to be not satisfied with peace of mind for the tribes under their control for fear that they would collaborate to oppose some of their rules. So they would incite the tribes and cause discord between them but this was done surreptitiously and in secret. p. 137

[220] "When the Sauds' strength became established in the days of Muhammad Ibn Saud, it was their habit in wars to appoint people to each tribe, village, or city to support their struggle. They did not even give them jobs, but, rather, they would say, 'This is your obligation and even ammunition is on those carrying out such struggles.' They would say to the chief of a group or prince of a country, 'Organize a group for the struggle wherever we wish and order.' And it was as they ordered." *Lam al-Shahab*, p. 137

The expertise of the rising Wahhabi emirate in the management of war evolved with the increase in invasions and raids, after having been limited at the

The Birth of Terrorism in Middle East

beginning. Muhammad Ibn Saud was not successful in these invasions and the Saudi historians acknowledged that. The author of *Lam al-Shahab* writes:

And Muhammad Ibn Saud was unable to be victorious on his own, but rather the leader and prince of his armies, his son Abd al-Aziz, was the victorious one. This was not due to a weakness in Muhammad Ibn Saud's forces but rather because he was not a mastermind in warfare. Abd al-Aziz's temperament was similar to that of Muhammad Ibn Abd al-Wahhab, and that was why the latter loved him excessively. He would say, "This imam, the champion of the religion…" and he would praise him. *Lam al-Shahab*, p. 125

In reality, these were exaggerations about the presence of Muhammad Ibn Saud's armies, ahead of Muhammad Ibn Abd al-Wahhab's arrival in Diriyah. The historian Ibn Bishar said, "The first raid was in 1160 AH, two years after the arrival of the Shaykh and it included seven camels with their riders who fell to the ground due to their lack of experience in riding camels."

[221] Ibn Bishar writes:

So one day I observed it, meaning Diriyah, from a high location known as the Baten and saw its houses and a group of women and all the gold, silver, weaponry, camels, and sheep. I saw buying and selling, giving and taking, and other such actions as far as the eye can see. It all sounded like the loud buzzing of bees. The shops were on both the eastern and western sides, and they had in them clothes, weapons, and material that cannot be described.

Amin al-Rayhani commented on Ibn Bishar's account about the prosperity in Diriyah by saying, "The word *monotheism* built Diriyah." *Tarikh Najd al-Hadith*, p. 42

[222] "They had in each town someone who scrutinized the affairs of the people by spying on the genuineness of their intent in their obedience to this religion as well as their worldly transactions."

"It was their practice to have spies in the towns that were not under their control, watching developments and keeping them informed."

References

Lam al-Shahab, p. 132

"He, Muhammad Ibn Abd al-Wahhab, ordered secret inquiries into the people's hidden money so he could forcibly take their tithing." Muhammad Ibn Abd al-Wahhab – Aziz al-Athama, p. 145

[223] I previously mentioned the text written by the author of *Lam al-Shahab* where he talked about the exceptional capabilities of Shaykh Muhammad Ibn Abd al-Wahhab.

Historians recounted many other details, too many to include here, that signal the treachery of Muhammad Ibn Abd al-Wahhab and his ability to maneuver in wars and negotiate with his enemies as he did with Arar, Ibn Dawass, Inb Muammar, and the people of Uyaynah. He also resorted to psychological warfare to beat his enemies.

Earlier I mentioned that the author of *Lam al-Shahab,* who was a supporter of the house of Saud, had noted that Muhammad Ibn Saud was incapable of conducting wars. Here I mention his note that Abd al-Aziz would not have been capable of the same at the beginning were it not for the help and support of Muhammad Ibn Abd al-Wahhab

In his first raid, Abd al-Aziz Ibn Muhammad Ibn Saud marched on the people of Washem and encountered them in the desert. They fought each other and he suffered heavy losses so he returned to Diriyah where he fortified his forces. He then carried out a surprise attack while they were partially guarded. He forcibly entered the town and killed all of its people… He was then told, "this is an act which does not please God. Do you kill those who do not fight?" *Lam al-Shahab,* p. 126

[224] Muhammad Ibn Abd al-Wahhab and the Saud family reportedly resorted to secretly bribing some of their helpers to persuade them in their wars with Ibn Dawass (who killed two sons of Ibn Saud). "This increased Muhammad Ibn Saud's and his son's, Abd al-Aziz, as well as Muhammad Ibn Abd al-Wahhab's fervor and ardor for the religion. It also increased their sense of preservation for

themselves and their honor. Therefore, they prepared large armies by secretly giving them some money. Some were from their own towns, some were from the other Bedouin Arabs, and included others who had pledged allegiance to their doctrine and proved their dedication." *Lam al-Shahab*, p. 125

Revenge was the motive propelling them to fight even though it was justified with love and fervor for the religion, especially since Ibn Dawass was a Muslim just like them and they had pacified him and maintained good relations with him for a long time as they had with others. Did he, in the blink of an eye, become a polytheist infidel?

No doubt this was a Bedouin excuse that took advantage of the religion in order to achieve its expansionary objectives as we will uncover in this study.

[225] *Lam al-Shahab*, p. 137

[226] As we saw in the excuses to which he had resorted to kill the prince of Uyaynah and destroy his city which continues to be in ruins into present day.

[227] Perhaps it is suitable to mention here the cruelty of Saud al-Kabir towards his enemies. Hafez Wahbeh, the advisor to king Abd al-Aziz, write in his book, *Jazeerat al-Arab Fi al-Karn al-Eshreen*:

Saud al-Kabir was famous for his cruelty towards criminals, or opponents. I repeatedly heard from his highness the king that he once imprisoned some Shaykhs from Mateer. Some of their elders came to mediate on their behalf. He felt they were too proud so he ordered the beheading of the prisoners. He had their heads brought to the table during a meal provided to their cousins who came to mediate on their behalf. He then ordered them to eat from that meal. This story was told by his highness king Abd al-Aziz to Shaykhs from Mateer who had come to mediate on behalf of Faisal al-Daweesh and he repeated the matter on April 13, 1913 AD when he invaded al-Ehsa and beheaded some people and served their heads. *al-Hokom al-Saudi*, p. 118

[228] *Al-Saudiyeen Wa al-Hal al-Islami*, Muhammad Jalal Keshek, p. 130

References

[229] *Lam al-Shahab*, p. 127

[230] Ibid., p. 134

[231] Ibid., p. 137

[232] Ibid., p. 122

[233] Ibid., p. 145

[234] Ibid.

[235] Ibid.

[236] Ibid.

[237] Reportedly, one day, Abd al-Aziz Ibn Muhammad Ibn Saud cursed a man in the council. When the council was adjourned, the man went to Muhammad Ibn Abd al-Wahhab complaining of the situation and said, "I want a judgment against the Prince of the Muslims." So he said, "What is your issue with him?" He replied, "He cursed me today." So Muhammad Ibn Abd al-Wahhab ordered one of his servants to summon Abd al-Aziz. When the servant arrived, he said, "There is a complaint against you." He asked him, "From whom?" He replied, "From a man you had cursed today for no reason." Abd al-Aziz, in no time and out of fear of Muhammad Ibn Abd al-Wahhab, went to him. When he arrived, he said to him, "Sit next to your friend and have a discussion with him for the religion has no room but for that." Abd al-Aziz then confessed his guilt to that man and said, "I offer to buy my honor from him for my insult to his honor for 50 gold pieces." He said, "This would be righteous if he agreed." He then asked the man, and the latter was not satisfied with that solution because he had his pride. So Muhammad Ibn Abd al-Wahhab ordered the stick that he uses to discipline some people brought to him and proceeded to hit Abd al-Aziz with it 20 times. Meanwhile, the latter was saying, "At the command of God and Islamic laws." He did not criticize Muhammad Ibn Abd al-Wahhab for that punishment, and neither did anyone from the people, but rather they complimented his actions. Many times

there were property disputes between ordinary and important people, as was typical among any people, and he never accepted any less than referring to the Islamic laws. His father Muhammad had done the same, as did his two sons Saud and Abd Allah Ibn Saud.

They conducted themselves modestly, sitting on the ground, without any cushions. They never expected people to rise for them when they passed by and if they knew that someone rose for them out of fear, they said, "We are just like you, except in authority. Never fear us and make yourself rise for us. If you wish to, you may honor us and if not, then refrain." *Lam al-Shahab*, p. 136

However, this modesty may seem questionable when one considers that this same author would write of the tyrannical practices and lavish lives of these rulers, including the vast fortunes they acquired as salaries or gifts in the days of Muhammad Ibn Abd al-Wahhab and after. He also told us of the legendary lavish lifestyle of Saud Ibn Abd al-Aziz, known as al-Kabir.

[238] This also occurred when Abd al-Aziz (the first) sought reconciliation with al-Najrani after he saw the might of his army. Al-Najrani remained bound to his accord in spite of the temptations of Arar, his ally.

This resulted in Abd al-Aziz raiding one of Shemer's tribes that had previously pledged allegiance to him. He killed many of its people and imprisoned two hundred of its men before returning to Diriyah on orders from Muhammad Ibn Abd al-Wahhab. This was an attempt to restore his dignity after the setback he had suffered.

[239] Observers noted that this same environment remained subject to the simplistic Wahhabi perceptions, especially since successive Wahhabi emirates seized control of Najd and Hijaz. It provided them with vast wealth to spread their doctrine in places such as Pakistan, Afghanistan, and elsewhere. They took advantage of the poverty afflicting the majority of the peoples in that region, their ignorance of the Arabic language, and the basics of the Islamic religion. They were able to buy speakers, preachers, authors, and others to spread their ideas.

References

Today, this situation has become critical. There has been an increase in the number of their supporters and those who are taking up arms to forcibly spread the Wahhabi religion. New generations, versed in modern sciences, have emerged. They pose a real threat in the future, especially since they have succeeded in striking select targets in America, Britain, and Spain.

[240] *Daeeyat al-Tawheed*, p. 114

[241] The author of *Lam al-Shahab* contradicted the other historians who talked about the poverty of the Shaykh of Diriyah. He went to lengths in talking about his alleged wealth and generosity:

He had a generous nature and he owned many properties, palms, and other crops, as well as some cattle. It was said that he was so generous that if a man came to him seeking his help in fulfilling a debt, he would oblige him, after confirming his need, even if the debt was significant… He also helped poor men get married and he would ready them from his own money… *Lam al-Shahab*, p. 131

[242] *Lam al-Shahab*, pp. 133–134

[243] Ibid., p. 136

[244] Ibid., p. 137

[245] Ibid., p. 138

[246] Ibid., pp. 174–176

[247] *Daeeyat al-Tawheed*, p. 95

[248] *Lam al-Shahab*, pp. 137–138

[249] *Lam al-Shahab*, p. 138

[250] *Unwan al-Majd Fi Tarikh Najd*, p. 106

[251] *Al-Dawlah al-Saudiyah al-Ula*, p. 267

[252] The author of *Lam al-Shahab* indicated that the Saudi forces used cannons early on. This was perhaps done with the assistance of Ibn Abd al-Wahhab's servants, the officers from the British Ministry of Colonies. Review *Lam al-Shahab*, pages 71, 72, 132.

[253] *Lam al-Shahab*, pp. 132–133

[254] Muhammad Ibrahim Mabrouk, an Islamic author who called for the return of an Islamic caliphate in his book *Mouwajahat al-Mouwajaha*, pp. 17–19, confirmed:

Jurisprudence in Islamic religious movements requires "adopting from the senior imams in Islamic history, especially from those who were near the primary Islamic resources."

Among those, he cited Ibn Taymiyyah, Imam Muhammad Ibn Abd al-Wahhab, Imam al-Mawdudi, and Imam al-Banna. He spoke highly of the emergence of Muhammad Ibn Abd al-Wahhab since "it was a shock to the Muslim world leading to shaking up the prevailing beliefs, concepts, innovations, and superstitions and to uprooting many of them from the hearts and minds… The Islamic movement was heavily influenced by the Wahhabi doctrine."

[255] In justifying Muhammad Ibn Saud's weakness and his lack of fighting experience, the author of *Lam al-Shahab* writes, "…In these invasions, Muhammad Ibn Saud did not prevail on his own, rather the leader and prince of the armies was his son Abd al-Aziz. This was not due to a weakness in Muhammad Ibn Saud's power but rather because he was not a mastermind of wars." *Lam al-Shahab*, p. 125

Even Abd al-Aziz himself was not experienced or strong enough, as we were told by the same author:

On the first foray led by Abd al-Aziz Ibn Muhammad Ibn Saud against the people of al-Washem, he confronted them in the wild. They fought him and killed many of his people, and he returned defeated back to Diriyah." *Lam al-Shahab*, p. 126

References

Shaykh Abd Allah al-Bassam also told us about Muhammad Ibn Saud's weakness:

…After the Shaykh moved to Diriyah and formed his agreement with the prince Muhammad Ibn Saud, Osman Ibn Muammar started mounting raids from Uyaynah against Diriyah. He would send battalions of horses and knights. Prince Muhammad Ibn Saud was so weak and powerless and mal-equipped that he could not confront Osman Ibn Muammar's campaigns. That is the reason that Muhammad Ibn Saud's daughter wrote in a popular poem about Ibn Muammar's forces coming up on the area of Zilzal, an area near the wall of Diriyah, every eve and saying that the fighting forces were not equitable so the raids on Diriyah should stop. *Ulama Najd Fi Khilal Sittat Qurun,* pp. 37–38

تطل على الزلال كل عشية	ما شاقني كود سرية لابن معتر
والا فزل عن شيخة الدَّرعيّة	يا ببه شوف للخيل خيل مثله

She is confirming that the raids by Ibn Muammar on the area of Zilzal near Diriyah are difficult for her and she is beseeching her father to send knights to face those attackers or give up the leadership of Diriyah since he is not worthy of protecting it.

[256] The author of *Lam al-Shahab* writes:

…The first war inflicted by Muhammad Ibn Saud on the orders of Muhammad Ibn Abd al-Wahhab was the war with Ibn Dawass. His forces at the time numbered 20 camels and seven knights. *Lam al-Shahab,* p. 125

This was further supported by Ibn Bishar when he talked about the weakness of Diriyah at the beginning, writing:

…The Shaykh then demanded jihad and they complied… The first army had seven mounts, and when they were mounted and they hastened in their pace, their riders fell because they were not accustomed to riding these mounts. *Unwan al-Majd Fi Tarikh Najd,* pp. 14–15

[257] Despite all that was said about the alliance at the beginning, the Saudi state historians stated that Shaykh Muhammad Ibn Abd al-Wahhab had taken control over all the situations in Diriyah, thereby becoming the top man. He managed everything and controlled the politics and affairs of this emerging nation. Despite the claims by the later historians about his need to use the sword to protect himself and spread his doctrine, there is no doubt that he did not need that method after realizing his power over his followers. They showed their willingness to march with him to the end. Diriyah was but a center to gather them until the crucial moments when he started his raids against the neighboring emirates and Shaykhs.

It could be argued that the Saud family was the beneficiary of the Wahhabi doctrine and that Wahhabism did not benefit from them except in one matter: They made Diriyah a center for their gatherings and the starting point for their expeditions and battles.

The author of *Lam al-Shahab* said about Shaykh Ibn Abd al-Wahhab being the sole controller of the affairs of the emerging nation:

…All matters were under the control of Muhammad Ibn Abd al-Wahhab, and if he favored a matter, so did they and if he did not favor a matter, they did the same without argument. The ongoing practice was that Muhammad Ibn Saud, along with his son Abd al-Aziz and the rest of his children, would visit the Shaykh twice daily, once in the morning and another time in the evening. They would sit silently, without speaking unless the Shaykh talked to them first. They would study under his tutelage his version of the science of monotheism, and he would also provide them special lessons separately. Muhammad Ibn Abd al-Wahhab became a very strong force and the people of Diriyah were all under his control, along with the people from neighboring villages. *Lam al-Shahab*, pp. 35–36

Hussein al-Shaykh Khazal writes of the influence of the Shaykh:

…Prince Muhammad Ibn Saud did not carry out any project or issue a significant decision without the consent of Shaykh Muhammad Ibn Abd al-Wahhab.

References

If he favored it, the prince favored it and if he refused it, the prince refused it… *Tarikh al-Jazeera al-Arabiyah Fi Aser al-Shaykh Muhammad Ibn Abd al-Wahhab*, pp. 265–271

This was also mentioned by Ibn Bishar:

…The khums and zakat, along with all small and big things that came to Diriyah, were personally given to him and he would put them wherever he wished. Neither Abd al-Aziz nor others took any of it except by his orders. He held all decisions of binding and discharging, giving and taking, and advancing or retreating in his own hands. The army would not advance and Muhammad Ibn Saud and his son Abd al-Aziz would not express any opinions unless they were aligned with the Shaykh's words and opinions… He furnished the armies, dispatched companies, and wrote to the people of other countries, and they wrote to him. Delegates and guests sought him and all comings and goings were to and from his place. *Unwan al-Majd Fi Tarikh Najd*, pp. 15, 19

[258] *Daeeyat al-Tawheed, Muhammad Ibn Abd al-Wahhab*, Abd al-Aziz Sayed al-Ahel, p. 12

[259] He concluded that "Wahhabism always arrived first to the regions that the Saud family targeted, and, as such, it played a big role in their victory over those regions…" *Al-Dawlah al-Saudiyah al-Ula*, p. 9

[260] Ibid., pp. 81–82. Even though Dr. Abd al-Raheem al-Rahman argued that the Saud family were the ones with power and influence and that the Shaykh was but a jurist who had a mission, he acknowledges that the power of the Saud family would not have been complete had it not been for the Shaykh's religious influence as well as the submission of his followers and their proliferation in the various regions and the fact that they were a fifth column that helped uncover the weak points of their enemies. This was also pointed out by Abd al-Aziz Sayed al-Ahel, despite his argument that the effective power was with the Sauds and not Shaykh Muhammad Ibn Abd al-Wahhab.

The Birth of Terrorism in Middle East

Abd al-Aziz Sayed al-Ahel writes, "The Saud conquests in the Peninsula progressed smoothly under the Wahhabi banner, and those who did not willingly submit to this *pure mission had to seek it out of fear and terror…" Daeeyat al-Ta-wheed, p. 77*

Sayed al-Ahel replaced the word "raids" with "conquests," perhaps in order to align the Wahhabi movement with early Islamic history. He also wrote that the invading Wahhabis resorted to instilling fear and terror to make their enemies, who were not convinced of the Wahhabi mission, submit to them.

[261] *Al-Dawlah al-Saudiyah al-Ula*, p. 9

[262] Ibid., p. 8

[263] In spite of this, the Saudi state historians indicated that the people of Diriyah, "who were very ignorant and had fallen into major and minor infractions such as polytheism, neglecting prayers and almsgiving, and rejecting the rituals of Islam…" were the ones who struggled with the Shaykh for two years after "the knowledge of monotheism settled in their hearts following their ignorance, and their hearts were saturated with love for the Shaykh and they loved and sheltered the migrants." (Ibn Bishar, p. 14) In a short period of time, they reportedly became dedicated soldiers, struggling in the way of the Shaykh who "commanded them to do so and urged them so they followed the orders". *Unwan al-Majd*, p. 14

The spoils of raids were, no doubt, an allurement. They embarked on the longest campaign of attacks in the history of the Arabian Peninsula. They swept through cities, towns, villages, oases, tribal gatherings, and neighboring regions in Iraq and elsewhere. Ibn Bishar wrote extensively about conquests, incidents, raids, and acquisitions, such that such accounts took up most of his history. Ibn Ghannam's history was also rife with the mention of hundreds of such terrorist raids.

In the largest campaign of revenge, the two allies resorted to executing their opponents and rivals and to eliminating prominent scholars, tribal chiefs, and princes. Ibn Muammar was among the first people touched by the Saudi

References

Wahhabi vengeful hand, and he was assassinated in a mosque after completing the Friday prayers. Afterwards, his prayers were invalidated under the pretext that he deviated from Islam, breached the covenant, committed treason, and fraternized with the enemies.

They resorted to indiscriminate murder in their raids, even the elderly and children. They violated their honor and property, demolished their cities, and uprooted their crops under the pretext that they were polytheists, outside the bounds of Islam.

The Shaykh used to join his followers in some of the raids and battles. He even marched on Uyaynah and ordered Ibn Muammar's palace destroyed along with the rest of the city. It remains in ruins to the present day.

Abd al-Aziz Ibn Muhammad Ibn Saud was the hero of most of the Wahhabi raids managed by the Shaykh. He was known for his harsh and violent methods. He was very close to the Shaykh who commended and praised him at every opportunity. He even recommended him to succeed his father. He did so, and ruled the emirate until his bloody era ended with his assassination. It was followed by an even bloodier era when his son, Saud Ibn Abd al-Aziz, known as Saud al-Kabir, succeeded him.

The Saudi historians do not condemn the gathering of massive spoils that arrived in Diriyah following the raids and they compared those raids to the invasions led by the early Muslim caliphs. They were also proud of the harsh methods that were used against the people of Uyaynah, Riyadh, al-Ehsa, al-Taif, and other cities.

Their raids on Karbala, the holy city in Iraq where the shrine of Imam Hasayn, grandson of the Prophet, is located continues to be a source of pride for them until today even though that was not a combatant city and its inhabitants were civilians and visiting pilgrims.

Ibn Bishar said in *Unwan al-Majd Fi Tarikh Najd*:

In 1216 AH, Saud marched his victorious armies and his famous thoroughbred horses targeting the land of Karbala and fighting the people of the city of

The Birth of Terrorism in Middle East

Husayn… The Muslims gathered around that city, scaled its walls, and forcibly entered it. They killed most of its people in the markets and homes. They destroyed the shrine and took all that was in it and around it. They also took the headstone from the grave and it was encrusted with emeralds, rubies, and other jewels. They took any types of money, weapons, clothing, furniture, gold, silver, and precious Korans they could find, along with other countless items. They were there for only one morning and they left around noon with all of that wealth, after they killed approximately 2,000 of the city's men… pp. 121–122

The Wahhabis destroyed a great amount of the ancient Islamic monuments and they used brute force with their opponents and victims, just like they did in Karbala, southern Basra, and elsewhere.

The guerrilla warfare style they adopted helped them in their attacks and quick escapes when they were faced with any army or organized force.

In all cases, we find ready Wahhabi justifications for these raids such as polytheism, treason, failure to observe religious duties, and harboring fabricators, along with other such justifications that had a powerful effect on the Wahhabi followers.

[264] *Lam al-Shahab*, Addendum, p. 122

[265] *Unwan al-Majd Fi Tarikh Najd*, p. 15

[266] Ibid., p. 83

[267] *Al-Hokom al-Saudi*, p. 118

[268] *Unwan al-Majd Fi Tarikh Najd*, p. 168

[269] *Ibid.*, p. 170

[270] The author of *Lam al-Shahab* wrote that Saud was accustomed to a life of luxury during his father's lifetime, before he became the heir to the first Saudi emirate. His comments were cited in a previous chapter.

[271] Review content in the two previous chapters.

References

[272] *Lam al-Shahab*, p. 37

[273] The author of *Lam al-Shahab* spoke of the orders of the Shaykh to Abd al-Aziz following nine years of occupation in al-Washem and after the atrocities committed to invade Uyaynah (which was not responding to Wahhabism despite the killing of its prince Osman Ibn Muammar). He said:

Abd al-Aziz marched on Uyaynah with 4,000 fighters. He entered it forcibly and killed many of its people. He wrote to Muhammad Ibn Abd al-Wahhab telling him of his feat. Muhammad Ibn Abd al-Wahhab ordered him to force the people out of their town, each and every one of them. He also ordered him to destroy the city's walls and houses, ruin its orchards, and cut down its palm trees. He told him to make their land just like the land of Thamoud. So he did as he was ordered and then some…

Muhammad Ibn Abd al-Wahhab and Abd al-Aziz behaved in such a manner toward the people of Uyaynah because these people were the most honorable of Najd and if there ever was a worthy leadership in the entire area of Najd, it was them. They were genealogically connected to the old Bani Hanifa who were the kings of the region. It was impossible for them to truthfully follow Muhammad Ibn Abd al-Wahhab and he knew that based on previous clear evidence. Therefore, he had to reject them under any circumstance.

When people knew of the severe impact of Abd al-Aziz Ibn Muhammad Ibn Saud and that he was set on that path with Muhammad Ibn Abd al-Wahhab and that together they were strong and to be dreaded, they submitted to them, accepting their religion. Some of them did so out of acceptance of the religion after they found it in themselves to do so. They felt that had this religion not been the right one, it would not have prevailed. Since it had prevailed, it must be the right one. Others accepted it gradually, but they did so out of fear.

Based on this, he started watching the people to reveal the degree of their acceptance. If he determined that someone's acceptance was both internal and external, he drew him closer, embraced him, gave him enough to support him, and listened to him. If he determined that someone's acceptance was out of fear and prudence, he gave him safety, but he was careful of him and he watched him from time to time... *Lam al-Shahab*, pp. 38–39

[274] Ibn Bishar spoke about the state of Diriyah before and after the arrival of Muhammad Ibn Abd al-Wahhab. He also went on and on to describe Saud's wealth:

He owned 2,400 thoroughbred mares and over 500 horses; some even said 600 while others said 1,000... He had 60 cannons, 30 of which were large. The amounts of money that came in to Diriyah from Katif, Bahrain, Oman, Yemen, Tahama, Higaz, and elsewhere, along with the revenues from Najd and other areas, were so vast they could not be counted. This is in addition to the incoming revenues from almsgiving which were even in higher proportions...

He owned black servants who had precious swords adorned with gold and silver... When he arrived at a council, people moved out of his way as not to be trampled by the servants... Once Saud was seated, he turned to the scholars and leaders. They would greet him and he would greet them in return. pp. 172–175

[275] Abd al-Aziz Sayed al-Ahel said in *Daeeyat al-Tawheed, Muhammad Ibn Abd al-Wahhab*:

For the first time in the modern history of the Arabian Peninsula, an emirate was established with an organized system where law prevailed, justice was structured, and the laws of religion were carried out... In this country, the poor and the rich were equal, as was mandated by Islam... The doors to exaggerations and praise were closed... The new spirit of the religion removed pompousness and luxury... And the rights of the good pious people and the martyrs from war were not forgotten... Their rights became sacred, and those with the means had to provide for them when the treasury failed to do so. The wealthy and those with honor fulfilled those needs willingly and happily and not out of fear or coercion... Islamic ethics and manners prevailed among the people... Sinful disagreements between the people ceased... Cursing and insults disappeared... Shaykh Muhammad Ibn Abd al-Wahhab was careful to spread the desired sciences, and he urged the people to learn them as he previously did... He also urged educators to learn in their

References

schools, homes, and communities the zealous poetry and poetry that incited good behaviors and the upholding of the religion… pp. 100–121

[276] *Daeeyat al-Tawheed, Muhammad Ibn Abd al-Wahhab*, pp. 5–56

[277] As cited by Ibn Bishar, Ibn Ghannam, and the author of *Lam al-Shahab* among others. We covered these in detail.

[278] *Tarikh al-Dawla al-Saudiyah Hatta al-Roubo' al-Awal Min al-Quarn al-Eshrin,* Dr. Madeehah Ahmad Darwish, p. 24

[279] *Al-Hukum al-Saudi*, Khalifah Fahed

[280] *Al-Saudiyeen Wa al-Hal al-Islami,* Muhammad Jalal Keshek, p. 112

[281] *Lam al-Shahab*, p. 137

[282] In spite of that, we find some who compare the Prophet and the Shaykh who wanted to spread his own understanding by use of the sword. It has been argued by some Saudi sympathizers that the intent was not to make the Shaykh like the Prophet but to showcase him as a reforming scholar who was renewing the effaced parts of the religion. It was claimed that there were similarities between the two eras. The era of the Prophet was one of corrupt idol worship when the Arabs were in decline. The era of the Shaykh was similar to that of those Dark Ages. God sent Muhammad a long time after the earlier prophets. Humanity was waiting for this noble mission. The Shaykh came at a time when the Peninsula was in dire need of a reformer so it could be on the righteous path.

And just as the Prophet was successful in his mission, so was Muhammad Ibn Abd al-Wahhab in renewing the mission.

And just as the Prophet emigrated from Mecca to Medina (where he found helpful, loving, and friendly supporters), so did the Shaykh when "he escaped with his religion and beliefs to Diriyah where he found loving supporters…after he encountered harm and abuse from his own family." *Shaykh Muhammad Ibn Abd al-Wahhab, Aqidatuhu al-Salafiyah Wa Dawatuhu al-Islahiyah*, pp. 95–98

The Birth of Terrorism in Middle East

Shaykh Butami goes on to say in his comparisons:

Just like the events that happened to the Prophet on the way to Medina, when Sourakah Ibn Malek wanted to kill him and his horses' feet were stuck to the ground, the Shaykh faced a similar situation when a knight wanted to kill him after he was expelled from Uyaynah and his hand became worn out dropping his sword. The Shaykh presented himself to the tribes such that they would support him just like the Prophet had done and he would get support from some and harm from others. The Shaykh prayed for these people just like the Prophet had done saying, "O God, guide my people for they do not know." The life of the Prophet was subject to danger and demise, and the life of the Shaykh was subject to scourges and disasters. And just like the Prophet would personally carry out invasions so did the Shaykh. The Shaykh also wrote to kings just like the Prophet before him and he was plagued by enemies who accused him of various charges… The Shaykh ultimately triumphed just like the Prophet did…

[283] Shaykh Nasser El-Deen al-Albani, who was one of the pillars of the modern Salafi line, said that the Salafis who were the followers during the three centuries called Salaf…, were the best people as indicated by the tradition included in al-Saheehain and other books, narrated on behalf of the Prophet, "The best of mankind are those in my time, followed by their successors and then their successors." He who belongs to the righteous Salafi line, in fact, belongs to immaculateness in general. It is not permissible for a Muslim to renounce affiliation with the Salafi line… The right approach, and there is no changing it, is that it is not sufficient to count on the Quran and the Sunna without the guidance of the Salafi doctrine clarifying them…" Review the book al-Manhaj al-Salafi Enda al-Shaykh Nasser El-Deen al-Albani, Amro Abd al-Meneim Saleem. Dar al-Deeya', pp. 9–10

[284] The Islamic university had Muhammad Ibn Saud hold conferences in the name of Shaykh Muhammad Ibn Abd al-Wahhab in 1976. It also formed a committee to prepare for this conference and to present a detailed account about the Shaykh.

References

The committee began its work by specifying the overall objective of the conference, namely: "Introducing the Shaykh and explaining the truth of his mission to the Islamic world and exposing the suspicions raised about that mission in some Muslim countries and under specific historic circumstances."

The committee gathered all of the Shaykh's writings, confirmed that they were written by him, and published them in a special edition in the name of the university. Copies of this edition could then be sent to committees and researchers who would be invited to participate in the conference.

The committee embarked on gathering all it could from the published writings and manuscripts by the Shaykh. It accumulated many copies of his books, published and manuscripts, and "these were the books or booklets that the committee was able to confirm as written by the Shaykh and they did not exceed one large volume." The committee examined those writings.

"The committee was careful to form each review subcommittee from the specialized scholars who had strong ties to the nature of the author being reviewed. It was also careful to have each subcommittee include a number of scholars with complimentary expertise in relationship to the task of correcting these writings and mastering them as much as possible. It resorted to using some non-member experts. Its efforts were intended to shed light on the truth of the Shaykh's mission, facilitating access to it, and reviewing his collection of writings in order to allow the fair-minded scholars in search of the truth to find it for themselves…"

Review the brief introductory biography of *Moukhtassarat Seerat al-Rassoul* by Shaykh Muhammad Ibn Abd al-Wahhab.

Darr al-Salam Lelnasher Wa al-Tawzee', Riyadh, first edition. This is a brief prophetic biography by Ibn Hisham.

[285] Those are *Keetabh al-Tawheed, Al-Usul al-Thalathah, Kashef al-Shoubouhat, Masa'el al-Jaheeleyah, Mokhtasar al-Ansaf Wa al-Shareh, Mokhtasar Zad al-Ma'ad,* and *al-Kaba'er,* in addition to edicts and letters.

The Birth of Terrorism in Middle East

286 The large volume entitled Jame' Shourouh Al-Usul al-Thalathah by the honorable Abd al-Rahman Ibn Quassem al-Najdi, Abd al-Aziz Ibn Abd Allah Ibn Baz, Muhammad Aman Ali al-Jamee', Muhammad Ibn Saleh al-Athemayn, Saleh Ibn Abd al-Aziz al-Shaykh, Abd Allah Ibn Saleh al-Fowzan, Saleh Ibn Saad al-Saheemi, Ali Ibn Khadeeer al-Khadeer, Numan Ibn Abd al-Kareem al-Watar, and Abou Obeida al-Masrati, was printed in a luxurious edition in color by Darr al-Quemma and Darr al-Eman in Alexandria, Egypt, 2004 edition.

These commentators employ a method by which the focus is verses of the Quran, and not the Shaykh's thought. Many such scholars demonstrate their own scholarly achievement more than that of the Shaykh.

287 "Most surely in the creation of the heavens and the earth and the alternation of the night and the day, there are signs for men who understand. Those who remember Allah standing and sitting and lying on their sides and reflect on the creation of the heavens and the earth: Our Lord! Thou hast not created this in vain! Glory be to Thee; save us then from the chastisement of the fire." Quran, 3:190–191

288 "(All) people are a single nation; so Allah raised prophets as bearers of good news and as warners, and He revealed to them the Book with truth, that it might judge between people in that in which they differed; and none but the very people who were given it differed about it after clear arguments had come to them, revolting among themselves; so Allah has guided by His will those who believe to the truth about which they differed and Allah guides whom He pleases to the right path." Quran, 2:213

289 "Say: I am only a mortal like you; it is revealed to me that your god is one Allah, therefore whoever hopes to meet his Lord, he should do good deeds, and not join any one in the service of his Lord." Quran, 68:4; "And We have not sent you but to all the men as a bearer of good news and as a warner, but most men do not know." Quran, 34:28

References

[290] God made the carriers of the message, specifically, the immaculate imams of guidance, "Then We gave the Book for an inheritance to those whom We chose from among Our servants." Quran, 35:32

[291] Review the book, *Al-Emara Wa al-Khelafa*, vol. 23 from Masnad Ahmad Ibn Hanbal, Egyptian edition, 1353 AH, p. 35 and thereafter.

[292] As was the case for others. Christians killed at the hands of other Christians exceed by tenfold those who were killed by Muslims during the Crusades or other wars. The First and Second World Wars clearly attest to the same.

[293] Some authors (funded by the Saudi State) have attributed the presence of petroleum in that land to the victory of the Wahhabi sect and its embracement by the people. One such example is the writings by the Egyptian author, Abd al-Aziz Sayyid al-Ahel, who writes:

The oil springing out has been attributed to the victory of the sect and its embracement by the people. This association is not an illusion nor is it groundless. God Almighty says to Noah, peace be upon him, "telling [them]: Plead to your Lord for forgiveness. Indeed He is all-forgiver. He will send for you abundant rains from the sky, and aid you with wealth and sons, and provide you with gardens and provide you with streams." *Daeeyat al-Tawheed, Muhammad Ibn Abd al-Wahhab* p. 148

[294] During my stay in one of the Emirates in the Gulf, I saw several television channels where presenters call for supporting those who are struggling for the sake of religion all over the world. It was as if the normal state in the world is one of war and as if it is their duty to escalate sentiments in that war and to incite the fighters and others to be a constant fuel for it.

In addition, no word of condemnation was heard from any imam or a Shaykh at a mosque about acts committed by Osama Ibn Laden or the al-Qaeda followers. In fact, when they mention Ibn Laden's name, it is done with reverence and veneration, using the title "Shaykh," similar to "Shaykh" Muhammad Ibn Abd al-Wahhab.

The Birth of Terrorism in Middle East

²⁹⁵ It was stated in an introduction of a brief biography of the Prophet attributed to the Shaykh, and it was a summary of the biography of Ibn Hisham:

…He clarified the truth of monotheism that God sent with Muhammad and that it is not just saying "There is no god but God." A person may be an infidel, whose blood and money are legitimate to violate, as he utters the testimony of monotheism. He used, as proofs of this, examples depicting precedents from the time of the companions such as them fighting Bani Hanifa and their exaggerated malice towards Ali, may God be pleased with him, and other such incidents after the companions. The followers also unanimously agreed on the desirability of killing al-Jaed Ibn Darham when he denied God's attributes, even though he pronounced the testimony to God's oneness and despite being known for his knowledge and worship. The scholars also agreed to declare the slaves as infidels for what they showed as evidence of their polytheism and hypocrisy, even though they also practiced the rules of Islam and they observed their Friday and congregational prayers. There is no doubt that it was necessity that forced the heeding of this principle which was concealed from a lot of the people, even those who were knowledgeable among them. This is the reason that the Shaykh was concerned with confirming this principle and clarifying it so he could use it to reply to those who opposed him from his contemporaries… pp. 9–10

The words "hostility" and "sanctioning money and blood" were frequently repeated in the Shaykh's booklets.

²⁹⁶ "As such, the monotheistic Wahhabis believed that any country that did not adopt the Wahhabi version of monotheism was theirs to plunder, violate, and capture. Therefore, spoils were legitimized for them. All regions with a religion which was tainted by a form of infidelity or polytheism were areas of war and not areas of peace." *Daeeyat al-Tawheed, Muhammad Ibn Abd al-Wahhab*, p. 114

By doing so, they classified all non-Wahhabi Muslims and the followers of all other faiths as blasphemous. They sentenced them to death, eradication, exile, and imprisonment, and they confiscated their wealth. Their mission continues

References

to be founded on the Shaykh's literature which continues to be taught in their schools, institutions, and mosques.

[297] "Do not fight the Kharijites after me because those who seek the truth and miss it are not the same as those who seek falsehood and realize it." A quote by Imam Ali, peace be upon him. *Nahj al-Balagha.*

[298] *Mouwajahat al-Mouwajaha Muhammad Ibrahim Mabrouk,* p. 17

[299] Ibid., pp. 18–19

[300] Take for example the Society for Revival of Islamic Heritage in Kuwait, as was stated in the guide to Islamic projects, the ninth edition, published in 2006. This society published Shaykh Muhammad Ibn Abd al-Wahhab's books in addition to its other projects. These included *Fath al-Majid Fee Ketab al-Tawheed, Ketab al-Tawheed, Moukhtassarat Seerat al-Rassoul, Maten Al-Usul al-Thalathah, Maten Kashef al-Shoubouhat, Maten Keetab al-Tawheed, Shareh Kashef al-Shoubouhat,* and others.

It also distributed approximately 5,000,000 booklets about which it said, "They aim to help establish libraries all over the Islamic world with a good complementary collection of books and pure Islamic references in all fields of Islamic laws such as monotheism, interpretation, traditions, biographies, and translations."

Over 5,000 libraries have been sent to various countries in the world, ranging in value from 300 to 2,500 Kuwaiti dinar, or $1,100 to $9,500. Contributions to this project are open-ended and without limits.

Audio libraries were also established. Each one is equipped with many lectures in various Islamic law sciences (creed, law books, biographies, etc.). These audio libraries are provided to Islamic centers, mosques, and schools where audio recordings have proven effective in spreading the mission.

Dozens of associations, like Jameeyat Ehya al-Turath, carry out similar activities beyond those carried out by the above-mentioned association. This was talked about in one of the association's statements urging the people to donate and volunteer for its charitable projects.

This association has a charitable endowment to fund large and charitable projects such as providing dedicated preachers, building schools and institutes, drilling water wells, building farms, establishing training centers and printing books for comprehensive Islamic libraries, providing transportation for its followers, and establishing schools, institutes and Islamic universities (so that more than 626 projects have been implemented between Islamic institutes and schools in Africa). Statistics on the number of working committees indicate that there are around 227 of them in Africa, 214 in Southeast Asia, 150 in the Indian continent, 25 in the Arab world, three in central Asia, and seven in Europe and the Americas. There are also projects for charity, services, and preaching, etc.

The parties concerned with fighting terrorism did not pay attention to the nature of this organization's activities until lately. They subsequently added it to the terrorist list of organizations, although it is still operating freely in Kuwait, Pakistan, Afghanistan, Indonesia, some African nations, and others under the pretext of raising funds for orphans, the poor, and for alms collections and its branches are scattered in various areas of these countries.

There are 39,000 religious schools in Pakistan and Afghanistan created from the donations of philanthropic and governmental associations and organizations in Saudi Arabia and the Gulf nations. These schools teach the Wahhabi doctrine with mechanisms that call for memorizing the Quran and understanding it according to the Wahhabi understanding. As such, these schools are suitable incubators for sleeper cells.